Unstable Populations, Anxious States

AF888694

Also from MCRG

Minorities in South Asia and Europe: The New Agenda
edited by *Samir Kumar Das*

Unstable Populations, Anxious States

Mixed and Massive Population Flows in South Asia

Edited by

Paula Banerjee

Samya

UNSTABLE POPULATIONS, ANXIOUS STATES:
Mixed and Massive Population Flows in South Asia
was first published in 2013 by SAMYA,
an imprint of Bhatkal and Sen,
16 Southern Avenue, Kolkata 700 026.

The support of UNHCR and the Government of Finland
is kindly acknowledged.

© 2013 by MCRG

ISBN 978-93-81345-06-1

Rs 575.00

All rights reserved. No part of this book may be reproduced
or utilized in any form or by any means
without prior written permission from the publisher.

Design by SAMYA and Krishna Gopal Das,
typesetting by Krishna Gopal Das,
74T Sultan Alam Road, Kolkata 700 033,
and printed at Roman Printers Pvt. Ltd.
37 Andul Road, Howrah 711109

Published by Mandira Sen for SAMYA,
An imprint of Bhatkal and Sen,
16 Southern Avenue, Kolkata 700 026.

Contents

Acknowledgements

I am grateful to the authors for sharing their thoughts with us. The papers are by practitioners who have been in the field for years. At times they do not follow the established scholarly style and this adds to the unique flavour of the book. I am grateful to Ranabir Samaddar for all his support. I remain indebted to Madhurilata Basu without whose meticulous editorial assistance this book would not have seen the light of day. I am grateful to Anwesha Sengupta, Suha Priyadarshini Chakravorty, Aditi Bhaduri, Patrick Hoening and Oishik Sircar who helped me unstintingly. Last but not the least, Atig Ghosh and Suhit Sen to whom I offer my heartfelt thanks. I learnt immensely by working with Mandira Sen and Madhuparna Banerjee. While for all the hitches and glitches I alone remain responsible; this has truly been a joint effort.

The impetus behind this book is the well-known Winter Course on Forced Migration under the aegis of the Mahanirvan Calcutta Research Group. The support of UNHCR and the Government of Finland is kindly acknowledged.

Introduction

Cartographic exercises have been the fulcrum of most geo-political boundary-making processes, perpetuating discriminatory territorializations and creating 'bordered existences' that have resulted in huge displacements in South Asia. In the context of South Asia, displacement is nothing new. From its inception, South Asia has been confronted by massive displacements. The liberation of much of South Asia was intrinsically attached to the partition of states, leading to huge flows interspersed with some of the worst cases of violence perpetrated against the fleeing population. In 1946-1947, South Asia witnessed population movement of sixteen million between only India and Pakistan.[1] Many more people were forced out of other parts of South Asia. From then on forced migration has remained intrinsically attached to any development in South Asia, be it political, economic or ecological. Very few regions of the world have witnessed, as South Asia has, not just massive inter-state but also intra-state movements of people. What makes the South Asian experience particularly poignant is that almost the entire process is attributable to human failures, imperial machinations, governmental failures and mismanagement of inter-communal relationships, and not merely economic factors which are largely applicable in the case of North America or Europe. Till the end of World War II, however, the impetus behind human flows in the West had much similarity with what we see in South Asia today. The developmental process in South Asia has led to large-scale displacement; even here the factors are more political than economic. And this is what makes the issue of protection so contentious.

Any discussion on forced migration in South Asia has to start with the situation of refugees. The partition of the Indian subcontinent in 1947 witnessed probably the largest refugee movement in modern history. About eight million Hindus and Sikhs left Pakistan to resettle in India while about six–seven million Muslims went to Pakistan. Such transfer of population was accompanied by horrific violence. Some 50,000 Muslim women in India and 33,000 non-Muslim women in Pakistan were abducted, abandoned or separated from their families.[2] Women's experiences of migration, abduction and destitution during partition and the state's responses to it are a pointer to the relationship between women's position as marginal participants in state politics and gender subordination as perpetrated by the state. In this context the experiences of abducted women and their often forcible repatriation by the state assumes enormous importance today when thousands of South Asian women are refugees, migrants or stateless within the subcontinent.

Following the partition refugees, the next group of forced migrants were the Tibetan refugees who came to India. In 1959 about 80,000 Tibetans fled to India and by 2007 their numbers had increased to 150,000. The next chapter in the saga of forced migration was written in the 1970s with the occupation of Afghanistan by the Soviets. Large number of anti-Soviet groups found their way into Pakistan. This flow continued for a long time. First it was the anti-Soviets, then the anti-Taliban and finally the victims of US bombings. While all these were continuing in the west of South Asia, in the southern side huge numbers were getting dislodged in Sri Lanka. In July 1983 when the civil war started in Sri Lanka displaced population began trickling into India. By 1987 the number of displaced Sri Lankans in India increased to 134,053. By 1989 about 25,585 refugees were repatriated to Sri Lanka, but after 1989 Sri Lankans again started coming into India. They kept coming progressively until 2009 when Mahinda Rajapakse's army defeated and annihilated the top leadership of LTTE. While the forced migration of Sri Lankan refugees was continuing, in 1988, after the crackdown in Myanmar, 3000 Burmese refugees came to India on its eastern front. Although UNHCR has given 2000 Burmese refugees the official status, the unofficial estimates suggest that there are about 40,000 displaced Burmese living in India. Apart from these there are some 9000 Afghan refugees in India, about 200 Somali refugee families, over a million forced migrants from Bangladesh and an indeterminate number of Lhotshampas.[3] In Pakistan there were huge numbers of Iraqi refugees following the bombing of Iraq by the United States. But still a particular issue of pertinence is that refugees are neither the only nor the largest group of forced migrants in South Asia. Side by side with the refugees are the internally displaced people (IDP) who hold an equal importance in the construction, determination, and delineation of the history of forced migration.

The situations of the IDPs are much more complex. These people, largely belonging to the vulnerable sections of the population such as religious and ethnic minorities, indigenous people, dalits, the urban poor, and so on, get displaced because of their vulnerability and often stay displaced for indefinite periods. The reasons behind these displacements are numerous, including conflict, controversial development projects, ecological problems, climate-related hazards, and change in laws such as forest laws and others. The largest numbers of displacements happen because of development projects such as dam building, mining, shrimping, urban beautification projects, and building theme parks and, most recently, formation of Special Economic Zones. The beautification of Dhaka during the SAF games displaced thousands from the slums and the brothels. The development paradigm favoured by much of the post-colonial world, including countries in South Asia, has inevitably resulted in massive displacements of the vulnerable sections of the population. This is because the cost of development is not borne equally by all sections of the society. The poor largely bear the cost but the rich benefit. The construction of over 4300 dams in India alone has resulted in the displacement of about 21 million to 40 million people according to one estimate.[4] Most of these are indigenous people. One of the main reasons for the displacement of the indigenous population is that over 80 per cent of coal and 40-50 per cent of other minerals are found in areas inhabited by indigenous people in South Asia. Much of their land is owned by the community so they have no papers for individual ownership of land. According to colonial law what belongs to the community is known as state property. Very often the indigenous people are considered as evicted and not as displaced once they are moved from their land because if they are termed as IDPs they automatically get certain rights within the legal system. The total number of those displaced due to development projects according to a number of researchers is as large as 50 million.[5]

That the whole process of displacing people for development projects and then rehabilitating IDPs was done in a flawed manner in much of South Asia became apparent from the results garnered from the first of these mega dam building projects. While building the Hirakud Dam, the first Indian mega dam, about 183,000 acres of land was submerged, affecting 294 villages. The displaced population got 7,216 acres of agriculture and 206 acres of homestead land, which was hardly enough for survival of so many people. Thus, many people remain yet to be relocated let alone rehabilitated. It has been over sixty years since this dam has been completed and yet about 10,000 people are still not rehabilitated.[6]

Apart from development-related displacement, there are many who are displaced due to conflicts. In the border between India and Pakistan an estimated 265,000 people are displaced. Thousands of people remain displaced in Northeast

India because of conflict. In 2008 itself the violence between Bodos and Bengali Muslims in Assam created 128,000 IDPs. The number increased manifold in the ongoing conflict in 2012. According to one estimate 'there were altogether 485,921 refugees in 340 relief camps during the height of the violence which began on July 19, claiming 96 lives.[7] Among others in the last count there are over 31,000 displaced Brus (Reangs) in Mizoram and Tripura. According to some estimates there are over 600,000 people displaced due to conflict in Northeast India alone. By 2008 there were 148,000 people displaced due to conflict with the Naxalites or Maoists in Chhattisgarh. Apart from IDPs caused by conflict, India faces periodic cyclones, earthquakes and floods including the tsunami of 2004 that have displaced thousands. Every year there are severe floods in the Bengal-Bangladesh border that displaces an indeterminate number of people. Also it has to be mentioned that IDPs cannot be boxed into a neat category. Often those who are displaced once can face multiple displacements, sometimes because of conflict, then for ecological disasters, and later for settling in a place that is marked for a developmental project. Therefore, sometimes it becomes impossible to know whether displacement was due to conflict, development or ecological conditions. What remains is the increasing vulnerability of population leading to protracted situations of displacement.

South Asia's list of forced migrants does not stop here. There are thousands living in India, Pakistan, Bangladesh, Nepal and Sri Lanka who are stateless, such as 28,000 Indian Tamil plantation workers who repatriated from Sri Lanka but never got their citizenship back. There are some 65,000 stateless Chakmas living in India according to the 1991 census and their numbers may have risen to 70-80,000 at present. There are also a number of Chinese, Bhutanese, Biharis from Bangladesh and Chitmahalis (people living in Chitmahals or enclaves in rivers in the border of Bengal and Bangladesh) who too are stateless. In Bangladesh there are many Bihari

Muslims who are stateless and in Nepal there are Bhutanese, known as refugees, who are actually stateless. Sometimes these stateless people are able to get access to ration cards or voter ids and their situation improves. Otherwise they remain in morbid situations of penury with a high risk of push back and deportation.

None of the South Asian countries are signatory to the 1951 Convention and the 1967 Protocol. Although most South Asian states are aware of the UN Guiding Principles on IDPs, none of them have enacted laws that protect IDPs. The National Human Rights Action plan developed by the Sri Lankan government in 2011 is currently being translated into both official languages prior to the approval of the cabinet of ministers. It focuses on avoidance, prevention from arbitrary displacement, calling for institutionalized focus in all development planning processes, a component on displacement, and that displacement must be justified by compelling and overriding public interest (the plan is in pursuance of undertakings by the government within the Universal Periodic Review of Member States and Human Rights). This is to be in accordance with a National Policy on Displacement. Yet till date full-proof protective measures could not be developed. Although India's record with refugees is not especially bad, its record with the IDPs is not as good, and it might be because their numbers are overwhelmingly large. India has an R and R (Resettlement and Rehabilitation) policy. At present an R and R bill is waiting to become an act for IDPs affected by developmental projects, where they are promised both land and jobs in the project. But to get that status the project-affected IDPs need to consist of at least 200 families (if affected in the hill areas) and 400 families (if affected in the plain lands). For the hills this is quite a large number, especially when one considers the situation of Northeast India where already thousands of people are displaced due to conflict and 300 dams are being planned that have a potential to displace entire hill tribes. Also, the Government of India is aware of the Guiding Principles; for IDPs affected by conflicts, it has the Communal Violence Bill. However, more than these measures, Articles 14 to 21 in the Indian Constitution promise many rights to people who are living in India even without citizenship and the most important of these is the Right to Life. Most courts in India are known to adhere to these rights even if it is regarding a non-citizen, refugee or forced migrant. However, more than the institutional response it is the kith and kin response that makes South Asia unique. Over two-thirds of the forced migrants are given resettlement by family and friends. This is slowly changing.

It is a sad truth that attitude to forced migrants has subtly changed all over Asia with fresh bouts of huge migrations, and after South Asian countries faced innumerable terrorist attacks now citizens have a threat perception about these foot-loose people. One of the reasons for the growing insecurity of the people about forced migrants is because it is very difficult to pigeon-hole them. It is getting more and more difficult to understand and categorize reasons for displacement. Conflict can make the oustees again face displacement; or they may be displaced because of ecological issues or because of purposes of development. Also with the growing number of displaced the political ability or will to handle the situation is dwindling. This is cause for worry indeed.

While this book was being written and even after the contributors had turned in their chapters, massive cases of displacement were occurring in South Asia while the political will to address it was being persistently challenged. The first of these was a natural disaster in the Sunderbans area caused by cyclone Aila. Newspapers carried stories about individual plights such as the following: 'Sabita Mondal, 32, Kanchan Sarkar, 28, and Saraswati Halder, 33, from Rangabelia village have become climate refugees ever since cyclone Aila hit the Sunderbans delta on May 25. Today, Sabita is living in a country boat with her two children and her cow, while Kanchan has taken shelter at a nearby relief camp along with her two daughters.'[8] Soon there were questions about why Aila had happened. The clearing of thick mangrove cover was considered an important reason for such massive devastations. Soon there were questions about the government's will to protect. It was reported that: 'The pradhan of Nagendrapur gram panchayat, Gopal Halder, alleged that the state government has not provided any relief money. "They have not sent any money. So the relief work has been poor in the area,"'[9] Aila was followed by recurrent floods in Sindh where it was reported that millions of people were being displaced every year because of these floods.[10] The latest in this series are the 2012 riots in Kokrajhar, which I have mentioned earlier. Attacks on minorities are a recurrent phenomenon in South Asia. In Pakistan and Bangladesh, the Hindus and other groups such as Ahmadiyyas, feel threatened; in Sri Lanka the Tamils; in India a few years back Christians were attacked in Kandhamal, and recently it is the Muslims who are perceived as 'outsiders' once again in Kokrajhar. Hence the timeliness of this volume as it is meant to analyse how best the mixed and massive displaced in South Asia can be protected both by the state, international communities and by the people. This remains the overriding concern regarding forced migration in South Asia.

THE ISSUE OF PROTECTION

Institutions, governments, inter-governmental organizations and people engaged in protection of human rights and humanitarian protection of the victims of forced migration are aware today that the situations they confront are not demarcated by clear typologies of forced migration. The situation is not only characterized by massive migration flows, but mixed flows. Refugees, asylum-seekers, illegal immigrants, internally displaced population groups, and other victims of violence, want, deprivation, hunger, homelessness, displacement, and other forms of persecution and discrimination have now become parts of massive and mixed flows in the face of which the old forms and principles of protection are often proving inadequate.

These early signs of transgression of boundaries in the map of forced migration have led governments and humanitarian agencies to adopt newer strategies to face massive displacements and unrest. The need to improve the humanitarian strategy is most visible in the international context where boundary transgressions appear as more pronounced. One can refer to, in this context, the recent move by the Office of the United Nations High Commissioner for Refugees (UNHCR) in the form of a 'Ten-Point Plan of Action for Refugee Protection and Mixed Migration'. The action plan towards protection of refugees in situations of mixed migration includes issues of cooperation among key partners, data collection and analysis, building protection-sensitive entry systems, reception arrangements, mechanisms for profiling and referral, differentiated processes and procedures, addressing secondary movements, return arrangements for non-refugees and alternative migration options, and finally, an appropriate information strategy.

Similarly, the International Committee of the Red Cross and Red Crescent (ICRC) in its Thirtieth International Conference has pointed out that the humanitarian assistance: for example, providing food, shelter, clothing, health care, first aid, psychosocial support, and so on, have to be increased and improved, that protection activities have to go deeper, and advocacy work has to be stronger. The ICRC followed this up with articulating its concern on escalating violence in the cities, once again where hordes of migrants converge. The concern has been of other humanitarian institutions too.

In this context of massive and mixed flows of forced migration, an analysis of the South Asian situation and protection strategies undertaken in South Asia becomes imperative. Such an analysis needs to respond to certain questions:

- What is the nature of the pronounced population flows in South Asia today?
- What are the consequences of mixed and massive flows in terms of erstwhile policies for the protection of the victims of forced migration?
- What are the protection strategies that are today adopted, and what are the best practices in this regard?
- How to ensure greater civil society participation in the protection of the victims of the abuses of human rights?
- What can be the architecture of such an appropriate new structure of protection that may require the participation of several agencies?
- What is the impact of resource crisis, environmental disorders and disasters, and climate changes on the patterns of migration?
- Finally, what impact can we envisage of such a dialogue on state, inter-governmental, and non-governmental protection strategies?

To address these questions Mahanirban Calcutta Research Group (hereafter MCRG) in collaboration with the UNHCR decided to hold a two-day dialogue on 'Protection Strategies in South Asia' on 14-15 December 2009. Some thirty experts (including UNHCR functionaries) participated in this dialogue from all over South Asia and Geneva. Among the experts there were both scholars and activists. This book is a product of research undertaken due to the dialogue, completed in two years following that dialogue. The dialogue was meant to help refocus the various protection strategies and needs in South Asia in the context of the new situation. South Asia has witnessed massive population exodus, transfer of population groups, creation of statelessness, all kinds of forced migration, massive cyclone and tsunami disasters, but at the same time unprecedented measures have been provided of relief, rehabilitation, refugee protection, and informal help to victims of various forms of displacement. And yet all these happen without a strong legal framework either to refuse or to offer protection. The South Asian experiences, in short, are worth observing closely so that appropriate lessons are drawn. These experiences have been chronicled both by social scientists, media analysts and civil society activists and so the writings bear their distinctive style.

MASSIVE FLOWS IN SOUTH ASIA: WHAT TO DO?

At the end of 2007, the total population of conflict-related IDPs, according to the Internal Displacement Monitoring Centre, stood at a staggering 26 million, while the number of refugees under UNHCR's responsibility, by its own estimate, amounted to 11.4 million. Roughly one-third of the global refugee population and 3.1 million IDPs were to be found in the Asia-Pacific region alone. The number of refugees in Asia would be significantly higher if one were to include the 'partition refugees'. The 'Ten-Point Plan of Action for Refugee Protection and Mixed Migration', a UNHCR policy paper, lays out a comprehensive system of identifying and addressing protection needs of refugees and other people of concern to the High Commissioner. Durable solutions discussed in the context of refugee protection traditionally include *voluntary* repatriation, local integration and resettlement in third countries. In the context of globalization and post-9/11 threat perceptions, however, the consensus on protection regimes, at the core of which lie the 1951 Refugee Convention and 1967 Optional Protocol, has begun to unravel. The principle of *non-refoulement* has come under intense pressure. Northern countries have been waiving immigration requirements for highly qualified professionals, while simultaneously curtailing the rights of refugees and asylum-seekers in favour of institutional guarantees, temporary protection schemes and third country procedures. Countries in the Global South, on the other hand, have voiced their incomprehension as to why they would be expected to abide by standards that the North no longer seemed to be willing to accept even though, in terms of both total numbers and proportion, the latter assumed only a fraction of the global responsibilities for refugees. Meanwhile, it is clear that any strategizing for comprehensive protection systems will only be meaningful in the framework of a participatory global dialogue, with substantial input from quarters of the Global South. The invitation to dialogue thus stands out as the central theme of the Ten-Point Plan of Action.

Dialogue has not come easy in a world of ideas cut into chunks and pieces befitting ideological convenience. It is surely no coincidence that the scenario of displacement reminds one of Frantz Fanon (1925-1961), a psychiatrist born in Martinique, a fighter for the independence of Algeria and a stout anti-colonialist. Fanon, in his book *The Wretched of the Earth* (1961), noted that both the 'colonizer' and the 'colonized' had their work cut out for them. The colonizer was busy making sure that the colonized found it impossible to do so much as dream of freedom; the colonized, on the other hand, was occupied with exploring even the remotest possibility of overthrowing the colonizer. The theory of the indigenous being 'bad in absolute terms' had found its mirror-image—so Fanon—in the theory of the colonizer being 'bad in absolute terms'. In Fanon's days, the dichotomy of the discourse on world governance could not be overcome. The creation of the *homme neuf*, the new man, with a skin not black and white but sensitive to the notion of justice, remained a utopian idea, a goal unattained.

Many of the contributors in this volume betray a lingering sense that aggression, oppression, domination and structural violence still constitute the cornerstones of the 'post-Fanon' world order. In terms of newer theories of protection, the text *Territory, Authority, Rights* (2008) by Saskia Sassen has highlighted the importance of developing 'democracy across borders' and 'participatory politics that decentre and sometimes transcend national political life', including the territorial fixation of the nation-state. But the contributors in this volume betray a sense of unease with such an argument. They caution against prematurely wishing the state away. In the face of a global financial meltdown, they say there was a strong possibility of world civil society having its funding dry up and programmes designed to meet protection needs significantly pruned. If that turns out to be the case, it is for the states to step into the fray and provide alternative funding in order to avoid a situation where protection gaps fuel another cycle of violence and displacement.

In this volume we will also find research on the complexities of globalization. Pockets of the First World can today be found in the Third World, and the global financial crisis, coming with a heavy loss of jobs, has removed any doubt (if proof was needed) that the Third World has made serious inroads into the First World, too. We have come to understand that as a result the fault lines of migration patterns are increasingly becoming blurred. And yet, empirical evidence shows that most refugees take shelter in countries neighbouring their own or, in any event, remain in the region. This finding is important because the outbreak of armed conflict along ethnic, religious or political lines is still very much the 'prerogative' of the Third World, along with the resultant flight from persecution. The concentration of displacement in the Global South brings home the urgency of burden-sharing, an issue which, despite all rhetoric to the contrary, has remained so far unresolved. The blame game between donor and refugee-hosting countries reminds us of pre-existing thinking patterns not unlike those in circulation in the colonial era, thinking patterns that block the search of overarching (just and fair) solutions.

The contributors touch on the question of how the imposition of the Western model of the state on large swaths of the Global South has triggered refugee flows of unprecedented proportions (partition) and entrenched the distinction between 'insider' and 'outsider' that is inherent in identity politics, albeit not just in South Asia. Rendering people stateless is an absurdity, but one that citizenship laws seem to have been universally fond of. It is also acknowledged that climate change knows no borders. The challenges of population movement resulting from global warming are unprecedented and cannot be met by the ratification of a treaty or policies devised on a national scale. So there is an increasing realization among practitioners and academics alike that massive and mixed migration flows, common in South Asia, elude existing definitions and protection frameworks. At the same time, it is undeniable that migrants of all strands require effective safeguards against violence, deprivation, exploitation and exclusion. New conceptual ground thus needs to be broken to translate the complex displacement realities of a new era into sound policies. Against that backdrop, the volume has attempted to do something very important: embedding local assessment of coping capacities and regional thinking on protection needs in global processes of decision making.

WAYS TO PROTECT

K. M. Parivelan in Chapter 1 'Protection Needs, Current Legal Avenues and New Legal Strategies: South Asian Perspective' underlined the need for clarifying the notions of ethnicity and (multiple) identity to be able to understand the reasons and consequences of forced migration in South Asia. He echoed Uttam Das (see Chapter 3) in regretting the absence of a legal framework for the protection of displaced populations, stating that the protection needs of the displaced were not adequately being addressed by a case-by-case approach. In policy terms, Parivelan highlighted the importance of nurturing a culture of hospitality in hosting populations, ensuring protection in regions of origin and establishing refugee camps at a safe distance from the border. Enumerating various categories of displacement in South Asia, Partha Ghosh in Chapter 2 'Mapping the Mixed and Massive Human Flows in South Asia: Impact on Women, the Stateless and Other Disadvantaged Groups' pointed out that confusion surrounding the terminology of forced migration made it difficult to examine its socio-political impact. He confessed that he found it hard to reconcile to the traditional paradigm of power-driven international politics with the notion of borderless regions, but expressed hope that people-to-people contacts would eventually overcome the walls being built by states in South Asia. Uttam Kumar Das in Chapter 3 'Refugee Protection in South Asia: Review of the Ad Hoc Mechanism and the Way Forward' explored possible avenues towards comprehensive protection of the displaced in South Asia. Noting that none of the states in the region had signed and ratified the 1951 Refugee Convention, he cautioned against viewing the international legal regime on refugee protection as a panacea for the problems of South Asia (it was 'too narrow', 'eurocentric' and 'insensitive to Global South concerns'). Instead, he advocated the adoption of a rights-based national legal framework for the protection of the displaced as well as a regional mechanism for status determination under the auspices of the South Asian Association for Regional Cooperation (SAARC).

In Chapter 4 'The Politics of "Belonging" and "Exclusion": A Note on Refugees in South Asia,' Nasreen Chowdhory pointed out that the tragedy that plagues the un-homed is that once removed they find it impossible to return to the home that they left behind; that is, once displaced, the refugee became essentially homeless, not just in their state of refuge but also when they were repatriated. When thrown out of their country of origin, the country of asylum looked upon them as unexpected guests and at worst they were seen as undesired infiltrators. In the country of asylum there is always the thought that these people will go back to their country of origin one day. Even UNHCR considers voluntary repatriation as the best among the suggested durable solutions. If by some remarkable stroke of fate the refugee is able to go back to her country of origin, she finds that it is no longer her own/her home, that there can be no return to that mythical home that they had dreamt of in their refuge. Thus, essentially, once homeless, a refugee is fated to remain an outsider. Working with similar assumptions and drawing on the South Asian experience, Bhavani Fonseka in Chapter 5 'Do the Displaced Have a Right to Return? South Asian Experiences' examined the concept of the right to return, in international and domestic law, as one option among others to be made available to refugees and IDPs. Fonseka insisted that national governments, assisted by UN agencies and international NGOs, take the lead in devising and implementing laws and policies designed to ensuring return, reintegration and rebuilding of lives and livelihoods in safety and dignity. In an important qualifier, she maintained that legislative measures were not going to help resolve situations if they were rushed into and ill-advised.

Hina Shahid, a young researcher and activist from Pakistan in Chapter 6 'Pakistan: Displacement Puts Thousands at Risk' wrote how processes of urbanization were effecting displacement and erecting markers of class, adding that the armed forces were major stakeholders in Pakistan's mega projects. She cited as examples Guadar Port City in Balochistan, the Liari Expressway (displacing people from a particular community) and Karachi beach. Those projects, rather than helping the communities concerned, were creating communal and ethnic tensions. And yet, whenever project-induced displacement took place, it was vocally justified in the name of the nation. In an obvious reference to James Scott's criticism of the concept of 'high modernism'[11] Shahid remarked that the sanctioning of Pakistan's dam projects on the heels of General Ayub Khan's introduction of five-year development plans spoke volumes of the disrespect of decision makers for the people on the spot. In conclusion, Shahid advised that the time had come for the myth of national development to be dismantled and the notion of 'collective good' be replaced by a democratic process of ascertaining the varied and contradictory interests of plural society, in Pakistan and elsewhere.

The contributors were of the opinion that trouble started at the borders both territorially and metaphorically. Recalling the burden of partition, Paula Banerjee in Chapter 7 'Humanitarian Aspects of Borders in the East and the Northeast' stated that despite '1001 linkages' security concerns overwhelmed 'all other equally legitimate concerns and values' in the way border regimes were enforced and borderlands 'managed' in South Asia. Borders, she said, were not just lines drawn on a map but places in which, with routine impunity, girls and women were trafficked and security forces engaged in shelling each other, destroying lives and livelihoods of civilians in the process. The media, rather than playing a constructive role in turning the borderlands into liveable areas, contributed to the threat perception associated with borders in the east and Northeast. Borderlands were portrayed as breeding ground for criminal activities and health hazards ranging from terrorism to drug smuggling and HIV/AIDS. Banerjee predicted that the situation of the borders in South Asia would not improve unless and until the plight of the people living in their vicinity was properly addressed.

Anuradha Bhasin Jamwal in Chapter 8 'Victims of Violence in the Borders and Humanitarian Tasks: The Jammu and Kashmir Case' argued that borders were not just delineations of territory but also 'zones of ambiguity' whose resident population took the brunt of a flawed security discourse focused on national assertiveness. Providing empirical evidence from Jammu and Kashmir, Bhasin showed how cross-border firing, landmines, fencing, interference and repression represented aspects of everyday life in the borderlands. While the nation asserted itself in the defence of symbols and the carrying out of rituals, people were forced to migrate across the international border, the Line of Control

(LoC) or further inland. What was the meaning of security, she asked, if people on the borders continued to be victimized, deprived of their identity and rendered homeless?

In Chapter 9 'Media and Displacement: Erasure, Aggravated Focus, Identity Building', Pamela Philipose judged the media coverage of disaster or conflict-induced displacement as 'episodic, fractured and insubstantial'. She juxtaposed the media's ability to cover events comprehensively in real time with a lack of attention to the story behind the story. Displacement was framed in 'entertainment-driven' narratives that would alternatively overexpose or trivialize the plight of affected people. Stories of displacement all too often also served the goal of constructing a 'national identity'. Philipose argued that the media was in a position to play a role much more conducive to generating understanding about the root causes of displacement if it were to stop viewing migration through the prism of 'national security' and to adopt a set of frames focused on 'people's security' instead. With that goal in mind, 'circular information' patterns and the 'immersion of the media in national security politics' had to be exposed, she ventured.

Providing case studies from South Asia, in particular Bangladesh, Subir Bhaumik in Chapter 10 'Climate Change, Environmental Refugees and Future Conflict Patterns in South Asia: Ominous Portents' maintained that the manifold manifestations of climate change, such as rising sea levels, melting glaciers, droughts and floods, were translating into a new pattern of conflict over resources, in particular water. To the extent that people affected by climate change chose to resort to the most radical means of adaptation, which was migration, they found borders getting fenced and their grievances dismissed (prawn cultivation, for instance, flourishes in saline water but needs much fewer people than farming).

Highlighting the diversified needs flowing from various strands of displacement in South Asia, Jeevan Thiagarajah in

Chapter 11 'Protection as Recovery: A Commentary from Sri Lanka' touched on the concept of human security (as enunciated in Armatya Sen's writing) and the role of the state, including its reluctance to take concerted, also legislative, action in the face of protracted displacement. What emerged from the paper and the following discussion was the paradox that even where the state had chosen to act, the waters had been muddled, more than root causes of displacement eradicated (notion of positive discrimination as a 'necessary evil'). Commenting on the massive displacement in Sri Lanka, Thiagarajah referred to the UN Guiding Principles on Internal Displacement as a 'useful' complementary tool 'to ensure the protection of IDPs' in contrast to Hina Shahid who in Chapter 6 has qualified the Guiding Principles as a reflection of 'weak policy'.

The contributors grappled with another phenomenon. This is the growth of Human Rights Commissions (HRCs) side by side with growing human rights abuse of the displaced. Explaining the proliferation of HRCs the world over against the backdrop of a 'new culture of governance', Shiva Dhungana in Chapter 12 'Policies and Practices of the National Human Rights Commission (NHRC) on the Internally Displaced Person (IDPs) in Nepal' pointed out that the Nepali HRC had come a long way since its inception in 1997. The HRC had not only become a constitutional body but also increased its presence in the field and its capacity to train staff and cooperate with civil society. On the other hand, the HRC still lacked a holistic approach and programme continuity, while having very limited reach and little investigative capacity. Dhungana lamented that recommendations were often not implemented ('no response by the government'), the compensation framework was inadequate, interaction with the media insufficient and data management in its infancy. Further obstacles were posed by political interference and undue politicization of human rights issues. NGOs continued to play a vital role in meeting the protection needs of the displaced, he said, be it with regard to assessing conditions or providing allocation for return or looking into issues of security, livelihood or return of property.

Explaining the proliferation of HRCs the world over against the backdrop of a 'new culture of governance', Mario Gomez in Chapter 13 'National Human Rights Commissions (NHRC)s and Internally Displaced Persons (IDPs): The Sri Lankan Experience' stated that the protection of IDPs had increasingly been incorporated into the mandate of HRCs. Among the IDP-related activities conducted by HRCs, he counted the following: monitoring the access of displaced populations to basic supplies and services; conducting camp visits and field surveys; handling complaints; engaging with the armed forces and militants to minimize consequences for the war-affected population as well as assisting in the drafting of policy and legislation. The Sri Lankan HRC, in his assessment, had capacity and potential but was faced by a host of difficulties. It was operating in adverse political conditions he said, aside from being handicapped by structural deficiencies, including the procedure for appointment of commissioners.

South Asia today is a region combining push and pull factors for migration. Economic growth rates and human development indices stand in stark contrast. The region boasts ethnic diversity, natural resources and human capital. At the same time, poverty is rampant, armed conflict endures and climate change threatens lives and livelihoods, especially in the 'low elevation coastal zones'. South Asia is the key to the success of global campaigns designed to meeting the Millennium Development Goals, mitigating the humanitarian consequences of asymmetrical development, including intra-state conflict, and reversing conditions leading to global warming. Success or defeat of these campaigns will make a world of a difference for millions of people. Maybe they will stay home. Or maybe they will be on the move. So what can be done? The contributors hoped that wherever these millions are forced to live, their lives and dignity will be protected without governments going into long-drawn analysis as to whether they are refugees, IDPs or economic migrants. The South Asian example portrays that such categorizations are no longer viable and displacement due to Tsunami and Hunger all amounts to the same, which is trauma of the vulnerables in a vulnerable region of the world.

Kolkata, December 2012

PAULA BANERJEE
MCRG

NOTES

1. There are many accounts that give a much larger number. For a discussion on numbers see Pradip Bose, 'A Review of Research in Refugee Studies', *Refugee Watch 36* (December 2010), p.4.
2. For a scholarly account of gender in the politics of partition refer to Ritu Menon and Kamla Bhasin, *Borders and Boundaries: Women in India's Partition* (New Delhi: Kali for Women, 1998) and Urvashi Butalia, *The Other Side of Silence: Voices from the Partition of India* (New Delhi: Kali for Women, 1998).
3. For an extensive discussion on refugee flows in India, see Ranabir Samaddar, *Refugees and the State: Practices of Asylum and Care in India 1947-2000* (New Delhi, Sage, 2003).
4. Bansuri Taneja, and Himangshu Thakkar, 'Large Dams and Displacement in India', Cape Town, South Africa: Submission no. SOC166 to the World Commission on Dams, 2000. http://www.dams.org/kbase/submissions/showsub.php?rec=SOC166
5. Sibaji Pratim Basu, 'The "Other" in the "Self": IDPs in India (A Status Report)', paper presented at the Regional Consultation of Citizen's Voices on 'The Challenges for South Asia: Human Rights and Democracy' organized by South Asians for Human Rights, held in Kathmandu, 27-29 Nov, 2010; available at http://www.southasianrights.org/wp-content/uploads/2012/03/IDP-Report-India.pdf. Last accessed on 5.12.12.

6. For an extensive discussion on the Hirakud Dam, see Arun Kumar Nayak, 'Development, Displacement and Rehabilitation in India and Bangladesh: A Comparative Study of Hirakud and Kaptai Dam', PhD Diss, South Asian Studies Division, SIS, JNU, 2008.
7. 'New Refugees Arrive in Kokrajhar Barpeta', *The Hindu*, Guwahati, 4 Sept 2012. file:///D:/Forced%20Migration The%20Hindu%20%20%20States%20%20%20Other%20 States%20%20%20Other%20States%20%20%20New%20 refugees%20arrive%20in%20Kokrajhar,%20Barpeta.htm; Last accessed on 5.12.12.
8. Soma Mitra, 'Aila, the Cry from Sunderbans', *The Times of India*, 23 Dec 2009. http://articles.timesofindia.indiatimes.com/2009-12-23/flora-fauna/28097464_1_potable-water-sunderbans-drinking-water. Last accessed on 6.12.12.
9. 'Cyclone Aila Affects Agriculture in Sunderbans', *The Deccan Herald*, 30 May 2010. http://www.deccanherald.com/content/72400/cyclone-aila-affects-agriculture-sunderbans.html. Last accessed on 5.12.12.
10. *The Express Tribune*, Islamabad. http://tribune.com.pk/story/448139/2012-floods-hit-sindh-the-hardest-ndma/. Last accessed on 6.12.12.
11. James C. Scott, *Seeing Like a State: How Certain Schemes to Improve the Human Condition Have Failed* (New Haven, Yale University Press, 1998).

PART I

Conflict-Induced Situations

1

PROTECTION NEEDS, CURRENT LEGAL AVENUES AND NEW LEGAL STRATEGIES: South Asian Perspective

K. M. PARIVELAN

In South Asia, we have mirror images of conflicts, displacements and forced migration, due to causes such as ethnic/religious strife, faulty developmental programmes, globalization or natural disasters. Refugees, asylum-seekers, illegal immigrants, internally displaced persons (IDPs) and other victims of violence and displacement have now become part of the migration flows in face of which the previous norms and principles of protection are often seen as inadequate. In this chapter an attempt is made to analyse and understand the causes of ethno-religious tensions in the region. The complex phenomena of other forms of forced migration which are due to non-protection reasons, such as poverty and environmental degradation, are adding complexity to the issues of concern pertaining to refugees, who deserve international protection. Mixed migration is of rising importance, both in terms of sheer numbers and with regard to its political significance at the national and regional levels. This reflects the tendencies for an increasing number of people to migrate at growing distances and with greater risks, in search of a better future in relatively affluent parts of the region. It also indicates that people are on the move for a combination of reasons that fundamentally are related to safeguarding physical and economic security. Thus, migration is very much linked to coping with livelihood problems caused by complex issues such as persecution, political turmoil and armed conflict, poverty, environmental problems arising out of climate change, population pressure and natural disasters. It is not only within this region that massive and mixed migration occurs; it also spills over to other parts of the world for purposes of work, education or family reunion.

In this context, an attempt will be made to unravel the current legal avenues working in the region in the absence of accession to the 1951 Refugee Convention or 1967 Protocol (with the exception of Afghanistan) and the possible new legal strategies vis-à-vis protection needs and human rights perspectives in approaching the problems in the intersection of asylum and mixed migration. The main focus is on the Indian experience of forced migration, though references to other parts of the South Asian region are also being made.

In December 2007, António Guterres, United Nations High Commissioner for Refugees (UNHCR), observed, 'Global refugee numbers have not increased dramatically in recent years. They had even decreased for a number of years prior to 2006. But the challenge of providing these and other displaced people with protection and solutions has not become any easier. This is particularly the case in situations where refugees are moving alongside people who are not in need of international protection.'

AN OVERVIEW OF SOUTH ASIAN ETHNICITY

The South Asian situation on ethnicity and related tensions is inevitably nebulous and shrouded in uncertainty. Max Weber defines ethnic group as 'one whose members entertain a subjective belief in their common descent because of similarities of physical type or of customs or both, or because of memories of colonization and migration'. Ethnicity consists of features shared by group members, such as same or similar geographic origin, language, religion, food, traditions, folklore, music and residential patterns. Also typical are special political concerns, particularly with regard to homeland, institutions to serve the group, and a consciousness of a kind or a sense of distinctiveness from others. Language is one of the pertinent markers to understand ethnicity. It is an intrinsic component of the socio-political realities of multi-ethnic states in South Asia, as in other parts of the world. Presently, ethnicization of politics and politicization of ethnicity have become very common and have diffused mutual toleration, thus, sharpening ethnic consciousness among various communities.

It may be necessary to dwell upon the factors that condition ethnic conflicts. The unequal power structure that exists in a state system (or even at the regional and global levels) could kick-off ethnic conflicts. In the event of the state structure being in the hands of a particular ethnic group, the dominant–subordinate group fights for power sharing for societal rewards and goods manifest themselves in ethnic terms. However, inequality in power sharing need not always lead to ethnic conflicts. Few pre-conditions exist for such conflicts—a socially mobilized population; the existence of a pool of symbols connoting its distinctiveness; the selection, standardization and transmission of such symbol pools to the community by the leadership; and a reference group in relation to whom a sense of relative deprivation (real or imaginary) is aggregated.[1]

'It is also evident that religion and language as components of ethnic identity are important in dividing as well as unifying groups in South Asia. For example, in Sri Lanka, language is a basis for intra-group unity amidst an internal cleavage along religious lines, whereas ethnic groups in Pakistan are divided along linguistic lines even though they share a common religion. In Bhutan, Buddhism tends to unify the linguistically divided Bhutanese and the Nepali-speaking migrants from Nepal. As regards India, language is a major unifying force for many groups in conflict, while religion remains the main source of conflict in a few cases—notably in Punjab and Kashmir. It is only in Bangladesh that both religion and language provide the basis for inter-group division and intragroup unity'.[2] This is the most significant trajectory in which ethnicity and related conflicts causing displacements add more complexity to the region.

The structural framework of the region—incorporating features such as close geographical proximity, socio-cultural linkages and interdependent politico-strategic relations of states—creates internal pressures for regionalization of ethnic conflict as an inevitable part of political life.[3] Table 1.1 provides an overview of the conflicts and the potential areas for conflict in South Asia, ranging from the autonomist to the secessionist and mixed variety.[4]

The colonial and post-colonial processes have tremendous influence on ethnic and religious identity shaping in South

Table 1.1 *Nature of Conflicts*

Autonomist	Secessionist	Mixed
Mohajir (Pak)	East Pakistan* (Pak)	Baloch (Pak)
Lhotsampa (BHU)	Sindh (Pak)	Pakhtun (Pak)
Chittagong Hill Tract (CHT) (Bang)	Eelam* (SL)	
Tripuri (Ind)	Kashmir (Ind)	
Bodo (Ind)	Khalistan* (Ind)	
Gorkha (Ind)	Dravidstan (Ind)	Assamese (Ind)
	Naga (Ind)	
	Mizo (Ind)	
	Meiti (Ind)	

* Autonomist conflict turned secessionist.

Source: P. Sahadevan, 'Ethnic Conflicts and Militarism in South Asia', *International Studies*, 39, 2 (2002), p.105.

Asia. There are widespread continuity and incongruities in language, culture and territorial boundaries as seen in the cases of those speaking Bengali in India and Bangladesh; Punjabi in India as well as Pakistan; Tamil in Sri Lanka and India; Nepali in India and Nepal; Sindhi in India and Pakistan; Kashmiri in India and Pakistan-occupied Kashmir (POK); and Urdu in India and Pakistan. Failure to appreciate multi-culturalism and pluralism in the political processes of South Asia in general and India in particular are the root causes to many of the ethnic tensions and forced displacements.

REFUGEE SCENARIO IN SOUTH ASIA

South Asia has witnessed forced movements of population in a huge manner. Countries in the region are both refugee-generating and refugee-hosting (*see* Introduction, p.viii). Colonial and post-colonial changes had tremendous impact on the forced migration situation in the region. The Partition of the Indian sub-continent in 1947 had produced nearly 15 million forced displacements. Other states in the region also had to deal with the problem of statelessness almost immediately after achieving political independence. In 1948, Burma (Myanmar) expelled an estimated 500,000 persons of Indian origin. During 1949-1950, the Government of Sri Lanka wanted India to take back Tamil plantation workers who were brought to the island by the British in the early nineteenth century and there were around 900,000 stateless persons in Sri Lanka. In 1971, during the Bangladesh War of Independence, an estimated 10 million out of a population of 70 million in East Pakistan sought refuge in India. Conflict between the inhabitants of the Chittagong Hill Tract (CHT) and the Bangladeshi government also led to influx of refugees into India. Bangladesh has been hosting the Urdu-speaking community or Biharis comprising about 2.5 million 'stateless persons', and about 258,000 Rohingya refugees from the adjoining Rakhine state (formerly Arakan) of Myanmar in the district of Cox's Bazar. Since 1991, Nepal has given refuge to more than 100,000 Bhutanese of Nepali origin from southern Bhutan (for details *see* Chapter 2).

Other challenges and protection issues

The mix of refugees and asylum-seekers along with the movement of people whose reasons for moving are different and not protection related is one of the most important challenges in forced migration, particularly more so in the context of increased terrorism and organized crimes in the region. More often than not, such movements are irregular, in the sense that they take place without the requisite documentation and frequently involve human smugglers and traffickers. The people who move in this manner often place their lives at risk, and are obliged to travel in inhumane conditions and may be exposed to exploitation and abuse. States regard such movements as a threat to their sovereignty and security.[5] We need to address this phenomenon in a coherent and comprehensive manner. Whether states have assumed or not the protection responsibilities for refugees under international instruments, it is their collective interest to address this issue more humanely either at the regional level or national level.

CHALLENGES FROM DEVELOPED COUNTRIES

Responding to the mixed migration trends and concerns, governments in the developed world have introduced a wide range of measures intended to obstruct or deter the arrival of people who intend to seek refugee status. These include more stringent visa and passport controls; restrictions on the rights and benefits provided to asylum-seekers; and the establishment of international agreements to address the situation of migrants who transit from one country to another.

In some respects, such measures appear to have had their intended effect, as the number of asylum applications submitted in the industrialized states seems to have declined in recent years. But there is also a growing awareness that restrictive asylum policies have fuelled the human smuggling industry because irregular entry is the only means of entry available. Such policies also seem to have encouraged new arrivals to go 'underground', rather than run the risk of detention and deportation by approaching the authorities and submitting a claim for refugee status.[6] Steps must be taken at the regional level as well as in the respective countries to establish organized legal frameworks to handle the massive and mixed flow of forced migration in South Asia.

These complex tendencies in the broad field of migration have contributed to increasing xenophobia in the receiving countries. This has been one of the key factors leading to the development of elaborate systems and barriers that regulate the movement of people across borders, in particular from the South to the North, but increasingly also within the South.[7] By themselves, these developments pose a challenge for agencies that deal with conflict-related displacement at a global level. We can rely on the definition of mixed migration as 'Complex population movements including refugees, asylum-seekers, economic migrants and other migrants'.[8] The term 'migrant' is usually understood to cover all cases where the decision to migrate is taken freely by the concerned individual for reasons of 'personal convenience' and without the intervention of any external compelling factor.[9]

In accordance with the human rights principle, no displaced person should be denied protection and durable solutions. Activities have traditionally focused on refugees—those internally displaced and those affected by conflict. However, in line with the above developments, it has become evident that these groups of concern are often mixed with other individuals and groups engaged in migratory movement. Distinguishing these groups from each other is increasingly difficult and perhaps even partially irrelevant, not only because of the mixed motivations for migrating, but also because of the frequent phenomena of changing status en route. A refugee may return to the place of origin to become an IDP again and later become a refugee in a neighbouring country or an IDP moving into a neighbouring country as a refugee, only to move on to other countries as a migrant in search of improved livelihood opportunities. This does not change the fact that he/she was forced to leave his/her country because of conflict and that he/she may not be able to return, but his/her legal status is nevertheless changing, depending both on own choices and on the policies of relevant authorities.[10]

CURRENT LEGAL AVENUES

A significant number of international instruments have defined and established standards for the treatment of refugees. The most important ones are the UN Convention Relating to the Status of Refugees, 1951 (hereafter 1951 Convention) and its 1967 Protocol. The Convention provides a general definition of the term 'refugee'. It defines any person as a refugee who 'as a result of events occurring before 1 January 1951 and owing to well-founded fear of being persecuted for reasons of race, religion, nationality, membership of a particular social group or political opinion, is outside the country of his nationality and is unable, or owing to such fear, is unwilling to avail himself of the protection of that country; or who, not having a nationality and being outside the country of his former habitual residence as a result of such events, is unable or, owing to such fear, is unwilling to return to it'[11] (*see* Chapter 3).

Although the refugee problem is a pertinent phenomenon in South Asia, none of the states did accede to the 1951 Convention or its Protocol of 1967, except Afghanistan. There is neither a regional framework nor any domestic legislation to deal with the issue. Here, refugees are subjected to the same laws as applicable under Foreigners Act, 1946. In the absence of any legal framework, asylum-seekers and refugees are dealt with through ad hoc administrative arrangements, which hardly take note of their individual protection needs. These arrangements given their very nature could be arbitrary and discriminatory (*see* Chapter 3). However, as the states in South Asia have been parties to major international human rights instruments, they are already under obligations despite of not becoming parties to the UNHCR Refugee Convention (1951).

NEW LEGAL STRATEGIES

UNHCR has spelt out a Ten-Point Action Plan to address the challenges emanating from mixed migration.

1. COOPERATION AMONG KEY PARTNERS
   Effective approaches to the dilemmas of mixed movements will inevitably depend upon full cooperation amongst the key actors concerned: affected states, governmental bodies, regional and international organizations with relevant mandates, for example, UNHCR, Office of the High Commissioner for Human Rights (OHCHR), the United Nations Children's Fund (UNICEF) and International Organization for Migration (IOM), as well as local and international non-governmental organizations (NGOs).

2. DATA COLLECTION AND ANALYSIS
   A key to any coherent and comprehensive strategy is the collection, analysis and exchange of data about the characteristics of the movement and the groups which make it up. Such data should typically include information related to conditions in countries of origin, motivations for movement, modes of transport, transit routes and entry points.

3. PROTECTION-SENSITIVE ENTRY SYSTEMS
   The establishment of a functioning entry system is an important element in any strategy related to mixed movements. Border control is essential for the purposes of combating international crime, including smuggling and trafficking, and averting security threats. Practical protection safeguards are required to ensure that such measures are not applied in an indiscriminate or disproportionate manner and that they do not lead to *refoulement* (*see* Chapter 3). In this respect, border guards and immigration officials would benefit from training and clear instructions on how to respond to asylum applications and handle the needs of separated children, victims of trafficking and other groups with specific needs.

4. RECEPTION ARRANGEMENTS
   Appropriate reception arrangements are needed to ensure that the basic human needs of people involved in mixed movements can be met.

5. MECHANISMS FOR PROFILING AND REFERRAL
   Once new arrivals have been registered and provided with temporary documentation, an initial determination will have to be made with regard to who they are, why they have left their own country and where their intended destination is. Counselling provides an opportunity to establish whether they wish to seek asylum and to identify other options available to them, including return, regularization or regular onward migration. This channelling arrangement would not constitute a refugee status determination.

6. DIFFERENTIATED PROCESSES AND PROCEDURES
   With respect to asylum claims, those which appear to be relatively simple (because they are well founded or manifestly unfounded) could be assessed in an expedited pro-

cedure. Other and more complex claims normally will require a more detailed assessment.

7. SOLUTIONS FOR REFUGEES
People who are recognized as refugees or as otherwise being in need of international protection require a protection-based response that includes a durable solution, the nature of which will depend on the opportunities and constraints inherent in each situation.

8. ADDRESSING SECONDARY MOVEMENTS
Addressing the situation of refugees and asylum-seekers who have moved on from countries where they had already found adequate protection requires a more defined strategy. This strategy should take into account both the legitimate concerns of states about irregular onward movement and the rights and well-being of the people concerned.

9. Return of non-refugees and alternative migration options
For people who are found not to be refugees, and for those who do not wish to seek asylum, expeditious return in safety and dignity is usually the preferred response of states. Efforts to address mixed population movements should also explore a place for regular migration options, temporary or even longer term.

10. INFORMATION STRATEGY
All the measures described earlier should be complemented by information campaigns in countries of origin, transit and destination. People need to be alerted to the dangers of irregular movement and the difficulties they might face upon arrival, as well as to any alternatives to irregular migration which might also meet their circumstances. UNHCR also has the capacity and interest to initiate public awareness activities about the plight of refugees

in order to promote tolerance and to combat racism and xenophobia.

Protection in regions of origin strategy

Seeking to resolve the mixed migration challenges, a growing number of governments in the developed world have expressed interest in the notion of 'protection in regions of origin'. Indeed, this concept was a dominant feature of the discussion at the October 2003 meeting of the executive committee of the UNHCR.

In simple terms, the notion of 'protection in regions of origin' is based on the principle that people who have fled from states that are affected by persecution, armed conflict, violence and instability should be able to find a safe refuge and enjoy acceptable living conditions in locations that are as close as possible to the borders of their own country. It is also based on the assumption that such refugees will try to move on to more prosperous parts of the world if they experience unacceptably high levels of physical and material insecurity in the regions of origin. According to its proponents, the 'protection in regions of origin' approach could, if effectively implemented, deter the need for refugees and asylum-seekers to make difficult migration journeys to distant parts of the world, whereas they could be made more comfortable in familiar cultural surroundings in the neighbourhood.[12]

In reality, this approach is not going to deprive human smugglers of their customers, as the reason for seeking asylum in a developed county is a mixed one. It is not going to reduce the pressures currently placed on the asylum and social welfare systems of the industrialized states, and in any case, it is not going to discourage the kind of xenophobic sentiments that have emerged in many parts of the developed world. It provides less opportunity for groups to interact and understand other cultures. There is nevertheless need for more rational debate on refugee policies and immigration. While the North expects the poor South to play host to refugees, it seeks to escape its obligations by constructing the non-entrée regime, and is now less than willing to share its financial burden. The central idea is to preserve unbelievable privileges for a section of its citizens.[13]

Firstly, arguments like by reducing asylum-related expenditures in the industrialized states, the 'protection in regions of origin' approach can make additional funding available for development assistance appears to be empty rhetoric and have a non-committal standpoint. Secondly, it has been suggested that if refugees can be accommodated safely in their regions of origin, they will be more likely to return to their country of origin once the persecution or violence that displaced them has come to an end. According to this argument, the tasks of repatriation and reintegration are also likely to be less expensive and simpler to organize in situations where refugees are located close to the borders of their own country. Here the question of cost or protection is to be answered. Take the example of the killing of K. Padmanabhan, leader of the EPRLF, a Sri Lankan Tamil group, in Chennai, allegedly by LTTE because of close geographical proximity. Thirdly, the argument that 'protection in regions of origin' approach would not necessarily prevent refugees and asylum-seekers from being admitted to countries in the developed world is not convincing because the scope for later resettlement automatically reduces when the asylum door is kept closed.

There is a tendency to shift from burden sharing to burden shifting itself. Experimentation with this model was made in northern Kenya, eastern Tanzania and northern Uganda, shifting the burden from East Africa which suffers from high levels of insecurity and low levels of development. The ideology of humanitarianism has used the vocabulary of human rights to legitimize the language of security in refugee discourse, blur legal categories and institutional roles, turn repatriation into the only solution and promote a neo-liberal agenda in post-conflict societies leading to the systematic erosion of the principles of protection and the rights of refugees.[14]

Significance of the 1951 Convention

The 1951 Convention (also *see* Chapter 3) has laid down a few significant clarifications:

- provided the foundational definition to the term 'refugee' (Article 1);
- embodied the principle of *non-refoulement* (*see* Chapter 3, p.65, note 20) according to which no person shall be returned to a territory where s/he may be exposed to persecution (Article 33);
- set the minimum standard of treatment of refugee, including the basic rights to be granted and the duties;
- contained provisions that concern their legal status, gainful employment and welfare;
- contained provisions regarding issues of identity and travel documents, naturalization and other administrative matters;
- required states to cooperate with UNHCR in the exercise of its functions, and to facilitate the task of supervising the application of the Convention.

When acceding to the Convention and/or Protocol, states may make reservations to certain clauses/articles, which they feel irrelevant or burdensome. There are, however, certain articles to which no reservations are permitted, and which acceding states must accept. They are as follows:

- Article 1 (refugee definition);
- Article 3 (non-discrimination as to race, religion or country of origin);

- Article 16 (1) (free access to courts);
- Article 33 (*non-refoulement*);
- Article 36–46 (information on national legislation; final clauses).

Reasons behind acceding to the 1951 Convention

Reasons that may inspire South Asian states to accede to the Refugee Convention of 1951 and the Protocol of 1967 are:

- South Asia accounts for nearly one-tenth of the global refugee population.
- States have already been hosting a significant number of refugees.
- Few states, for example, India and Bangladesh, are active members of the Executive Committee of the UNHCR (EXCOM) thereby playing a leading role in providing direction to UNHCR on global strategies and policies.
- States are already parties to major human rights instruments and have incorporated human rights protection as fundamental rights in its Constitution and other legislations.
- It is very important for aspiring global players like India to claim the UN Security Council seat. They need to demonstrate their global humanitarian commitments to uphold refugee rights in an exemplary manner. Besides making these issues a priority, there can be national legislations and regional framework convention as an additional or initial step.

PROTECTION: A CHALLENGE AND AN OPPORTUNITY

Irrespective of their legal status, many migrants included in these movements are vulnerable to hazards and violations of their human rights, including trafficking, human smuggling, inhuman treatment and loss of life. Such abuses and sufferings are strongly reflected in reports on migratory flows in South Asia. These developments have amplified the need for national governments and civil society to address the plight of people involved in mixed migration through a comprehensive approach that tackles protection gaps and identifies durable solutions. With rights-based vision for responding to violations and vulnerabilities throughout routes of mixed migration, we need to understand and evolve a national and/or regional framework.

With regard to the interface between asylum and mixed migration, specific issues relate to protection problems arising from the possibly growing presence of irregular migrants in India. Similarly, the forced return of rejected asylum-seekers continues to be of concern, in part because it, in some cases, may result in protection problems for the returnees and others in countries of return. The interface between integration and mixed migration constitutes both a challenge and an opportunity.

Following Afghanistan, India along with her neighbours needs to be guided in her response to the protection needs arising from mixed migration. It is of key importance for India to strive towards ensuring that none of its action has any negative impact on concerned individuals and groups either within the country or in the region. India has to base its strategies on a comprehensive analysis of the causes and effects of protection gaps in countries of origin. A collaborative approach is necessary at the regional level involving institutions, governments, inter-governmental organizations and people to ensure an appropriate, comprehensive and sustainable response to the broad range of protection problems arising from mixed movements.

NOTES

1 Urmila Phadnis, *Ethnicity and Nation-building in South Asia* (New Delhi: Sage Publications, 1989), p.27.
2 P. Sahadevan, 'Ethnic Conflicts and Militarism in South Asia', *International Studies*, 39, 2 (2002), p.103.
3 Ibid., p.104.
4 Autonomist states emphasize on gaining autonomy as permitted within the framework of the Constitution of India; secessionists, however, insist on abandoning the constitutional parameters.
5 'Refugee Protection and Mixed Migration: A 10-Point Plan of Action', Geneva: UNHCR.
6 Jeff Crisp, 'Refugee Protection in Regions of Origin: Potentials and Challenges', Migration Information Source, Washington, DC, December, 2003.
7 World Bank classifies the countries of the South as low- and middle-income countries and the high-income ones as those of the North.
8 Policy on Mixed Migration, Danish Refugee Council (DRC), Copenhagen, May 2008.
9 Glossary on Migration, International Organization for Migration (IOM), Geneva, 2004.
10 Policy on Mixed Migration.
11 Article 1, 1951 Convention.
12 Jeff Crisps, 'Refugee Protection in Regions of Origin'.
13 B.S. Chimni, 'Globalisation, Humanitarianism and the Erosion of Refugee Protection, RSC', Working Paper, 3, February 2000, University of Oxford.
14 Ibid.

2

MAPPING THE MIXED AND MASSIVE HUMAN FLOWS IN SOUTH ASIA: Impact on Women, the Stateless and Other Disadvantaged Groups

PARTHA S. GHOSH

The phenomenon of human flows, that is, movement of people, both as individuals or groups, from one place to another, is as ancient as humans on earth. Even recorded history talks about people changing their places of residence, like birds building their nests from one tree to another, or animals demarcating their territories, a subject dramatically highlighted by Nayan Chanda.[1] It is estimated that in 2005 there were about 190 million migrants worldwide that accounted for about 3 per cent of the global population.[2] The United States alone, which is one of the most attractive destinations for all international migrants, recorded the presence of 11.6 million illegal immigrants in 2006 of which 7 million were from Mexico. In other words, 4 per cent of the American population constituted of illegal immigrants.[3] The corresponding Indian figure would be 40 million, which is of course not the case, nor for the entire region of South Asia.

Still, the South Asian regional scene makes an interesting case to analyse for several reasons. Firstly, the region has witnessed massive inter-state and intra-state movements of people as no other region of the world has. In the last six decades, about 50 million people have been involved in the inter-state process alone and, if the intra-state processes are added, the numbers will swell multi-fold. Secondly, what makes the experience different is that almost the entire process is largely attributable to human failures, imperial machinations and mismanagement of inter-communal relationships (*see* Introduction) and not economic factors which are applicable in the case of North America or Europe.

The phenomenon has affected both political—domestic and inter-state—and social relationships in the region. Such is the reality in all such cases, the greatest victims are women and children. This chapter intends first to capture the process by mapping all the waves of migration and displacement in the region, both across the nations as well as within them, and then to underscore their socio-political impacts. Two categories of human flows, one, the rural–urban migration, and, two, the blue-collar labour migration to West Asia and the white-collar labour migration to the West, however, have been excluded from this analysis. Our explanations are as follows: one, both are structurally temporary phenomena; two, both are essentially voluntary acts, motivated by economic interests and three, no agency, state or non-state initiated this happening. One may argue that all economic migrations in the ultimate analysis fall within the category of forced migration but that logic is too far-fetched and will obfuscate effective policy interventions. Also, if one argues that rural–urban migration is not necessarily temporary, then one's methodological tools of analysis should probably be urbanization theories and not those of migration.

DELINEATING SOUTH ASIA

The origin of the idea of South Asia as a region can be traced to the late 1970s when South Asian regional cooperation was first mooted. Earlier notions in this regard were diffused both in terms of geography as well as conceptualization. The seven conferences that took place between 1947 and 1955, namely, the Asian Relations Conference (New Delhi, March 1947), Conference on Indonesia (New Delhi, January 1949), Baguio Conference (Baguio, Philippines, May 1950), Colombo Plan (July 1950), Colombo Powers Conference (Colombo, April 1954), Afro-Asian Conference (Bandung, Indonesia, April 1955), and the Simla Conference (May 1955) included countries from beyond the region. It was only during 1977–1980 when President Ziaur Rahman of Bangladesh suggested that the seven states of South Asia should work out a cooperative arrangement to ameliorate the economic problems of the region that the concept of South Asia as a region became popular. For many years thereafter, South Asia meant the seven nations that constituted the South Asian Association for Regional Cooperation (SAARC) which came into being in 1985. These nations were: Bangladesh, Bhutan, India, Maldives, Nepal, Pakistan and Sri Lanka. In 2008, Afghanistan was formally added to the group raising its membership to eight. Since Myanmar (Burma) was part of British India till mid-1930s and in many respects matters importantly for South Asia, several scholars suggest that it too should be included for a better understanding of the region. For the purposes of the present chapter, therefore, South Asia will connote the above nine states.

DEFINITIONAL CLARIFICATION

In discussing human flows, several words and phrases occur routinely. Since some of them are often used inter-changeably they create confusion. For example, 'migrants', 'refugees', 'illegal settlers' and 'displaced' persons are casually used to mean one for the other. The displaced Kashmiri pandits of the Valley are referred to as 'Kashmiri migrants' as much as illegal Bangladeshi settlers in India are called 'Bangladeshi infiltrators' or simply 'Bangladeshis'. Similarly, the IDPs are generically termed as 'refugees'. Even the Indian state, for example, the Government of West Bengal in the context of migrants from East Pakistan/Bangladesh, kept changing their designation from 'displaced' to 'migrants', to 'refugees' (*see* Chapter 1) and then to 'new migrants'.[4] Since each term has a specific definition, it must be understood individually.[5] However, as this chapter is concerned with the broad phenomenon of human flows in the region, all the categories have been merged under the comprehensive notion called human flows, or population movements. These movements are essentially involuntary, at least circumstantial, if not forced, and generally long term, at least not too short term by pre-meditation.

MAPPING THE MOVEMENTS

From a strictly conceptual and methodological point of view, all inter-state human traffic in South Asia can be put in just one category, that is, the failure of nation building and its fallout. For example, whether it is the question of Hindu–Muslim migration after India's Partition, or that of the Bengali refugee influx in India in the wake of Bangladesh Liberation War, or of Tamil or Arakanese refugees—all fall in the same broad category. But this helps neither in our understanding of the causes of migrations, nor their socio-political impacts. To make the exercise simpler and more meaningful, it is proposed to subdivide the category into several sub-categories based on the cause–effect dialectics giving full allowance to the inevitability of mutual overlaps. The sub-categories are as follows:

- colonial legacy of Partition;
- majoritarian nation-building approach;
- democratic deficit;
- open, or virtually open, borders;
- war-related migration;
- developmental and environmental migrants;

- stateless or the virtually stateless;
- extra-regional interventions;
- position of the IDP.

Colonial legacy of partition

Migrations that took place across India–Pakistan borders immediately before and after India's Partition, and which continued for several years thereafter, fall in this category. It is estimated that about 13 million people were involved in the process. During the 1950s, another 4 million each of Hindus and Muslims migrated to India and Pakistan (*see* Introduction).[6] The frequent communal strife in East Pakistan in the 1960s caused further exodus of Hindus to the Indian states of Assam, Tripura and West Bengal. Till 1964, the number of all such refugees was estimated to be 5.5 million.[7]

Majoritarian nation-building approach

Bengali Refugees: The exodus of millions of Bengali refugees to India during the Bangladesh Liberation War of 1970–1971 falls into this category. The denial of democratic rights to the East Pakistan-based Awami League to form the government following the general election of 1970 sharpened the already existing divide between the Punjabi-dominated Pakistan government and the Bengali population of East Pakistan. The liberation struggle invited an unprecedented repression from the Pakistani military junta causing an exodus of about 10 million East Pakistani refugees to India.

Bengali Hindu Refugees: Bangladesh, which was created in opposition to Punjabi majoritarianism, soon gave rise to Bengali Muslim majoritarianism targeting the minority Hindus. The Vested Property Act of Pakistan (1965) which had been reinforced by the Enemy Property (Custody and Registration) Order of 1965 in the aftermath of the Indo-Pak war of 1965 was not only retained, but actually consolidated by the Bangladesh Vesting of Property and Assets Order, 1972. It seriously disadvantaged the minorities, most notably the Hindus, who started leaving for India. The same happened to the Christians as well; although they were very small in number, not even 1 per cent of the country's population and constituting a better-educated lot, they mostly migrated to Kolkata.

Lhotsampa Refugees: In the late 1980s and early 1990s the majority Drukpas (Ngalongs and Sarchops combined), who controlled the Bhutanese state, forced about 90,000 ethnic Nepalis (Lhotsampas) to leave Bhutan and seek refuge in Nepal. About 20,000 went to India to places like Arunachal Pradesh, Assam, Sikkim and West Bengal. Out of them 7,000 in the Bomdila region of Arunachal Pradesh were at one point of time under threat of deportation because of the anti-foreigner campaign launched by the All Arunachal Pradesh Students Union. According to June 2007 statistics, there were 106,690 Bhutanese refugees in Nepal sheltered in seven camps.[8]

Indian Repatriates from Myanmar: Before 1937, Burma (present Myanmar) was part of British India. There were about 900,000 ethnic Indians holding important commercial and professional positions. After Burma's independence in January 1948, Burmese was made the official language, virtually forcing most of the Indians (mostly Hindus) to return. This process continued till 1960s when yet another exodus of about 150,000 Indians was triggered by the policy of nationalization of trade, industry, banking and commerce.[9]

Arakanese Refugees: In the 1970s, the same majoritarian policy forced the Arakanese, who were mostly Muslims, to leave for Bangladesh. The 1963–1964 census had revealed that the Arakanese Muslims had spread to the Yangon (Rangoon) and Delta areas. This alarmed the Bhama Buddhist authorities. To arrest the trend the Ne Win government prohibited the movement of Muslims beyond the Akyab district towards the east. The policy, however, failed. It not only impoverished the region badly, giving rise to youth unrest and insurgencies, but it also could not prevent the Muslims from settling in the area. The 1974 census revealed the hard reality of Muslims having spread to the eastern border and commercially important areas such as Mandalay, Pegu, Prome, Moulmein, Bassein, and so on.[10] A policy of repression of the Arakanese rebels followed, leading to large-scale migrations of Muslims to Bangladesh. Starting from 1977, about 260,000 such refugees arrived in Bangladesh.[11] By the end of 1996, almost all were repatriated.

Afghani Hindu/Sikh Refugees: From within the massive influx of Afghan refugees in Pakistan in the wake of the Soviet intervention in 1979, there was a fringe section that arrived in India. It consisted primarily of Hindus and Sikhs who had settled in the country for generations. According to the World Refugee Survey 1996, published by the United States Committee for Refugees, India hosted about 20,000 such Afghan refugees.

Democratic deficit

Tamil Refugees: The failure of the Sri Lankan state to solve the Sinhala-Tamil ethnic conflict within a democratic framework has led on the one hand to the deterioration of communal relationship between the majority Sinhalas and the minority Sri Lanka Tamils, and, on the other, to a long-drawn war between the government and the militant LTTE. Both these processes have resulted in insecurity among the Tamils, forcing many of them to flee to India and some Western countries for safety. The first batch of such refugees numbering about 30,000 came immediately after the anti-Tamil riots of July 1983. By May 1985 their number had increased to 100,000, by 1990 to 125,000, and by 1997 to 164,000. While almost half of them lived in refugee camps, the remaining half lived outside, with relatives (*see* p.39).[12] Many of the refugees have settled in India permanently.

Some refugees were identified as militants and particularly after the assassination of Rajiv Gandhi in May 2001, the refugees in general were seen with suspicion by the Indian state, so much so that they were virtually threatened to leave. For example, the collector of Tiruvanamalai district accompanied by the district police chief visited camp after camp to announce through the public address system: 'Aren't there any Tamils living on the island? Is only *your* life precious? We do not want you to be cowards and we do not want you to be unwelcome guests. We want you to go back because no education, nor work facilities, will be given to you.' The Home Ministry of the Government of India, however, intervened and the policy was toned down. In any case, by 1997, there were about 270 refugees who were identified as militants and they were put in three special camps.[13]

Bhutanese Political Refugees: The absence of democracy in Bhutan had also resulted in many Bhutanese, belonging to the same ethnic group as the ruling elite of Bhutan, leaving the country and seeking refuge in Nepal and India. This was apart from the ethnic Nepalis, referred to earlier. These exiles mostly belonged to the Sarchop community. The Druk National Congress, an exile political group of Sarchops, operated from Kathmandu and fought for the democratic rights of the Bhutanese people. In 1996, the organization claimed to have 32 active workers in Nepal, besides 977 'registered' members in Bhutan.[14]

Chin-Burmese Refugees: There has been some flow of Myanmarese refugees to India also on account of the repressive policies of the State Law and Order Restoration Council (SLORC). Most of these refugees belong to the Chin tribe and have settled in Mizoram, some are Nagas who have taken shelter in Arunachal Pradesh and Nagaland. There were only 267 Burmese refugees in India as recognized by the UNHCR though the actual number could be about 2,000. Ever since the junction of India-Myanmar-Bangladesh has become an integrated economic corridor, the migration and settlement of the Chin-Burmese people in India has been a continuous phenomenon. It is estimated that in 1996 there were 40,000 Chin-Burmese in India.[15]

Kashmiri Refugees in Pakistan: The disturbed situation in Kashmir has resulted in the migration of some Kashmiri Muslims to Pakistan. By 1996, 13,000 Kashmiri Muslims were reportedly living in Pakistan.[16]

Open, or virtually open, borders

India-Nepal: The open border between India and Nepal has resulted in Nepalese and Indian migrations across the borders. The Nepalese have migrated largely to four states of India—Assam, Bihar, Uttarakhand and West Bengal. The Indian census reports show that the Nepal-born population in India increased significantly after 1951. According to the 1971 census, there were 1.3 million Nepal-born Nepalis living in India. Migrant organizations such as the Emigrant Nepali Association claim that this figure reached three million by mid-1970s.[17] Till 1991, India accounted for almost 90 per cent of Nepal's emigration. But the 2001 Census of Nepal registered a sharp fall to 77.3 per cent, accounting for 589,050 Nepalis migrating to India.[18]

Like the Nepalis in India, the Indian population in the Terai region of Nepal has also been growing. While part of the growth in the Terai is attributable to the migration of people from the hill regions, it has also been caused by the Indian migrations. According to the 1991 census, there were 439,488 foreign-born people in Nepal of which India accounted for 418,982.[19] Some Nepalese press reports have suggested that on account of the ineptitude of the Nepal government, thousands of Indians from neighbouring districts of Katihar, Arariya and Supoul in Bihar are constructing houses on public land in Biratnagar and Morang in Nepal. According to the Biratnagar municipality, there were 10,000 such migrants in 1994 and by 1999 the number had increased to 15,000.[20] According to Nepal's Census of 2001, 2.7 per cent of the population, that is, 608,092 were foreign born of which 96 per cent were India born. Of the total foreign-born population, 81 per cent have become Nepalese nationals.[21]

India-Bangladesh: Unlike the Indo-Nepal open border, the India-Bangladesh border is not supposed to be open. But at many places it is virtually open. This has resulted in large-scale movements of Bangladeshis into India. Due to the hurried job of partitioning India that Cyril Radcliffe performed and on account of the inherent difficulty of trying to demarcate areas in mixed Hindu–Muslim localities which exist almost along the entire border, the international boundary hardly gives the impression of being one. Economic and social interactions across the border are as common as they were before the Partition in most places. As a result, many people have settled on the Indian side of the border as a matter of routine. The 1981 census revealed that in the eight border districts of West Bengal the population grew at over 30 per cent between 1971 and 1981 whereas the remaining districts reported growth rates below 20 per cent. An extreme case was of a town in northern West Bengal where the population leapt from 10,000 to 150,000.[22] According to the Indian census, the number of people who have migrated illegally from Bangladesh to India was 1,729,310 in 1961–1971 and 559,006 in 1971–1981. These figures do not include the estimated 600,000 who entered Assam between 1971 and 1981. It is possible that many of the Bangladeshi infiltrators were the so-called Biharis.[23]

To these infiltrators one should also add those Bangladeshis who enter India with forged travel documents or even with valid ones but do not return to their country after the expiration of their validity. A decade ago, it was revealed by the West Bengal government that at least 400,000 passport holders from Bangladesh who entered West Bengal during the previous ten years had disappeared into the Indian community without any trace. In a status report on illegal immigration submitted to the Supreme Court in January 1999, the government of West Bengal admitted that 1,240,000 Bangladeshis who entered the state with travel documents had melted into the local population while 570,000 had been pushed back into Bangladesh between 1972 and 1998. The document said that till 1997, the intercepted infiltrators were summarily pushed back, but after 1997, this practice was discontinued.[24]

At the moment, there are millions of unauthorized Bangladeshis living in various parts of India generally doing small and menial jobs. Demographers agree that such out migrations of people from poorer regions to neighbouring less poor ones are as natural as water seeking its own level. The density of population per square kilometre is close to 800 in Bangladesh as against 287 in Assam and just 7 in Arunachal Pradesh. Earlier, these settlements were concentrated in states neighbouring Bangladesh such as Assam and West Bengal but of late even far flung areas, such as Mumbai, Delhi, Haryana, Punjab, western U.P., and so on, have started getting illegal Bangladeshi immigrants.

It is difficult to figure out the extent of Bangladeshi immigration to India. Based on Indian census reports, the following conclusions can be drawn. Based on the criteria, 'place of birth' and 'place of last residence', the 2001 census revealed that Bangladesh accounted for about 60 per cent of all immigrants in India, which is 3.1 million. The corresponding figures for 1991 and 1981 were 3.4 and 3.2 million, respectively.[25]

India-Pakistan: In no sense, the border between India and Pakistan is open, yet there are cases of clandestine movements of people across it through the Rajasthan-Punjab and the Gujarat-Sindh borders. The first is 512 km long, the second 1335 km. People living in these bordering areas often have kinship ties across the border. Smuggling is a way of life there, and trafficking in drugs and arms, particularly after the intensification of the Punjab crisis in India and the Mohajir crisis in Pakistan in 1980s, is a problem causing serious concern to both the Indian and Pakistani authorities. Many bordering villages—Barmer, Bikaner, Ganganagar and Jaisalmer in Rajasthan—have registered higher rates of growth compared to other villages which is attributed to migrations from Pakistan.[26]

Indian Migrations: So far as the migration of Indians into neighbouring Bangladesh and Pakistan is concerned, it is much smaller in scale. Except in the aftermath of the Partition when many Urdu-speaking Muslims from Bihar and U.P. left for Pakistan, there has been no evidence of migration into Bangladesh. However, taking advantage of the porous border, there has been a constant flow of Muslims from India, again mostly from Bihar and U.P., to Pakistan some of whom must logically be the so-called 'Biharis' of Bangladesh.[27] A 1995 police survey revealed that there were 1 million undocumented Bangladeshis in Karachi. Most of the migrant workers in Pakistan arrived after the creation of Bangladesh and are treated as illegal immigrants. Their status is determined by the Foreigners Act of 1946.[28] Due to the politically sensitive nature of the matter, on account of its fallout on the Sindhi–Mohajir relations, the subject has not received much scholarly attention in Pakistan. However, most of the Pakistanis this author has interacted with are aware of the phenomenon. According to one estimate, the number of such illegal immigrants had touched two million during the 1960s and the 1970s.[29]

India Bhutan: In a limited sense, the border between India and Bhutan is open. The commercial capital of Bhutan, Phuntsholing, which houses the headquarters of the Bank of Bhutan and the Royal Insurance Corporation, is almost totally in the hands of Indian businessmen. Even the entry of Indians to this town in the district of Chukha is free. The immigration check-post is situated only at the northern edge of the town, so only those seeking to enter into Bhutan beyond Phuntsholing are required to obtain the necessary permit.

India-Myanmar: A virtually open border exists between India (in Mizoram) and Myanmar. Eastern Mizoram adjoins Myanmar and the western part touches Bangladesh. As a result, there are infiltrations into the state from both Bangladesh and Myanmar, more so from the latter. According to the Mizoram police records, between 1994 and 1997 about 3,500 foreigners were arrested in the state.[30] The data, however, did not give the breakup as per their nationalities. As such, one is not sure how many of them were Bangladeshis and how many were Myanmarese. But since people from Myanmar visit the Chhimtuipui district in southern Mizoram as a matter of routine to work as daily wage labourers or for shopping and medical treatment, one may surmise that many were Myanmarese. It may as well be noted that the Chins who live across the border in Myanmar are ethnically Mizos.

War-related migration

There was some migration of Hindus from Pakistan to India in the Rajasthan sector during the 1971 Indo-Pak war. Following the Simla agreement of 1972, when the Indian troops were withdrawn from areas occupied by them across the Rajasthan border, Hindus living in those areas migrated to India along with the withdrawing Indian troops. They feared that once Pakistan's authority was restored in the area they would be subjected to prosecution and violence. At least 100,000 such people belonging mainly to three communities, namely, Sodha Rajputs, Bhil tribals and Meghawat dalits came to India. During the 1965 war exactly the opposite had happened but on a lesser scale. At that time, a few colonies of Muslims in Rajasthan had crossed over to the other side of the border with similar fears.[31]

Developmental and environmental refugees

Environmental refugees, according to Eassan Hinnawi who coined the word in a report prepared for the United Nations Environment Programme (UNEP) in 1985, are 'those people who have been forced to leave their traditional habitat, temporarily or permanently, because of a marked environmental disruption, natural and/or triggered by people that jeopardize the existence and/or seriously affect the quality of their life.' On the basis of this definition one may identify three categories of refugees as environmental refugees, namely, *a)* those displaced temporarily because of an environmental stress such as an earthquake or a cyclone and who *will* return to their habitat once conditions normalize; *b)* those who have been permanently displaced because of a permanent change caused to their habitat such as the establishment of dams and associated man-made lakes; and *c)* those who migrate permanently or temporarily in quest of an improved quality of life because their original habitat can no longer meet their basic needs.[32] Since we are concerned here with permanent or semi-permanent migrations, the last two categories are relevant. As internally displaced persons have been discussed here under the head 'IDP', we are concerned here with the categories *b)* and *c)* insofar as their cross-border components are concerned.

Bangladeshi Developmental Refugees: The large-scale migrations of Bangladeshis into India, particularly from the Khulna and Rajshahi divisions are largely attributed to the construction of the Farakka Barrage in India on the Ganga near the India-Bangladesh border. It is alleged that it led to the impoverishment of the people of these divisions. Khulna was traditionally a high growth division but after the construction of the Barrage it has registered a drastic fall because of the negative impact of the dam on Khulna's agriculture. The exact number of out-migrants from these divisions to India cannot be established but it may be in the tune of about two million.[33]

Chakma Refugees: The construction of Karnafuli (Kaptai) hydroelectric project in 1962 in the Chittagong Hill Tracts (CHTs) of East Pakistan submerged 54,000 acres of settled and cultivable land affecting about 100,000 people, 90 per cent of whom were Chakmas and other tribals.[34] Besides, the state-sponsored schemes to settle people of the plains in these areas also made them alien in their own habitat. All this led to disaffection, civil strife, militancy, and eventually, state repression resulting in the flight of these tribals to neighbouring India for safety. By 1987, there were about 33,000 such refugees spread over several camps in India's Northeast. In Arunachal Pradesh, the Chakmas were given permanent residence as early as 1966 (also discussed in the following section).

Stateless or the virtually stateless

In this category fall three cases, namely, the Indian Tamils of Sri Lanka, the so-called 'Biharis' of Bangladesh, and the Chakmas and Hajongs of Arunachal Pradesh. There is also a fourth category in the practical sense, though neither in strict legal sense nor in the sense of human flows, which this chapter addresses. It includes people in the enclaves that dot the India-Bangladesh border.

Stateless Indian Tamils: According to the Sri Lankan census of 1981, which is the last official one, Indian Tamils were 825,233 in number, constituting 5.6 per cent of the island's population. According to the Shastri-Sirimavo Pact of 30 October 1964, it was decided that of the 1953 estimate of 975,000 stateless persons of Indian origin in Sri Lanka, 300,000 (together with the natural increase in that number) would be granted Sri Lankan citizenship, while 525,000 (including the natural rise in that number) would be provided with Indian citizenship. The status and future of the remaining 150,000 people (including the natural rise in that number) would be decided later by a separate agreement. In 1974, through another agreement between the two countries, it was decided that both the governments would grant citizenship to the 150,000 persons left undecided by the 1964 Pact according to a 50:50 ratio.[35]

The agreements, however, could not be implemented for

years because of inherent problems. But eventually, Sri Lanka did honour its commitment. On 9 November 1988, the Sri Lankan parliament unanimously passed the bill entitled 'Grant of Citizenship to Stateless Persons (Special Provisions) Act', which conferred Sri Lankan citizenship on all stateless persons lawfully residing in the country and those who had not applied for Indian citizenship.[36] But the Indian component could not be implemented. In April 1997, S. Thondaman, the president of the Ceylon Workers' Congress, alleged that while Sri Lanka had granted citizenship to all stateless Indian Tamils who had opted for Sri Lanka, India had not honoured its commitment. According to him of the 200,000 Indian Tamils who had applied for Indian citizenship most had since died but their children still remained stateless.[37]

Stateless Biharis: The 'Biharis' of Bangladesh are stateless. Because of their mother tongue Urdu and doubtful loyalty to Bangladesh they are suspect in the eyes of the Bangladeshis. Major Ziaur Rehman, who became president of Bangladesh, is said to have remarked in 1971: 'Those who speak Urdu are also our enemies because they support the Pakistan army. We will crush them.' On 28 March 1971, when his troops brought some Bihari prisoners before him, he said: 'Take the men out and shoot them' and with women 'you can do what you like with them'.[38] Successive Pakistani governments have reiterated their commitments to repatriate the Biharis but the problem has not been fully solved though most of the young Biharis have become Bangladeshi nationals.

Stateless Chakmas: The Chakmas of Arunachal Pradesh are stateless. In 1964, the Government of India settled about 66,000 Chakma and Hajong refugees in North East Frontier Agency (NEFA) which is now Arunachal Pradesh. While the Chakmas had migrated from the CHT of the erstwhile East Pakistan after the construction of the Kaptai Hydroelectric Project, the Hajongs had migrated from Mymensingh and Sylhet districts to escape religious perception (*see* p.41). According to the Assam Accord of 1985 all infiltrators who came from East Pakistan prior to its becoming Bangladesh were to be granted Indian citizenship. As such, these Chakmas and Hajongs of Arunachal Pradesh are entitled to citizenship. But due to the opposition of the All Arunachal Pradesh Students' Union (AAPSU), this has not been possible. Citizenship means inclusion into the voters' list and hence a share in political power, which the AAPSU is not willing to concede in spite of the Supreme Court rulings in their favour. Political leaders of Arunachal Pradesh across the board are also in favour of evicting the Chakmas. It is not only an AAPSU demand.

The 'Stateless' Enclave People: This category has more to do with the redefinition of borders than with the actual movement of people. Van Schendel estimates that there are 123 Indian enclaves in Bangladesh and 74 Bangladeshi enclaves in India.[39] On account of the problems faced by the people of these enclaves to move freely in and out of the enclaves, particularly in respect of their movements to the countries they legally belong, they are stateless in all practical purposes. Their split identity as *chhitmoholia* (enclavians) is virtually their citizenship. They say that it is others outside the enclaves who consider them to be Indian or Bangladeshi. To them, their statelessness is the unifying identity.[40] For want of census in these enclaves on account of logistical and political difficulties, it is not possible to estimate the exact number of these *chhitmoholias*.[41]

Extra-regional interventions

There are three cases of this variety: one, the Tibetan refugees in India and Nepal following the Chinese annexation of Tibet; two, the Afghan refugees in Pakistan (and also some in India) following the Soviet intervention in Afghanistan in 1979; and three, the same following the US and NATO intervention in Afghanistan after 9/11, in October 2001.

Tibetan Refugees: Tibetan refugees started arriving in India first in 1950. It was during this year that the People's Republic of China started asserting its sovereignty over Tibet. It was, however, only in 1959 that a large number of Tibetans began to flee to India and Nepal in the wake of the Chinese military action on the plateau. The reports of the International Commission of Jurists (ICJ), published in 1959 and 1966, documented several cases of religious persecution, torture, forced sterilization, destruction of families, and so on, perpetrated by the Chinese authorities, thereby causing forced migration. It is difficult to ascertain the exact number of such refugees; by 1966, about 80,000–90,000 Tibetans had taken refuge in India.[42] The flow was more or less continuous and according to press reports during the first nine months of 1998, 2300 Tibetans, mostly monks and nuns, poured into India following reports of a Chinese crackdown.[43]

The Chinese presence in Tibet also resulted in some refugee influx in Nepal after 1959. About 30,000 Tibetans took shelter in Nepal then. The flow continued and about 50 Tibetan refugees arrived in the country every week.[44] It may be noted that the Chinese invasion also resulted in the eviction and deportation of the small number of Chinese families settled in the urban centre of Upper Assam and Kolkata for generations. They were deported to China.[45]

Afghan Refugees: The Soviet intervention in Afghanistan in December 1979 resulted in a huge inflow of Afghan refugees into Pakistan. Although many Afghans had come to Pakistan as refugees even before the Soviet intervention (by Hafizullah Amin's time some 400,000 Afghan refugees had reached Pakistan), there was a great increase in the flow after the intervention and reached up to 10,000–15,000 heads per month. By the time the Geneva Accords were signed in 1988, the number of Afghan refugees had crossed 3.5 million.[46] Of the registered Afghan refugees in Pakistan some 67 per cent were in the North-West Frontier Province (NWFP), 28 per cent in Balochistan and the rest scattered all over the country.

By the beginning of 1997, 2.6 million Afghan refugees had returned from Pakistan, 1.9 million of them with repatriation assistance from UNHCR. Another 1.3 million had returned from Iran, taking the total number of Afghan refugees who went home to around 3.9 million—the largest repatriation of a single refugee group since UNHCR came into existence and one of the largest ever.[47] The situation, however, changed after the events of 9/11.

US–NATO Intervention: Following the collapse of the Taliban regime in the aftermath of 9/11, the refugee situation changed in the sense that the border between Afghanistan and Pakistan which was already unenforceable became even more open leading to uninterrupted cross-border movements. The US-led bombing campaign that started in October 2001 not only prompted thousands of Pathans to take refuge in Pakistan in a fresh wave but also affected the process of UNHCR-sponsored repatriation drive. For several ethnic and political reasons, the Pathan, Tajik, Uzbek and Hazara refugees sheltered in Pakistani and Irani camps refused to go back. According to an October 2008 report, there were still two million Afghan refugees in Pakistan and more than one million in Iran and Tajikistan.[48]

Position of the IDP

Displacements in India: Internal displacements in India that are caused by man-made factors fall primarily into two categories—development induced and strife induced. Dams and mining projects figure prominently in the first category. (The migration of the rural poor to the urban areas which is a major component of this category is not within the purview of this chapter as has been explained in the beginning.) Migration of people in search of physical and material security in times of inter-communal, inter-ethnic or ideological strife falls in the second.

It is estimated that between 1950 and 1990 about 18.5

million Indians were subjected to resettlement on account of development projects. In Orissa alone, by 2000, about 200,000 people were directly affected by development projects.[49] Of the various dam projects that have caused massive displacement, particular mention may be made of the Narmada project. The Narmada Valley Development Project comprises 3000 dams of which 30 are large and five of them are on the Narmada itself. These five dams are: Bargi, Omkareshwar, Maheshwar, Narmada Sagar (all in Madhya Pradesh) and Sardar Sarovar (in Gujarat). According to the activists of the Narmada Bachao Andolan (NBA—Save Narmada movement), the last-mentioned dam displaced about 200,000 people. Mining activities also have resulted in massive displacements. Jharkhand as a mineral-rich state is particularly affected. Following the New National Mineral Policy (1993), private and multinational investments were encouraged, which aggravated the problem.[50]

Displacement due to social and political strife is also massive. The Naxalite violence which is active in large parts of central and south India and the counter insurgency actions led by the states' security forces, including the Salwa Judum in Chhattisgarh, have uprooted thousands of villagers, 50,000 in Chhattisgarh alone.[51] Frequent inter-communal, inter-caste and inter-tribe conflicts are routinely displacing scores of Indians. The involuntary migration of large numbers of Punjabi and Kashmiri Hindus to Delhi, Jammu and other parts of India in search of security from the separatist terrorists was a highly emotive issue in the 1980s and 1990s. The anti-Muslim riots in Gujarat in early 2002 that displaced thousands of Muslims and contributed to their ghettoization, together with other similar experiences, do not augur well for India's inter-communal politics.[52] In the Northeast, inter-ethnic conflicts have been causing displacements consistently. The conflict between Bodos and Adivasis in western Assam has turned hundreds of thousands of Adivasis into refugees (*see* Chapter 7). Also affected in the strife are Bengali-speaking

Muslims and Hindus. A 1996 memorandum of the Kokrajhar and Bongaigaon Saranarthi Committee claimed that there were more than 20,000 Muslim refugees in 18 relief camps since 1993.[53] The recent Bodo–Muslim conflicts have again displaced thousands of people (*see* Introduction).

Displacements in Pakistan: In Pakistan, the evidence of internal displacement on account of internal disturbance and developmental activities is less but the rural–urban migration which is significant has the overtones of regional disparities and ethnic conflicts (*see* Chapter 6). For example, the poor quality of life in the NWFP had encouraged heavy migration of Pathans from rural to more prosperous urban areas, most notably Karachi, causing severe complications in the ethnic politics of Sindh. Migrations have also taken place from such economically stressed urban areas as Peshawar, Malakand, Rawalpindi and Sargodha. Of the internal displacements on account of developmental activities, mention may be made of the Ghazi-Barotha hydropower project which aims to use the drop of the Indus river between the tailrace of the Tarbela dam and the confluence of the Indus and Haro rivers. The project will reduce the flow downstream by 12 per cent, causing hardship to the people of these areas and eventually forcing many of them to migrate.[54]

Lately, particularly after the 9/11, on account of the counter al Qaeda offensive launched by Pakistani security forces in areas bordering Pakistan, large-scale displacement has been reported. The Wana Operations in southern Waziristan, which commenced on 16 March 2004, displaced over 100,000.[55] The UNHCR refused to undertake relief measures on the ground that while in the case of Afghan IDPs 'there was no functional central government in Afghanistan', in case of Pakistan 'there was a functional central authority'.[56]

Displacements Due To Indo-Pak Cross-Border Shelling: Both India and Pakistan routinely shell across the Line of Control (LoC) in Kashmir (*see* Chapter 8). This causes occasional displacement of people living in villages on both sides of the

LoC. The problem reached a flashpoint in May–June 1999 when in response to infiltration by the Pakistan army regulars in the Kargil sector, the Indian Army and Air Force stepped up their operations to drive out the intruders. The exchange of fire between the Indian and Pakistani armed forces created panic amongst the villagers in the border areas leading to their exodus to safer areas. About 20,000 people left their homes in Dras and Kargil to avoid Pakistani shelling. There was displacement also on account of preparations for combat by the Indian Army. About 400 people were evacuated from Pandras, 140 km northeast of Srinagar and 12 km from the LoC, after the Indian Army took over their village for operational purposes.[57]

The anxiety about an impending war between India and Pakistan in 1999 also caused panic flights of villagers near the international border in Punjab. Fear particularly gripped the border towns of Khem Karan and Khalda and villages in the Khem Karan and Bhikiwind sectors. These movements had demonstration effect on nearby Wan village and Rajoke, in the Attari sector, where also the residents fled from their homes in panic. All assurances by Prakash Singh Badal, chief minister of Punjab, that there was no reason to panic, fell on deaf ears.[58]

There was similar reaction in Pakistan too. The Pakistan Army evacuated about 4,000 villagers living close to the border near Sialkot in Punjab as the Indian Army had moved troops close to the border and the Indian Air Force had activated the forward operation bases. Flights of panic-stricken villagers were particularly pronounced opposite India's Samba sector, which includes Kathua district bordering Punjab and part of Jammu district, and the Chicken Neck area, which is a narrow piece of Pakistan territory jutting into the Akhnoor sector of Jammu district. The Chicken Neck area is considered highly vulnerable by the Pakistanis at the time of hostilities.[59]

Displacement in Sri Lanka: In the 1990s, Sri Lanka witnessed large-scale internal displacements on account of the policies and activities of the LTTE and the Sri Lankan government's response thereto. Earlier, during the 1958 and 1983 riots also there were displacements. The anti-Tamil riots of 1983 alone caused the displacement of 100,000 Sri Lanka Tamils. Between 1985 and 1990, approximately 300,000 Tamils were displaced from the North-Eastern Province due to fights between the LTTE and the government forces. An important aspect of this displacement was the fate of Muslims. Owing to LTTE highhandedness, at least 100,000 Tamil-speaking Muslims had to leave their homes and take shelter with friends and relatives and in refugee camps in the Puttalam and Kurunegala districts of the North-Western Province and in the Anuradhapura district of the North-Central Province.[60]

Huge displacements also took place following the government offensive against the LTTE in the Northern Province which resulted in the government regaining control of Jaffna town in November 1995. The LTTE itself had asked the people of Jaffna to evacuate. All this resulted in 1,017,181 displacements and the involuntary movement of Jaffna Tamils to Vanni, south of Jaffna.[61] The intensification of war around 2003–2008 had once again brought the issue of internal displacement to the fore. The Internal Displacement Monitoring Centre (IDMC) estimated that 200,000 people had been displaced since January 2006 and the IDPs were again in excess of 500,000. Some recent reports suggest that Colombo and its suburbs had registered the arrival of more than 37,000 Tamils from the Northern Province of whom more than 2,000 were new arrivals.[62]

Besides, there have been displacements of people on account of developmental plans such as the Mahaveli Project as also the displacement of the Sinhalese people from certain areas in the Eastern Province. The ethnic break-up of the total number of displaced people is 78 per cent Sri Lanka Tamils, 13 per cent Muslims and 8 per cent Sinhalese.

Displacements in Nepal: Nepal's wildlife conservation

projects and national parks have caused some internal displacements. The Chitwan National Park and the Bardia National Park, for example, have also displaced thousands of people.[63] Particularly affected communities are Taru, Chepong, Limbu and Sunuwar. But the real problem of displacement arose in the wake of the conflict between the Maoists and the state security forces that started in the mid-1990s. It claimed more than 13,000 lives, intensified migration to India and internally displaced about 200,000 people.

Displacements in Bangladesh: In Bangladesh, too, every year tens of thousands of people are displaced on account of developmental activities like dams, shrimp projects, and so on. In a populous country like Bangladesh, where the density of population is 800 per square kilometre, any project inevitably displaces a large number of people. During the Pakistan days, the Kaptai hydroelectric project, completed in 1961, displaced about 90,000 tribals of the CHTs many of whom migrated to India. Other displacements are also reported from the area due to jungle cleaning and logging carried out by the security forces for the purposes of counter insurgency. The high-profile Jamuna Multipurpose Bridge, which was opened in 1998, did not directly require any land acquisition but its related facilities did. They directly or indirectly resulted in displacement of about 82,000 people.[64]

MARGINALIZED GROUPS

Most migrants and refugees in South Asia belong to poorer sections of the societies, which of course is the case anywhere. Since in South Asia being poor on the one hand and belonging to the lower castes or tribes on the other are more or less coterminus, the latter forms the bulk of the displaced. The Hindu refugees/migrants from East Pakistan and later Bangladesh mostly belonged to the scheduled castes. Similarly, most of the displaced people due to the construction of dams in India and Bangladesh are tribals. The *29th Report of the Commissioner of Scheduled Castes and Scheduled Tribes (1990)* noted that although only about 7.5 per cent of the Indian population was tribal, over 40 per cent of the displaced came from this category. The ongoing militancy of the Naxalites and the state's response to counter it has been displacing tribal people in huge numbers in central India. In situations of international migrations most migrants become virtually stateless because they do not hold valid papers. The *char* areas (river islands that emerge due to change of riverine courses or silting) provide best locations for these stateless people.[65]

WOMEN AS VICTIMS

Since patriarchy dominates in almost all societies in the world, it will be tautological to say that women are greater sufferers as refugees, forced migrants or displaced persons. In the case of migrants by choice also the decision to migrate is generally a male decision. The female migration that follows is largely due to the requirements of family reunion. The fact that female migrants are less in number globally, and in South Asia particularly, because of its additional cultural reasons, underscores the point. In 2000, the global percentage of female migrants was 48.5 but in South Asia it was 44.4.[66] Till recently, migration research was generally silent on the issue of gender but it is not so any more. A volume of literature has emerged on the subject the focus of which is to have a gendered view of the processes involved in the human flows.[67]

There are several ways in which women suffer more than their male counterparts. While their physical vulnerability exposes them to sexual abuse and maltreatment at work places, they are discriminately paid as well. At home, the real burden of resettling in new abodes primarily falls on women. Whether it is the Afghan, Bangladeshi, Indian or Pakistani experience, the story is the same.[68]

POLICIES, POLITICS AND SOUTH ASIA

In South Asia the problem of refugees is relatively less strident compared to those of migrants and the internally displaced, who constitute the bulk. Yet, relatively more concern is shown for having uniform refugee laws. Since other issues get embroiled in domestic politics, they become more intractable.[69] Just to take the example of India, three political developments are likely to complicate problems further. First, growing communalization of Indian politics is making the Bangladeshi migrant issue more complicated for decision makers. Second, regionalization of Indian politics—'now, the region has become the centre' is the phrase—will increasingly make any central response to such pan-Indian problem more problematic. And third, the delimitation of Indian parliamentary constituencies (still incomplete, five states are yet to have delimitation) has already added five more reserved (SC and ST) constituencies making the depressed classes and tribals more exposed to cut-throat politics. Since there are about 35 tribal constituencies where both the Naxalites and the Hindutva forces are at loggerheads for domination, more violence and resultant displacement seems inevitable.

A wave of democracy is inundating South Asia. But democracy has its own dilemma. As Samaddar's study[70] had shown that democracy sometimes victimizes the marginalized even more, one may extend the logic further and argue that the South Asian states that are heading towards democracy, and yet are fragile political entities in terms of democratic institution building, will be even more dangerous for the weak and the marginalized. The journal *Foreign Policy* composed 'Failed States Index 2008', which surveyed 177 states, and found Afghanistan, Pakistan, Bangladesh, Sri Lanka and Nepal (in that order) as failed states. The records of the remaining three—Bhutan, Maldives and India were not too encouraging either. India's ranking was 98 (Norway is least failed, ranking 177).[71] If at all this index is correct, the problem that we are discussing in this chapter does not seem to be over at all. Who will care for the stateless migrants when the states are not able to take care of their bona fide nationals?

LOOKING BEYOND BOUNDARIES

The enormity of the problem of migrants, refugees and the IDPs defies all theories of governance because it inevitably gets politicized, making the solution complex. The only redeeming feature is that because of social and familial networking the state alone is not the service provider. For example, the Sri Lanka Tamil refugees in Tamil Nadu, the Afghan refugees in the NWFP of Pakistan or the Bangladeshi Hindu refugees in West Bengal often depend, in the initial stages of their arrival, on migrants who had come earlier. Many Bangladeshi Hindus have confessed to this author that because of the deteriorating communal situation in their country they often try to have one of their children located in India so as to fall back upon in days of crisis. Since the borders in general are porous there is always a sense of having dual belongingness, which actually underlines the artificiality of the borders in the Indian subcontinent.[72] Besides state interventions based on legal regimes, what is required more is civil society's contributions both ideationally as well as in terms of activism. Mercifully, people-to-people contacts in the region are growing in spite of higher walls that are being built by the states to prevent academic seminars and conferences. The path has hurdles, but they will have to be overcome.

NOTES

1 *Bound Together, How Traders, Preachers, Adventurers, and Warriors Shaped Globalization (*New Haven, CT: *Yale University Press,* 2007).

2 World Migration Report 2005, 'International Migration Trends'; for further details see: http://imges.gmanews.tv/htm/research/2007/12/wprld_migration_r., last accessed on 8 October 2008.

3 *The World Almanac and Book of Facts 2008* (New York: World Almanac Books), p.601.

4 Abhijit Dasgupta, 'Refugees in India: Repatriation and Resettlement', in *India as a Refugee Host Country: Management, Practices and Policy Options* Mahendra P. Lama (ed.), (New Delhi: SIS/JNU, 2000), pp.78–79.

5 Partha S. Ghosh, *Unwanted and Uprooted: A Political Study of Migrants, Refugees, Stateless and Displaced of South Asia* (New Delhi: Samskriti, 2004), pp.1–7.

6 See P.H.K. Spate, *India and Pakistan: A General and Regional Geography* (London: Methuen, 1957) and Kingsley Davis, 'India and Pakistan: The Demography of Partition', *Pacific Affairs* (Vancouver), 22 (1949) pp.254–64.

7 The Indian Commission of Jurists, 1965, *Recurrent Exodus of Minorities from East Pakistan and Disturbances in India: A Report to the Indian Commission of Jurists by its Committee of Enquiry* (New Delhi), pp.309–12.

8 *Complex Emergency Database (CE-DAT)* (Brussels), 7 March 2008, p.12.

9 Myron Weiner, 'Rejected Peoples and Unwanted Migrants in South Asia', *Economic and Political Weekly* (21 August 1993), p.1738.

10 Shwe Lu Maung, *Burma: Nationalism and Ideology: An Analysis of Society, Culture and Politics* (Dhaka: University Press, 1989), pp.61–62.

11 Swapna Bhattacharya (Chakraborti), 'Bangladesh-Myanmar Relations: A Study of the Problem of Refugees in Bangladesh', in *Integration, Disintegration and World Order: Some Perspectives on the Process of Change* Arun Kumar Banerji (ed.), (Calcutta: Allied, 1995), p.69.

12 *Hindustan Times*, New Delhi, 20 January 2009.

13 V. Suryanarayan, 'Sri Lankan Tamil Refugees in Tamil Nadu', *The Hindu*, 28 July 1997.

14 Author's conversation with Rinzin Dorji, an active member of the Druk National Congress, in Kathmandu on 21 November 1996. Dorji is the editor of the Dzongkha publication *Lhoyi Khuju*

(Kathmandu). One of his colleagues secretly informed this author that it was printed by the Indian embassy at Kathmandu, a fact which cannot be authenticated.

15 Tapan Bose and Rita Manchanda (eds), *States, Citizens and Outsiders: The Uprooted Peoples of South Asia* (Kathmandu: South Asia Forum for Human Rights, 1997).

16 'US Committee for Refugees', *World Refugee Survey,* 1997, p.129.

17 *Himal South Asia* (Kathmandu), January–February 1997, p. 12.

18 Bal Kumar K.C., 'Migration, Poverty and Development in Nepal', *Asian and Pacific Migration Journal* 13, 2 (Manila, 2004), pp. 217.

19 *Population Census—1991: Social Characteristics Tables,* 1, 4 (Kathmandu: His Majesty's Government of Nepal, Central Bureau of Statistics, 1991).

20 *POT (Public Opinion Trends),* Nepal Series, 5, 31 (9 June 1999), pp.316–17.

21 Ibid.

22 Ashis K. Biswas, 'The Unchecked Influx', *The Hindu* (Madras), 17 February 1982.

23 Imtiaz Ahmed, 'Refugees and Security: The Experience of Bangladesh', in *Refugees and Regional Security in South Asia* S. D. Muni and Lok Raj Baral (eds), (New Delhi: Konark, 1996), pp.143, 150.

24 *Asian Age,* 8 February 1999.

25 Aswini Kumar Nanda, 'Immigration from Bangladesh to India Based on Census Data', *Asian and Pacific Migration Journal,* 14, 4 (Manila, 2005), pp.489–90.

26 Partha S. Ghosh, *Unwanted and Uprooted: A Political Study of Migrants, Refugees, Stateless and Displaced of South Asia* (New Delhi: Samskriti, 2004), pp.31–33.

27 On 11 May 1999 the BSF arrested 64 Biharis near the border outpost of Ala Mai Kothi in R. S. Pura sub-sector of Jammu when they were trying to enter Pakistan. *The Hindu,* 12 May 1999.

28 Imtiaz Ahmed, 'Refugees and Security', p.346.

29 The estimate is that of Mohammad Irfan of the Pakistan Institute of Development Economics, Islamabad, who at one point had studied the subject but did not publish anything. Hard data on the subject is difficult to find, partly on account of the political sensitivity of the subject and partly because demography is a largely ignored subject in Pakistan. Author's conversation with

Irfan, Islamabad, 15 October 1996.
30 Ghosh, 2004 , pp.34–35.
31 P. Sainath, 'The Borderlines of Caste', *The Hindu*, 4 July 1999.
32 C. R. Abrar, 'Environmental Security and Migration in South Asia', in *Sustainable Development: Environmental Security, Disarmament and Development in South Asia* D. D. Khanna (ed.), (New Delhi: Macmillan, 1997) p.412.
33 Ashok Swain, 'The Environmental Trap: The Ganges River Diversion, Bangladeshi Migration and Conflicts in India', Report No. 41, Sweden, Department of Peace and Conflict Research, Uppsala University, 1996.
34 Thomas Homer-Dixon and Valerie Percival, 'Environmental Security and Violent Conflict: Briefing Book (Toronto: American Association for the Advancement of Signs and the University of Toronto, 1996), pp.10–16.
35 Partha S. Ghosh, *Cooperation and Conflict in South Asia*. (New Delhi: Manohar, 1989), pp.155–61.
36 T. Sabaratnam, 'Out of Bondage: The Thondaman Story' (Colombo: Sri Lanka Indian Community Council, 1990).
37 *Asian Age*, 22 April 1997; *The Hindu*, 23 April 1997.
38 Taj-ul Islam Hashmi, 'The "Bihari" Minorities in Bangladesh: Victims of Nationalism', in *Islam, Communities and the Nation: Muslim Identities in South Asia* Mushirul Hasan (ed.), (New Delhi: Manohar, 1998), p.402.
39 'Stateless in South Asia: The Making of the India-Bangladesh Enclaves', *The Journal of Asian Studies* (Ann Arbor), 61, 1 (February 2002), pp.117–18.
40 Ibid., p.134.
41 Author's discussion with Willem van Schendel in Amsterdam on 3 July 2002.
42 Dawa Norbu, 'Refugees from Tibet: Structural Causes of Successful Settlement', paper presented to the Fourth International Research and Advisory Panel Conference on Forced Migration, Oxford University, 5–9 January 1994, pp.1–3.
43 *Asian Age*, 28 October 1998.
44 Hari Phuyal, 'Nepal's Refugee Burden', in *States, Citizens and Outsiders: The Uprooted Peoples of South Asia* Tapan Bose and Rita Manchanda (eds), (Kathmandu: South Asia Forum for Human Rights, 1997), p.238.

45 Monirul Hussain, 'Fear of Being Killed, Violated and Displaced: An Incomplete Dossier of Terrorism in Post-Colonial Assam', paper presented to the seminar on 'Dynamics of Identity and Intergroup Relations in North-East India', Indian Institute of Advanced Study (Simla, 12–14 November 1996), p.9.

46 P. I. Cheema, 'The Afghan Refugees and Pakistan's Internal Security Problems', in *Refugees and Regional Security in South Asia* S. D. Muni and Lok Raj Baral (eds), (New Delhi: Konark, 1996), pp.179–90.

47 Monique Malha. 'Eighteen Years in Exile: The Situation of Refugees in Pakistan', *Liberal Times*, 5, 1 (New Delhi, 1997).

48 *People's Daily Online* (Beijing), 7 October 2008.

49 Mathew Areeparampli, 'Displacement Due to Mining in Jharkhand', *Economic and Political Weekly* (Mumbai, 15 June 1996), pp.1524–28.

50 Ibid.

51 Anasua Basu Ray Chaudhury, 'Sabarmati: Creating a New Divide?', *Economic and Political Weekly* (24 February 2007), pp.697–703.

52 Ibid.

53 See Monirul Hussain, 'State, Identity Movements and Internal Displacement in the North-East', *Economic and Political Weekly* (Mumbai, 16 December 2000), p.4522. For information of all kinds of IDP in North East, see Samir Kumar Das (ed.), *Blisters on their Feet: Tales of Internally Displaced Persons in India's North East* (New Delhi: Sage, 2008), and Monirul Hussain, *Interrogating Development: State, Displacement and Popular Resistance in North East India* (New Delhi: Sage, 2008).

54 Peter Gizewski and Thomas Homer-Dixon, *Environmental Security and Violent Conflict: The Case of Pakistan* (New York: American Association for the Advancement of Science, 1996), pp.21–28.

55 Saba Gul Khattak, 'Post-9/11: Terror, Terrorists and Women', A. D. Shrestha and R. Thapa (eds), *The Impact of Armed Conflicts on Women in South Asia* (New Delhi: Manohar, 2007), pp.137–66.

56 Ibid., pp.151–57.

57 *Asian Age*, 16 June 1999.

58 *The Hindu*, 14 and 15 June 1999.

59 *Asian Age*, 16 and 17 June 1999; *The Times of India*, 16 June 1999.

60 H. S. Hasbullah, 'Ethnic Conflict and the Prospects for Rehabilitation and Reconstruction: The Eastern Province', in *Pursuit of Peace in Sri Lanka: Past Failures and Future Prospects* K.M. de Silva and G.H. Peiris (eds), (Kandy: ICES, 2000), p.335.
61 *Sri Lanka: State of Human Rights 1995* (Colombo: NHRC, 1996), p.225.
62 *The Hindu*, 23 September 2008.
63 Hari Phuyal, 'Nepal's Refugee Burden', in *States, Citizens and Outsiders,* Bose and Manchanda (eds), p.247.
64 Chirantan Kumar, 'Development, Displacement and Rehabilitation in Bangladesh: A Comparative Study of Kaptai Dam and Jamuna Multipurpose Bridge Project', M. Phil. dissertation, School of International Studies, JNU (2007), p.54.
65 Kuntala Lahiri-Dutt and Gopa Samanta, 'Fleeting Land, Fleeting People: Bangladeshi Women in a *Char* land Environment in Lower Bengal, India', *Asian and Pacific Migration Journal,* 13, 4 (Manila, 2004), pp.482–89.
66 Meenakshi Thapan, 'Series Introduction', in Navnita Chadha Behera (ed.), *Gender, Conflict and Migration* (New Delhi: Sage, 2006), p.9.
67 For example, the five-volume DCRC series *Women and Migration in Asia*, edited by Meenakshi Thapan.
68 See the country-specific case studies in Navnita Chadha Behera (ed.), *Gender, Conflict and Migration* and Shrestha and Thapa (eds), *The Impact of Armed Conflicts on Women in South Asia*;
69 Ghosh, *Unwanted and Uprooted*, pp.63–104.
70 *The Marginal Nation: Transborder Migration from Bangladesh to West Bengal* (New Delhi: Sage, 1999), p.132.
71 A failed state has several attributes. Common indicators include a state whose central government is so weak or ineffective that it has little practical control over much of its territory and population. There are debates on what changes a working state into a failed state. Sometimes it might be a severe economic down swing. Whatever the crisis maybe, it has to be strong enough to abort any kind of possibilities of administration and governance. For more details see http://www.fundforpeace.org/web/index.php?option=com_content&t, accessed on 31 October 2008.
72 K.Lahiri-Dutt, 'Imagining Rivers', *EPW*, 35, 27 (1 July 2000), p.490.

3

REFUGEE PROTECTION IN SOUTH ASIA: Review of the Ad Hoc Mechanism and the Way Forward

UTTAM KUMAR DAS

This chapter aims to review the mechanism related to refugee protection in South Asia, taking Bangladesh and India as case studies. It looks into the current avenues for the protection of refugees. It assesses the UN Convention Relating to the Status of Refugees 1951 in the present global and South Asian context and examines the possibility for South Asian states towards accession to the instrument. The potentiality of a new protection regime including adoption of a national and regional framework to deal with asylum and refugee issues will also be examined.

REFUGEES IN INTERNATIONAL LAW

International Refugee Law is an emerging branch of international law. There is a set of international instruments, which have defined who a refugee is and established a standard for their treatment. The most important instruments related to refugees are the UN Convention Relating to the Status of Refugees, 1951 (hereafter, 1951 Convention) and its 1967 Protocol. In addition, other human rights instruments including the Universal Declaration of Human Rights (UDHR) 1948 have also supplemented the international legal regime for refugees.[1]

The 1951 Convention was adopted following the recommendation from the newly established UNCHR. This development is considered as a landmark in setting standards for the treatment of refugees.[2] The 1951 Convention sets out the minimum standards for treatment including the basic rights to which they are entitled. It also establishes the legal and juridical status of refugees and contains provisions on their rights to gainful employment and welfare, issue of identity papers and travel document, applicability of fiscal charges, and right to transfer their assets to another country where they have been admitted for the purposes of resettlement.

REFUGEES AND HUMAN RIGHTS

The concept of international protection of refugees has evolved gradually.[3] Presently, it involves a series of institutional and legal responses. The UN General Assembly through a resolution decided to establish the office of the UNHCR,[4] set up as a subsidiary organ of the General Assembly on 1 January 1951, initially for a period of three years. It succeeded the International Refugee Organization (IRO).[5] The mandate of UNHCR has routinely been extended until 2003. Through a resolution adopted by the General Assembly at the end of 2003, the time limit of UNHCR's mandate has been extended indefinitely.[6] This is considered as a strong sign of support to the organization by the concerned parties of the state.

The main task of the UNHCR is to provide international protection to refugees and to seek durable solutions for them by assisting governments in facilitating the voluntary repatriation of refugees, or their reintegration within new national communities, or resettlement to third countries.[7] These functions are entirely non-political, humanitarian and social.[8] The activities of the UN in the field of human rights and that of UNHCR are inextricably linked in the sense that they both share common purposes, which include safeguarding of human dignity. The UN's human rights programme deals with the rights of individuals within a state. On the other hand, UNHCR aims to provide minimum rights to a person in the country where he/she seeks asylum or refuge. The task of international protection includes the prevention of *refoulement*,[9] assistance in processing and screening of asylum-seekers, providing legal counsel and aid, promoting arrangements for the physical safety of refugees, promoting and assisting voluntary repatriation, and helping refugees to resettle.[10] Thus, international protection of refugees has a legal basis, and its exercise is mandatory for UNHCR. The right to protection, although not defined as a separate right as such, is implicit in the 1951 Convention[11] and its fundamental provisions, particularly the principle of *non-refoulement* (*see* below).

The Universal Declaration of Human Rights provides that 'Everyone has the right to seek and enjoy in other countries asylum from persecution'.[12] Many universally recognized human rights are also directly applicable to the refugees. These include among others: right to life, protection from torture and ill treatment, right to a nationality, right to freedom of movement, right to leave any country including one's own and return to one's country, and the right not to be forcibly returned.[13] The rights, which include civil, political, economic, social and cultural rights, are affirmed for all persons, citizens and non-citizens alike in different international human rights instruments.[14]

PROTECTION FOR REFUGEES

The refugees are a vulnerable group of people. They are deprived of the protection from the state from where they originate. In most cases, the concerned state authority is the perpetrator for the persecution.[15] The necessity and urgency for the protection of refugees may be briefly summarized as follows:

- Refugees are individuals or groups of persons fleeing persecution based on race, religion, nationality, membership of a particular social group or political opinion, and so on.[16]
- Refugees are unable to avail the protection of their country of origin, hence need international protection, that is, protection of the host state that they may have entered or may be seeking to enter. Hence, refugees need to be treated differently from other foreigners.
- Given the absence of a refugee protection regime for individual refugees, they fail to receive the protection they need and instead fall within the purview of the laws governing foreigners in general.[17]
- Involuntary return of refugees or *refoulement*[18] (with or without the knowledge of the government) may result in grave human rights violations to the returnees.

THE 1951 CONVENTION AND THE 1967 PROTOCOL: A BRIEF OVERVIEW

The 1951 Convention is the key legal instrument in defining who a refugee is. It lays down the rights and legal obligations of the state parties with regard to the treatment of refugees.[19] The 1967 Protocol removes geographical and temporal restriction from the original 1951 Convention. It is, however, important to note that all states are not signatories to the international instruments protecting refugees. Nevertheless, the general principles of interna-tional human rights law apply universally.

A significant number of refugee-hosting countries did not sign the 1951 Convention or its 1967 Protocol in South Asia, Bangladesh, Pakistan, India, Nepal, Thailand and Malaysia are mentionable.[20] These states, nonetheless respect the principles of International Refugee Law, to some extent, especially with regard to the principle of *non-refoulement*.[21]

Limitations of the 1951 Convention

The 1951 Convention was adopted at a special United Nations conference on 28 July 1951. The Convention is the basic instrument of Refugee Law (that is, it defines the term 'refugee', specifies her/his rights and obligations and outlines the responsibilities of the state party). The Convention also sets out who do not qualify as refugees, such as war criminals or those who are involved in serious non-political crimes, and so on.

When the 1951 Convention was adopted, the participating states were concerned about focusing mainly on the existing refugee problems, and necessarily not to assume obligations for the future, the extent of which could not be foreseen. This resulted in two major limitations: *a)* the dateline of 1 January 1951; and *b)* its applicability only to Europe. The benefits of the 1951 Convention were not applicable to persons who corresponded to the definition, but who became refugees because of events occurring after 1 January 1951 (Article 1 of 1951 Convention). The 1951 Convention needs further revisions due to increased complexities in the process of refugee generation, protection and progress in the field of refugee studies.

The 1951 Convention is essentially 'Eurocentric',[22] and insensitive towards the internecine racial, ethnic and religious conflicts in the Third World, which has resulted in the creation of refugees in large numbers. Thus, states had the possibility of making a declaration, when becoming a party to the 1951 Convention, limiting their obligations (under the 1951 Convention) to European refugees only.[23] The 1951 Convention, further, is unable to extend its protection coverage to the need of the IDPs, unlike the refugees (who could or would be allowed to be able to cross the border of the country of origin). The same also goes for the victims of global warming, the climate refugees.[24] The instrument mandates, among others, the protection for those whose civil and political rights are violated. However, it does not protect persons whose socio-economic rights are at risk.

The 1951 Convention has been the point of contention for the developed and developing countries. While developed countries are bidding for a rights-based approach, developing countries on the other hand have been voicing their incomprehension as to why they would be expected to abide by the standards that the North no longer seems to accept.[25] It is likely that now the Northern countries assume only a fraction of the responsibilities for refugees.[26] Given the post-9/11 scenario, most of the developed countries have tightened their borders. By the end of 2004, only two out of the top ten receiving countries were developed ones. Developed countries have already introduced and imposed the concept of 'third country protection' or 'offshore asylum system'. These types of initiatives are contradictory to the spirit of the Convention.[27]

Experts also find various dilemmas in the 1951 Convention with regard to refugees: its definition, material assistance, shared responsibilities, and lack of consensus in observing the standards of international law.[28] Some have argued to extend the definition of refugee, incorporating issues like 'human security' at the forefront.[29] Senior officials of UNHCR publicly support modifications in the Convention saying, '. . . the Convention has to be looked into from different angles/ perspectives considering the present scenario.'[30] In this scenario it is unlikely that South Asian states will accede to the 1951 Convention in the near future.

PROTECTION MECHANISM IN SOUTH ASIA

The refugee problem is almost a permanent phenomenon in South Asia. However, none of the states (except Afghanistan) has acceded to the 1951 Convention or its 1967 Protocol,[31] nor have the states developed any domestic legislation to deal with the issue. Again, there is no regional initiative by the states so far on the issue.[32]

In South Asian states like Bangladesh and India, refugees are subjected to the same laws as applicable for aliens. In the absence of any legal framework, asylum-seekers and refugees are dealt with through an ad hoc administrative arrangement, which hardly takes note of the individual protection needs. These arrangements given their very nature could be arbitrary and discriminatory.[33] Following is a brief discussion on the position of International Refugee Law in the domestic legal regime of Bangladesh and India and their implications accordingly.

Bangladesh

Bangladesh has been managing the Rohingya refugee problem without any legal framework for years. None could say under what authority the Government of Bangladesh (GOB) granted 'refugee status' (through an executive order) to about 258,000 Rohingyas in 1991.[34] In practice, the GOB has been providing protection against *refoulement* to those who fled from the country of origins fearing persecutions. However, there is no instance of granting refugee status routinely. In fact, there is no procedure in place and the GOB has never conducted any refugee status determination (RSD). No national asylum procedure means that asylum-seekers do not have a scope to approach the GOB for status determination and protection related issues. In Bangladesh, the major laws relevant to refugees are: Passport Act, 1920;[35] Registration of Foreigners Act, 1939;[36] Foreigners Act, 1946;[37] and the Extradition Act, 1974.

As a result of the broad application of domestic legislation controlling the entry and stay of foreigners, many bona fide asylum-seekers and refugees may run afoul of the law and be charged with any number of offences including:

- illegal entry chargeable under the Foreigners Act, 1946;
- illegal stay chargeable under the Foreigners Act;
- illegal departure with false passports chargeable under the Foreigners Act, Passport Act, 1920; and the Penal Code, 1860.[38]

In addition to specific charges, which refugees may risk under national laws, many asylum-seekers and refugees face difficulties with being granted asylum or being allowed to remain in Bangladesh once they have entered. This may result in their being forcibly returned to a country where they face persecution. Despite the generally 'good practice of the Government of Bangladesh' in granting asylum and protection to a large number of refugees, there is cause for concern that certain individuals have been denied the ability to secure refuge in Bangladesh as a result of the conflicting requirements of national legislation in the absence of formal recognition of the legal status of refugees.[39] Since Bangladesh does not have any specific and separate law in its statute book to deal with refugees, the laws of the land in general such as the Criminal Procedure Code 1898, the Penal Code 1860, the Evidence Act 1872 and the Code of Civil Procedure 1908 would apply to asylum-seekers and refugees.

Further, according to the Constitution of Bangladesh, the refugees are also entitled to certain rights. These are: right to protection of law (Article 31); protection of the right to life and liberty (Article 32); safeguards as to arrest and detention (Article 33); prohibition of forced labour (Article 34); protection in respect of trial and punishment (Article 35); freedom of religion (Article 41); and right to enforcement of these rights (Article 44).

According to the Constitution, only citizens have the right

to freedom of movement (Article 36), freedom of assembly (Article 37) and freedom of association (Article 38). Therefore, the refugees who fall in the category of non-citizen do not enjoy such rights as a matter of right.

The refugees in Bangladesh do not have the right to acquire, hold, transfer or otherwise dispose of property—a right that can be exercised by the citizens only (Article 41). According to Article 20, 'Work is a right, a duty and a matter of honour for every citizen', therefore, refugees as non-citizens do not have the right to work. However, under Article 17, the state is obliged to establish 'a uniform mass-oriented and universal system of education and extending free and compulsory education to all children . . . .' Therefore, any children who are for the time being in the territory of Bangladesh, shall have the right 'to education'.

Unlike India, judicial decisions having bearing on asylum or refugee issues in Bangladesh are significantly few. Among the reported cases, the mentionable one is *Sailful Islam Dilder* vs. *Government of Bangladesh*,[40] which has relevance in this context. This was about an attempted extradition of Anup Chetia[41] and others by the Government of Bangladesh (GOB). Here the petitioner sought issuance of a rule as to why the decision of the GOB to extradite Chetia and others should not be stayed.

The High Court Division of the Supreme Court of Bangladesh relying on the Special Powers Act, 1974 and the Extradition Act 1974 rejected the claim of the petitioner. Section 3(1) of the Special Powers Act empowers the government to make an order directing any person to remove himself from Bangladesh in such a manner as it may specify in the order to prevent him from doing any prejudicial act. Section 2(f) has given meaning of the expression 'Prejudicial act'. According to section 2(f)(ii), 'Prejudicial act' among others means 'act to prejudice the maintenance of friendly relations of Bangladesh with foreign states'.

The Court thus observes:

> In a case where a citizen of a foreign country intends to stay in Bangladesh and if the Government is satisfied that extradition of such person is called for in order to maintain friendly relations of Bangladesh with foreign states, the Government can on the strength of section 3(1) read with section 2(f)(ii) of the Special Powers Act, 1974, extradite such citizen to his own country in absence of any extradition treaty between the Government and such foreign states.

In a writ petition in the High Court Division,[42] the petitioner sought direction upon the respondent not to release the convicts on completion of their sentence till their applications seeking political asylum filed on 3 September 1998 was disposed off by the GOB (Respondent No. 1). The court issued a rule directing the respondents to allow the convicts to stay inside the prison as a measure of safe custody or protective custody until the applications for political asylum was disposed off. The matter is still pending before the court and, accordingly, the convicts are staying in jail. Further, the government has taken no decision yet as to political asylum.

India

India, like other South Asian countries, is neither a party to the UN 1951 Convention relating to the status of refugees nor its Protocol of 1967. There are no national laws, which define and regulate the status of refugees in the countries of South Asia. Thus, in India, refugees fall under the purview of the legislative framework that addresses foreigners in the same way. In reality, the international human rights are not enforceable in courts of law unless specific provisions are incorporated into existing municipal laws or given effect through separate legislations.

The Indian Constitution comprises fundamental rights, some of which guarantees protection to 'citizens' as well as 'non-citizens' or 'persons'. For instance, while Article 14, which guarantees equality before law or the equal protection of laws within the territory of India, is applicable to 'person' which would also include the 'citizen' of the country and the 'non-citizen' both, Article 15 speaks only of 'citizen'.

But it is very interesting to see, how, the Indian judiciary has through its verdicts benefited the marginalized sections of the society. In the Chandrima Das case (2000), the court had extended the right to life as guaranteed under Article 21 of the Indian Constitution, to a foreigner. Hanuffa Khatoon, a Bangladeshi national, was gang-raped by many, including employees of the railways, in a room at Yatri Niwas at Howrah Station of the Eastern Railway. Since, she was a Bangladeshi national she could not seek justice on the ground that her fundamental rights were violated. Article 21, of the Indian Constitution guarantees the fundamental right of 'Protection of life and personal liberty'. Further, in the case of *Zothansangpuri* vs. *State of Manipur*, the Guwahati-Imphal bench of the Guwahati High Court, ruled that refugees have the right not to be deported if their life was in danger. Again, in *Malvika Karlekar* vs. *Union of India*, the Supreme Court held that authorities should consider whether refugee status should be granted and until this decision was made, the petitioner should not be deported.

The word 'life' has also been used prominently in the Universal Declaration of Human Rights, 1948. The Fundamental Rights under the Indian Constitution are almost in consonance with the rights contained in the Universal Declaration of Human Rights as also the Declaration and the Covenants of Civil and Political Rights and the Covenants of Economic, Social and Cultural Rights, to which India is a party.[43]

The domestic application of international human rights and norms was considered by the judicial colloquia at

Bangalore in 1988. It was later affirmed by the colloquia that it was the vital duty of an independent judiciary to interpret and apply national constitutions in the light of those principles. Further the colloquia at Zimbabwe came up with the Zimbabwe Declaration 1994, which stated: 'Judges and lawyers need to familiarize themselves with the growing international jurisprudence of human rights and particularly with the expanding material on the protection and promotion of the human rights of women.' One cannot forget that the recognition of the dignity of all individuals and of the equal and inalienable rights of all members of the human family are the foundation of freedom, justice and peace in the world.

THE WAY FORWARD

From the preceding discussion, it is very unlikely that states like Bangladesh and India would accede to the 1951 Convention in the near future. It is also evident that the current legal regime on refugees in both Bangladesh[44] and India is not conducive to the protection of refugees. Therefore, there is a need to have a comprehensive legislation[45] for the protection of refugees, which among others would ensure a standard and humane treatment.

At the same time, the phenomenon of imposing restrictions by the developed nations against the very principles of the 1951 Convention also makes a point. Therefore, there is also an argument for an extension of the definition of refugee incorporating issues like 'human security' at the forefront.[46]

Pending the accession to the 1951 Convention or 1967 Protocol, South Asian states should go ahead for adoption of a rights-based national legal framework to deal with asylum and refugee issues immediately. In this regard, the Model Refugee Law adopted by the Eminent Persons Group (EPG) in 1997 could be a foundation. The law should be drafted in such a manner, which would reflect on the basic principles of the 1951 Convention and its 1967 Protocol, and among others, the Bangkok Principles Concerning Treatment of Refugees, adopted by the Afro-Asian Legal Consultative Committee in 1966. A regional legal framework under the auspices of SAARC should also be explored.

The benefits of a national legal framework for South Asian states could be summarized as follows:

- create a rights-based mechanism in place to deal with asylum-seekers and refugees instead of the present charity-based ad hoc mechanism;
- facilitate a system distinguishing between migrants and refugees;
- make an avenue for avoiding diplomatic tensions between states over status determination;
- prevent *refoulement*, unlawful detention of asylum-seekers and refugees;
- provide for uniform treatment between refugee groups;[47]
- promote a mechanism to address the specific needs of refugee women and children;
- spell out rights and obligations and duties of refugees;
- make provision for cessation of refugee status.[48]

International commitments by the states oblige them as well to develop an effective domestic legal framework that protects the rights of the refugees in accordance with the standard of protection outlined in the international human rights law. A rights-based approach to domestic legislation is to give '. . . weight within a framework that recognizes the distinctive essence of humanitarian problems and gives legal recognition to the fact that every person, alien or national, is of equal moral worth, and worthy of treatment that does not violate his/her dignity'.[49] The law should have provisions, among others, on the definition of refugees, asylum procedure, rights and obligation, status of mixed marriages, cancellation and cessation processor of refugee status, and so on.[50]

The absence of a legal framework has created so many

problems to deal with the refugees in the region, as reflected in the case of Bangladesh and India. With regard to Bangladesh in dealing with Rohingya refugees, it is also evident that 'mismanagement' could contribute to security concerns as well. As the population does not see any future for them in the country of origin and in the host country, due to the absence of a framework, they, therefore, are vulnerable to various kinds of exploitation. Some of them may take resort to other means like getting involved in militancy and guerilla activities. For the harmonization of the legal standard, the South Asian states should also vie for a regional legal framework on asylum and refugees. SAARC should take the lead in this regard. The civil society groups and human rights organizations should come forward for advocacy in this regard.

NOTES

1 Other supplementing human rights instruments include International Covenant on Civil and Political Rights (ICCPR) 1966; International Covenant on Economic, Social and Cultural Rights (ICESCR) 1966; Convention on the Elimination of All Forms of Discrimination against Women (CEDAW) 1979; Convention against Torture and Other Cruel, Inhuman or Degrading Treatment or Punishment, 1984; Convention on the Rights of the Child (CRC) 1989, and so on.

2 For definition of refugee, *see* Chapter 1, p.8.

3 Interventions have been made by states or UNHCR on behalf of asylum-seekers and refugees to ensure that their rights, security and welfare are recognized and safeguarded in accordance with international standards. Such interventions include: ensuring respect for the principle of *non-refoulement*, admission to safety, humane standards of treatment, and the implementation of durable solutions. UNHCR is the only United Nations agency with a mandate for the protection of refugees (*Protecting Refugees:*

A Field Guide for NGOs, UNHCR, Geneva, 1999, p.131).

4 Resolution no. 319 A (IV) of 3 December 1949.

5 IRO was established by the UN General Assembly in 1946. It took over the tasks of the UN Relief and Rehabilitation Agency (UNRRA). Its temporary mandate was to register, protect, resettle and repatriate refugees from some 30 countries, especially from the Eastern Europe. From July 1947 to January 1952, the IRO facilitated resettlement of over one million refugees in third countries; repatriated 73,000; and made arrangements for 410,000 who remained displaced in their home countries, as reported in the *UN Human Rights Fact Sheet,* No. 20.

6 Presentation of Hitoshi Mise, the then deputy director for the Bureau for Asia and the Pacific of UNHCR at the Eighth Informal Regional Consultation on Refugees and Migratory Movements in South Asia, Islamabad, 23–24 January 2004.

7 Article 1 of the Statute of the Office of UNHCR.

8 Article 2 of the Statute.

9 The removal of a person to a territory where he/she would be at risk of being persecuted, or of being moved to another territory where he/she would face persecution. *Refoulement* constitutes a violation of the principle of *non-refoulement*, and is, therefore a breach of refugee law and of customary international law (*Protecting Refugee: A Field Guide for NGOs*, UNHCR, 1999).

10 Article 8 of the Statute of the Office of the UNHCR.

11 Adopted in Geneva on 28 July 1951 by the UN Conference of Plenipotentiaries on the Status of Refugees and Stateless Persons held in Geneva from 2–25 July 1951. It came into force on 22 April 1954. The preparation of the Convention took place from 1947-1950, following a recommendation of the UN Human Rights Commission that early consideration be given to the 'legal status of persons who do not enjoy the protection of any government'.

12 Article 14.

13 Articles 9, 13, 14 and 15 of the Universal Declaration of Human Rights. Presentation of Md. Akhtaruzzaman, Deputy Director (Joint District Judge), Bangladesh Judicial Service Commission Secretariat at the Residential Training on Refugee Law (19-21 September) organized by ELCOP at Koitta, Manikganj on 20 September 2006.

14 The instruments include the Universal Declaration of Human

Rights, 1948, International Covenant on Civil and Political Rights, 1966, and International Covenant on Economic, Social and Cultural Rights, 1966.

15 In the refugee context, persecution refers to any act by which fundamental rights are severely violated for reasons of race, religion, nationality, political opinion or membership of a particular social group. However, this violation has to be sustained and systematic.

16 As defined in Article 1 of the 1951 Convention. Also see Article 4 of the Model National Law on Refugees, adopted by the Fourth Informal Consultation on Refugees and Migratory Movements in South Asia held in Dhaka in 1997; as contained in the revised Bangkok Principles on the Status and Treatment of Refugees of the Asian-African Legal Consultative Committee (AALCO), February 2001.

17 Ibid.

18 *Non-refoulement* meaning 'non-expulsion' is an accepted principle of customary international law and applies to refuge protection. In the *Agiza* v. *Sweden*, the UN Committee against Torture stated that *non-refoulement* under the Convention against Torture is absolute even in the context national security concerns. UN Doc. CAT/C/34/D/233/2003 (2005), 20 May 2005.

19 Borhan Uddin Khan, 'Towards a Refugee Law Regime in Bangladesh', unpublished research paper, UNHCR, Dhaka 2004.

20 Afghanistan is exception, which has acceded to the 1951 Convention in 2006.

21 With the meaning that no person shall be returned to a territory where s/he may be exposed to persecution. For significance of the Convention, see Chapter 1, p.14.

22 *International Refugee Law* (New Delhi: Sage Publications, 2000).

23 Borhan Uddin Khan, 'Towards a Refugee Law', p.5.

24 Etinne Piguet, 'Climate Change and Forced Migration', UNHCR Research Paper No. 153, Geneva, January 2008.

25 For North-South differentiation, see Chapter 1, p.17, note 7.

26 Patrick Hoenig, presentation at the Fifth Winter Workshop on Forced Migration, organized by MCRG at Kolkata on 5 December 2007.

27 Report of the Fifth Winter Course on Forced Migration (2007), MCRG.

28 Ibid.

29 For details see Mehreen Afzal, '"A Violation of His or Her Human Security" New Grounds for the Recognition of Refugee Status: A Proposal for Reform', UNHCR Research Paper No. 140, December 2006.

30 Carol Batchelor, Chief of Mission of UNHCR in India (former Head of agency's Stateless Unit in Geneva), presentation at the Fifth Winter Workshop on Forced Migration organized by MCRG at Kolkata on 5 December 2007.

31 Afghanistan has become a party to the Convention in 2005. The number of state parties to the Convention and Protocol separately is 144. State parties to both the instruments is 141. State parties to one or both the instrument is 147 (as on 1 October 2008).

32 There are few advocacy initiatives by the civil society groups and NGOs for accession to the 1951 Convention and adoption of national legislation. The mentionable initiative is the informal dialogues organized by the EPG, which was patronized by UNHCR. EPG has drafted a draft Model Law on Refugee in 2007.

33 C. R. Abrar, 'Legal Protection of Refugees in South Asia', *Forced Migration*, April 2001, p.21.

34 C. R. Abrar, 'State, Refugees and the Need for a Legal Procedure', in *Towards a National Refugee Laws in South Asia,* C. R. Abrar and Shahdeed Malik, (eds), (Dhaka: Refugee and Migratory Movements Research Unit, October 2000), p.45.

35 Amended by the Government of India (Adaptation of Indian Laws) Order, 1937; The Adaptation of Central Acts and Ordinances, 1949 (G.G.O..4 of 1949); The Passport (Amendment) Act, 1950 (13 of 1950); The Central Laws (Adaptation) Order, 1961 (P.O. 1 of 1961); The Bangladesh Laws (Revision and Declaration) Act, 1973 (8 of 1973), as amended by The Bangladesh Laws (Revision and Declaration) (Amendment) Act, 1974 (53 of 1974).

36 Amended by The Adaptation of Central Acts and Ordinances, 1949 (G.G.O.4 of 1949); The Registration of Foreigners (Amendment) Act, 1949 (8 of 1950); The Registration of Foreigners (Amendment) Act, 1957 (35 of 1957); The Repealing and Amending Ordinance, 1961 (1 of 1961); The Bangladesh Laws (Revision and Declaration) Act, 1973 (8 of 1973), as amended by The Bangladesh Laws (Revision and Declaration) (Amendment)

Act, 1974 (53 of 1974).

37 Amended by the adaptation of Central Acts and Ordinances, 1949 (G.G.O.4 of 1949); The Adaptation (Security Laws) Order, 1956 (PO 8 of 1956); The Foreigners (Amendment) Act, 1957 (35 of 1957); The Central Laws (Statute Reform) Ordinance, 1960 (Ord. No. 21 of 1960); The Preventive Detention Laws Amendment Act, 1962 (4 of 1962); The Foreigners (Amendment) Act, 1965 (9 of 1965); The Bangladesh Laws (Revision and Declaration) Act, 1973 (8 of 1973), as amended by The Bangladesh Laws (Revision and Declaration) (Amendment) Act, 1974 (53 of 1974).

38 Borhan Uddin Khan, 'Towards a Refugee Law Regime in Bangladesh'.

39 Ibid., p.13.

40 50 DLR, 1998, p.318.

41 Anup Chetia and others were arrested on 21 December 1997 under section 54 of the Code of Criminal Procedure and was confined in Dhaka Central Jail on 28 December of the same year. He was sent to Jail Hajat (custody) on 1 January 1998. They applied for political asylum on 3 September 1998.

42 No. 5558 of 2003 between Bangladesh Society for Enforcement of Human Rights *vs*. Bangladesh and Others.

43 For a comprehensive outline on the issue please see, 'Time for Change: The Legal Framework for the Rights of Refugees in India', Human Rights Features, HRF/190/08;
see http://www.hrdc.net/sahrdc/; last accessed on 13.11.11.

44 In the absence of a legal framework, there is no direction regarding the consequences of mixed marriages between a Rohingya male and Bangladeshi female and citizenship of their children thereof. However, an amendment was made in November 2008 according to which the child of a Bangladeshis mother and non-Bangladeshi father would have Bangladesh citizenship. There is nothing about the citizenship opportunity of the non-Bangladeshi husband. Apart from that the Birth and Death Registration Act 2004 has provisions for birth registration of a refugee child.

45 A broad-based legal framework covering criteria and procedure for admission of refugees, rights and obligations, cessation criteria, implication of refugee status, role of international solidarity, burden sharing, and so on.

46 For details see Mehreen Afzal, '"A Violation of His or Her Human Security" New Grounds for the Recognition of Refugee Status: A Proposal for Reform', UNHCR Research Paper No. 140, December 2006.
47 Given the refugee caseloads in India and Bangladesh, for example, there are no uniform mechanisms to deal with protection of refugees. The role of UNHCR is also not uniform in dealing with refugee groups; for details see http://www.thedailystar.net/story.php?nid=39222; last accessed on 8.10.11.
48 Uttam Kumar Das, 'The Protection of Refugees: Quest for a National Legal Framework in South Asia', unpublished paper (2007).
49 B. S. Chimni (ed.), *International Refugee Law: A Reader.*
50 Udatta Bikash, 'Why Bangladesh Needs Refugee Law', *The Daily Star*, Dhaka, 3 June 2008; see http://www.thedailystar.net/law/2008/06/03/index.htm.

Bibliography

Abrar, Chowdhury R. 'Legal Protection of Refugees in South Asia', *Forced Migration*, April 2001.

Afzal, Mehreen. '"A Violation of His or Her Human Security" New Grounds for the Recognition of Refugee Status: A Proposal for Reform', UNHCR Research Paper 140, December 2006.

Alam, Shah. 'International Refugee Law: A Critical Review', *Bangladesh Journal of Law*, 1, 1, June 1997.

Chimni, B. S. *The Law and Politics of Regional Solution of the Refugee Problem: The Case of South Asia,* Colombo: Regional Centre for Strategic Studies, 1998.

——. *International Refugee Law.* New Delhi: Sage Publications, 2000.

Das, Uttam Kumar. 'Refugees' Rights: Legal Position and Practices in Bangladesh', in *Human Rights and Domestic Implementation Mechanism*, Mizanur Rahman (ed.), Dhaka: Empowerment through Law of the Common People (ELCOP), 2006.

——. 'International Protection of Refugees', in *Human Rights and Non-State Actors,* Mizanur Rahman (ed.), Dhaka: Empowerment through Law of the Common People, 2005.

——Michael J. Shapiro and Hayward R. Adler, 'Legal Protection of Refugees: Bangladesh Perspective', in *Human Rights and Good Governance*, Mizanur Rahman (ed.), Dhaka: Empowerment through Law of the Common People, 2004.

Doerfel, Jan. 'The Convention against Torture and the Protection of Refugees', *Refugee Survey Quarterly*, 24, 2, 2005.

European Commission and UNHCR. *Refugees: Protection Gaps, Framework for Analysis, Enhancing Protection of Refugees*, Geneva, 2006.

Feller, Erika, Volker Turk and Frances Nicholson. *Refugee Protection in International Law*, Cambridge University Press, 2003.

Goodwin-Gill, Guy S. *International Law and Movements of Persons between States*, Oxford: Clarendon Press, 1978.

——. *The Refugee in International Law*, Oxford: Clarendon Press, 1996.

Gorlick, Brian. 'Human Rights and Refugees: Enhancing Protection through International Human Rights Law', UNHCR Working Paper No. 30, October 2000.

Haider, Naima. 'Understanding the Meaning of "Persecution" from "Gender" Perspective', *The Dhaka University Studies*, F, 15, 2, December 2004.

Hathaway, C. James. *The Law of Refugee Status*, Toronto: Butterworths, 1991.

Islam, Mohammad Towhidul. 'Protection of Refugees against Refoulement', *The Dhaka University Studies*, F, 15, 1, June 2004.

Trakroo, Ragini, Aparna Bhat and Samhita Nandi. *Refugee and the Law*, New Delhi: Socio-Legal Information Centre, Human Rights Law Network, undated.

UNHCR and Inter-Parliamentary Union. *Refugee Protection: A Guide to Refugee Law*, undated.

United Nations. *Human Rights and Refugees*, UN Fact Sheet No. 20.

4

THE POLITICS OF 'BELONGING' AND 'EXCLUSION': A Note on Refugees in South Asia

NASREEN CHOWDHORY

This chapter draws from a diverse literature—refugees, migration, state formation and citizenship—to analyse the impact of refugee behaviour and the lack of their recognition in countries of origin and asylum upon repatriation.[1] In a period of globalization, population movements across international borders due to political and economic conditions presuppose the rights of mobile groups. In respect to refugees, such a presupposition of rights has little meaning.

In South Asia, state formation and the subsequent nation-building project, aimed at including people of multi-ethnic origins, went forward, but succeeded only in a few instances. The state is viewed as an abstract entity with an extensive reach towards people within certain territorial boundaries.[2] It seems like 'an illusion and organ' 'super-imposed on society' with 'organized political forces'.[3] The state-building processes in postcolonial societies were responsible for developing a particular trajectory of accommodation for minority rights. The state exists within two kinds of boundaries: the first is based on territoriality and the other is the state–society divide that tends to co-opt the state structure within the societal framework. The structural features in state formation should be an ongoing process rather than a one-time phenomenon. The structural features of states include the entire set of rules and institutions involved in making the state function as a unit, with regard to managing day-to-day affairs and policy making. Despite misgivings regarding the functioning of state power, the state as an institutional structure remains in a position of authority to determine the membership of those living within the territorial domains of its state structure.

Despite the shared colonial history in the South Asia region, the experiences of Sri Lanka, East Pakistan and later Bangladesh vary remarkably from that of India, which has a clearly stipulated need to be multicultural in order to accommodate pluralist tendencies. Countries like Sri Lanka and Bangladesh failed to accommodate certain minority groups completely. Whereas the states of Sri Lanka and Bangladesh adopted a unitary model as opposed to a federal system with a bifurcation of power distribution, India adopted a federal system. In India, the strong party system and the accommodation of linguistic demands rather than religion (with the exception of religious laws) facilitated the process of nation building where the degree of state autonomy was different. Rudolph and Rudolph[4] characterize the Indian state as semi-autonomous or 'constrained'. But Kohli denies that the Indian state had complete autonomy and asserts that it is 'weak';[5] however, Bardhan[6] disagrees with Kohli's assertion and points out that the Indian state was able to develop policies independently of 'goals and aspirations of propertied class'.[7]

This chapter explores the links between the rights of certain groups of people in postcolonial societies (Tamils in Sri Lanka and Chakmas in Bangladesh); state formation and refugee-generation; and later, the lack of formal recognition in the country of asylum and in the motivation to repatriate home while exploring the following three sets of interrelated questions. Firstly, why do refugee studies emphasize on repatriation yet overlook problems of integration in post-repatriation context? Secondly, what is the rationale of asylum states for denying status to refugees in exile? Thirdly, under what conditions does 'home' assume significance in the 'refugee narrative'? In the following sections, these questions will be addressed by engaging with the literature on repatriation and citizenship, and how the concept of 'home' is interwoven into repatriation. This discussion leads to the section on framework to understand the problems of belonging among refugees in South Asia.

PROTECTION AND REPATRIATION IN THE INTERNATIONAL REFUGEE REGIME: THE OFFICIAL PERSPECTIVE

The 1951 Convention Relating to the Status of Refugees[8] and the 1967 Protocol[9] do not explicitly refer to the repatriation of refugees (*see* Chapter 3). Article 1(C)(4) of the 1951 Convention stipulates that refugee status ceases if refugees voluntarily re-establish themselves in their country of origin. Furthermore, the successful completion of a voluntary repatriation programme would indicate that the circumstances that caused the refugees to flee no longer exist. Voluntary repatriation could occur only when certain conditions have been met by countries of origin, which in turn facilitates the safe and dignified return of refugees. However, repatriation becomes a tool to suspend the status of refugees in asylum states, where a cessation clause may be applicable; it may also represent another way to prevent *non-refoulement* (*see* Chapter 3, note 20) under Article 33, whereby the refugee status only ceases when there is either voluntary re-establishment (not just return), or when a change of circumstances has been shown to exist in the country of origin. In this process, states may find an ally in an unusual place, the UNHCR. The UNHCR has agency-based standards of repatriation that often conflict with the true meaning of cessation clauses. Hathaway observes that the UNHCR has adopted 'a spectrum of institutional positions on repatriation which explicitly includes the facilitation of return "even where UNHCR does not consider that objectively it is safe for refugees to return"'.[10] Zieck disagrees with Hathaway's argument of institutional overreaching by the UNHCR but concedes that it might be possible. Zieck holds the Convention responsible for a lack of proper guidance in the modalities involved in voluntary repatriation. The 1951 Convention did not make any reference to voluntary repatriation, not in terms of solutions 'for it can be argued that the fourth cessation clause is predicated on voluntary repatriation'.[11] Article 35 of the 1951 Convention provides a specific obligation on the part of states that accords certain carte blanche for the UNHCR. This article stipulates clearly that states need to provide ultimate cooperation to facilitate the functions of the UNHCR. Article 2 of the 1967 Protocol also requires states to work toward complete cooperation with the UNHCR in matters related to refugee determination. In essence, Zieck disagrees with the concept of institutional overreaching but holds the Convention responsible for any misuse by the UNHCR.

The Organization of African Unity (OAU) 1969 Convention Governing the Specific Aspects of Refugee Problems in Africa is one of the binding documents between signatory countries and the international agency, the UNHCR, that explicitly treats some of the issues related to 'voluntary repatriation'. It recognizes the voluntary character of repatriation and specifies the responsibilities of both the country of asylum and the country of origin.[12] The Cartegena Declaration also includes provisions that relate to repatriation. The principle includes a range of issues such as the provisions of adequate information to refugees, freedom of movement, non-discrimination, access to means of subsistence and land, as well as access of the UNHCR to the returnees. None of the documents directly addresses the regional component of repatriation other than a few treaty provisions in the 1969 OAU Convention,[13] which refers to 'new circumstances prevailing in [the] country of origin' that enable refugees 'to return without risk and to take up a normal and peaceful life without fear of being disturbed or punished'.[14] But some of these changes in countries of origin are less discernible.

Repatriation can occur based on the terms and conditions involved in return. The decision to repatriate often requires a sense that the return would be long lasting or durable. The durability of repatriation is due to a 'change in circumstance in the country of origin' that would make repatriation a feasible and preferable option for refugees. However, certain assumptions are involved in the notion of 'change' that can be difficult to ascertain, which leads to an emphasis on the 'voluntariness' of return.[15] Scholars of international refugee law emphasize the changes in the historical and political context of the Convention to stress the importance of the 'voluntariness' of repatriation. The notion of voluntary repatriation operates within the boundaries of refugee law (based on interpretation of both the Statute and Convention): it relies on the ability of the country of origin to use it to its own advantage. The UNHCR asserts, '[a] voluntary repatriation programme presumes there are refugees who return to country of origin based on change in conditions in their country'.[16] Elsewhere, the UNHCR describes voluntary repatriation as 'a practical technique for affecting the safe and dignified return of repatriation once the conditions that forced them to flee or to remain outside their country no longer exist'.[17] The UNHCR can legally determine when repatriation will occur, and it can also send refugees back based on the provisions stipulated in cessation clauses. The UNHCR's Protection Guidelines on Voluntary Repatriation states, 'the idea behind promoting and subsequently encouraging voluntary repatriation is to give the refugee an opportunity to voluntarily return home with UNHCR protection and assistance before he or she formally ceases to be a refugee'.[18] The drive to resolve refugee problems is accomplished when refugees make a voluntary and conscious decision to return. The countries of asylum are obliged to help refugees repatriate in accordance with the accepted standards for voluntary repatriation. The concept of 'safe return' has gradually replaced the concept of 'temporary protection' that had legitimized instances of 'involuntary return'. The idea of 'safe return' in repatriation literature has a 'lower threshold' than voluntary repatriation, so it is applied when countries of asylum seem inclined to apply the cessation clause and promote only safe return.[19] International norms require states to acquire voluntary consent from refugees prior to the repatriation process. The process begins with a visit by UNHCR officials to refugee camps; they request that the refugees complete questionnaires to verify their consent and the voluntary nature of their return. In some cases, refugees have affirmed their consent without being properly informed of the changes in their countries of origin or other such manipulation.[20]

Chimni examines the shift in the focus of international agencies from voluntary repatriation to the concept of safe return; and in doing so he challenges the normative basis of voluntary repatriation.[21] Chimni argues that voluntary repatriation has been replaced by 'sustainable return', an expression that describes the status of refugees upon their return to the homeland. 'Sustainable return' includes the physical and material security of returnees as well as their integration with the given civil society and state. The Convention Relating to Status of Refugees does not explicitly include provisions related to the 'voluntary' nature of repatriation. Chimni claims that it was the Statute of the UNHCR that had some provisions, a claim supported by Hathaway: 'It is wishful legal thinking to suggest that a "voluntariness" requirement can be superimposed on the text of the Refugee Convention'.[22] Hathaway further opines, 'once a receiving state determines that protection in the country of origin is viable, it is entitled to withdraw refugee status'.[23] However, countries of asylum have their own impetus to create conditions for 'safe return'. Under these circumstances, refugees have no option but to follow the asylum state's bidding and 'go back'. The idea of return is based on subjective opinions of refugees living in countries of asylum. Goodwin-Gill observed that such views 'effectively substitute "objective" (change of) circumstances for the refugee's subjective assessment, thereby crossing the refugee/non-refugee line'.[24] The assumption that repatriation occurs when all conditions are favourable is, in fact, how it is intended that asylum states should deal with refugees prior to the use of the cessation clause. In other words, it is assumed that the cessation clause will only be used by asylum states when 'the circumstances in connection with which he has been recognized as a refugee have ceased to exist'.[25] Thus, the criteria that must be understood for repatriation are as follows: firstly, there should be a decision made by refugees that is explicitly expressed to the host state to return; secondly, there should be certain minimum changes in the country of origin; and thirdly, the UNHCR facilitates the return (which might go against the very tenets of its mandate).

The UNHCR determines the 'voluntariness' of repatriation. The UNHCR acts in an advisory capacity, providing information and assistance to refugees in order that they may make informed decisions, to facilitate, promote, or certify self-repatriation. The UNHCR defines modalities of assistance in guidelines[26] on voluntary repatriation, or what it calls 'refugee-induced voluntary repatriation', indicating that its facilitation of voluntary repatriation is defined as: 'Assisting refugees, *in situations where UNHCR cannot [promote] voluntary repatriation* to make an informed decision reflecting their own priorities and standards and, once they decide providing them with the necessary support and guidelines so that they can achieve the goals of their decisions.'[27]

Initially, the UNHCR had been reluctant to facilitate the repatriation of refugee groups who explicitly desired to return. However, officials who were then involved were convinced that 'the overall assessment of the situations in the country of origin' was such that repatriation 'is *not* in the best interest of the refugees concerned'.[28] The initial mandate of the UNHCR changed in 1996, when repatriation was re-interpreted to respect 'the refugees' right to return to their country at any time, UNHCR may *facilitate voluntary repatriation* . . . when refugees indicate a strong desire to return voluntarily . . . [and] it is safe for most refugees to return.'[29]

The 'promotion' of voluntary repatriation in the Handbook seems to represent an evolution of the UNHCR, with a move from an advocacy role, with 'actions taken from the very outset of a refugee situation which could not foster a climate for return,'[30] to one that promotes repatriation. The earlier definition was much more elaborate: 'Furthering or advancing the development and realization of voluntary repatriation as a durable solution to the *refugee problem* on the basis of the principles of international co-operation and state responsibility to create conditions conducive to the safe and dignified return of refugees.'[31] The concept of 'promotion' now involves 'planning and organizing the voluntary repatriation of refugees under conditions which are conducive to their safe return and durable reintegration'.[32] Since the mid-1980s, the UNHCR's right to initiate the organization of repatriation was accepted and endorsed by the executive committee (and the General Assembly).[33]

'REPATRIATION' IN REFUGEE STUDIES: THE REFUGEE PERSPECTIVE

Most literature pertaining to refugees tends to focus either on their resettlement or on their integration. Earlier studies tended to indicate a particular trajectory in research on refugees. During the 1970s, the literature tended to study the initial phase of refugee experience: specifically, the causality and patterns of flight that created the conditions for refugees.[34] During the 1980s, the literature focused on refugee resettlement and integration in the countries of asylum.[35] Scholars like Rogge and Akol have focused on the repatriation of refugees.[36] The earlier approaches to refugees placed the responsibility on the host-state to solve refugee problems rather than on the states from which they had fled. Previous approaches to refugee studies were reactive, exile-oriented and refugee-specific as opposed to the present discourse on refugees, which seems to be more proactive, homeland-oriented and holistic.

Most traditional academic research on refugees relates either to the causes of refugee flow or to the development of mechanisms to prevent the outflow of refugees to neighbouring countries. In view of the inherent inadequacies in such traditional research, recent scholars have studied the political context of refugees.[37] Other researchers such as Bascom and Rogge[38] have studied the socio-economic fallout of refugees. Scholars[39] have also examined the perspectives of refugees' long-term interests and possible rehabilitation. Motivations for the repatriation of refugees and their alleged ties or links to their countries of origin and their ability to regain status through repatriation have also been studied. Little academic research focuses on the aspects of reconstruction and rehabilitation among returnee-refugees in their countries of origin.[40] Bascom[41] analyses the dynamics of the repatriation process of Eritrean refugees from Eastern Sudan and contends that the mass movements of human beings symbolize a changing world order. Rogge[42] emphasizes the importance of the social transformation of refugees in exile as a contributory factor in their repatriation. The variation in decision making within two or three generations of refugee groups is significant. The fundamental preconditions for 'voluntary repatriation', according to a minimalist interpretation, are the cessation of military conflict, regime change (where applicable), and the stability of the home government.

To understand why refugees may be hesitant to repatriate, it is necessary to begin with an analysis of the country of asylum. 'Location-specific mobility' is a generic term that denotes any or all of the factors that 'tie' a person to a particular place.[43] In addition to community ties, affinity factors may be factors for refugee repatriation that depreciate over time. Kunz has identified two basic categories of refugees who are inclined to return: the 'event-related refugees' and 'majority-identified refugees'.[44] The 'event-related refugees' are less likely to return home because of the lack of fundamental changes in their countries of origin if groups become well integrated economically and socially in their countries of asylum. The 'majority-identified refugees' are most likely to repatriate when the opportunity arises, which seemed evident in the context of Africa. A few studies on repatriation focus on these challenges faced in the countries of origin after repatriation.[45] These challenges are particularly problematic in contexts where refugee movements have been spurred by civil conflict and over a longer period of exile. Also, most studies on refugees tend to be territory-based,[46] and until recently, the discourse on repatriation had overlooked integration problems involved in the post-repatriation context.

The literature also tends to overlook the nexus between the legal position of refugees in their countries of asylum and their choice to repatriate. Therefore, it is imperative to understand the conditions for the 'voluntary' repatriation of refugees. It is possible that refugees could return home after considering their options, but their repatriation would depend on their personal aspirations and the available information on the wider structural changes that may have occurred in their countries of origin; however, most refugees do not have the experience of such a balanced decision-making process when they repatriate. Stein and other scholars suggest a classification of repatriation along the continuum of conflict resolution in countries of origin.[47] The different classifications are: ricochet repatriation, with almost immediate return; relocation-stimulated, when host governments try to move refugees into camps; alienated-induced, when some refugees cannot identify with the emerging refugee community; secondary relocation-stimulated, when host governments try to move refugees to settlements a long way from the border; and the major repatriation, where the UNHCR promotes mass return. The literature does not address the lack of political status of refugees in the countries of asylum and the consequences upon refugees' decisions to repatriate. The gap in the literature is manifested in several ways: firstly, the resolution of refugee crises seems to be more homeland-oriented, which means little to refugees; secondly, studies on repatriation have failed to address why refugees are inclined to repatriate; and thirdly, the linkages between refugees as 'temporary' exiles encourage notions of repatriation. This chapter will address these gaps and provide an alternative rationale for why refugees are inclined to repatriate.

Determinants of belonging in exile and 'home' in refugee narratives

The notion of 'belonging' within a state is determined by membership. Citizens belonging to a territory are politically accepted and acknowledged and are legal members of the state. These citizens are admitted on the basis of rules of admissions determined either from birth, domicile, or marriage. The conventional notion of belonging is typically dictated by these rules of membership. Citizenship constitutes the basis of the relationship between the individual and the state. The countries of asylum and origin determine the nature of rights of refugees and other individuals who live within a particular demarcated territory. The spheres of inclusion/exclusion of rights are thus determined by the state. In search of recognition, refugees are faced with a dilemma regarding whether to continue to reside in exile or to repatriate 'home', which leaves them with choice.

But non-citizens, like citizens, can make claims to belonging: there exists a correlation between the identities of people residing within a territory and the sense of belonging they derive from it. People residing in a territorially demarcated area tend to derive their identity based on their sense of belonging to that territory. The sense of belonging in turn depends on a perceived sense of attachment to a certain land and a resulting identity. Soguk asserts refugees or 'moving people' tend to 'transgress political or cultural borders' and seek to 'reaffirm' the proposed boundaries of belonging.[48] Refugees, as per the rule of statist claims on belonging, remain outside the ensemble of rights that prioritize rights to citizens over similar rights to non-citizens. In a general sense, the capacity of individuals to move into or away from a state effectively challenges the capacity of the state to control the 'status of the border'. In a practical sense, migration empowers those who move as they challenge the government's ability to impose 'difference' by patrolling the 'dynamics of bodies' in the border areas since 'moving bodies' represent a cluster of people in search of transcontinental rights.

But states determine the characteristics of belonging within a geographically demarcated territory and provide rights to those who are legally entitled to belong. The state provides different rights to members as opposed to granting a 'free-for-all' to inhabitants and outsiders. The state engages in strategies of accommodation to incorporate outsiders. Two such strategies are the assimilationist and the pluralist models of incorporation. The assimilationist model includes one-sided policies adopted by the state to reduce the social, linguistic and cultural distinctiveness of immigrant communities, which allows members to assimilate or merge with the dominant community with the promise of citizenship. Membership in these situations enhances the dominant culture while eradicating the peculiarities of immigrant communities. The pluralist model accepts immigrant communities as ethnic communities with distinguishable characteristics, such as language or culture, and accepts them as citizens. Pluralism would imply that immigrants are given complete access to all spheres of society. Comparing the two, the pluralist model has a higher level of inclusion than the assimilationist model. However, both models have faced many problems in practice and have limited application in relation to determining refugee rights.

In citizenship literature, scholars have debated the significance of membership and the ability to accommodate the changes that globalization has brought to the world. The membership issue within citizenship literature is predominantly based on the legal and formal acceptance of members within the state. States tend to determine membership based on nationality. Globalization literature asserts that despite the tendency in the literature to prefer nationality-based membership, it has made some strides in accommodating a few changes. Globalization literature tends to be optimistic on the reach of the state in determining nationalized-based rights as the role of the state is decreasing. The traditional approaches to citizenship that are typified by rights-based understandings such as Marshall,[49] Black[50] and Shklar[51] have expanded to accommodate other notions such as 'citizen-as-desirable-activity' and 'citizen-as-identity', or group identity and group participation in a multicultural society.[52] However, the traditional approach to citizenship is limited to a 'formal-national-membership', which tends to prioritize the rights of members over those of non-members. While the concept of citizenship rights has expanded from an approach that is based on the individual to one that may include group-based demands, the trajectory of the change nonetheless overlooks the need to include the category of non-citizens. It has failed to address or acknowledge the rights of the stateless and non-nationals, aliens, and refugees.[53] Bosniak concurs that previous theories of citizenship overlook the immigrant 'alien' context of citizenship.[54] Bosniak and Sassen[55] both discuss citizenship rights through the lens of a globalized world and assert that the present literature does not address citizenship rights beyond nationality, that is, the concept of *denationalized*[56] or *postnational*[57] citizens.

Multiculturalists in the citizenship literature argue that 'citizen as identity' should take precedence over citizenship as a legal status of membership. Soysal argues that 'decoupling in citizenship between rights and identity' is necessary to understand claims beyond nationality.[58] Identity-based claims tend to be more particularistic in nature. Brubaker argues that it is impossible to 'decouple' the rights and the identity aspects of citizenship.[59] For Brubaker, rights and identity are interconnected within citizenship while the politics of citizenship is about nationhood that fashions and shapes the distinctive kinds of political social membership. Another school of thought focuses on the decreasing role of the state due to globalization. Soysal and Sassen[60] posit that the significance of the state is decreasing in the globalized world as rights acquire universal meaning; as a result, rights that were previously enjoyed by citizens are now also enjoyed by non-citizens, which demonstrate a shift in focus from a state-based conception of rights to one that is universal. But as rights assume universal meaning, identities of individuals can express specific traits as determined by the state. Hammer asserts that foreigners who reside in countries for long periods of time should be entitled to substantial rights.[61] Both Hammer and Brubaker contend that the rights of immigrants should be based on residence rather than nationality. The territorial location of citizens remains the main focus of citizenship rights, which are sometimes accommodated based on the duration of residence as opposed to other ways of gaining membership to a state such as 'nationality' or marriage.

Thus, the multiculturalist citizenship literature permits two conclusions about how globalization has affected citizenship. Firstly, the decreasing importance of the state, especially as a result of globalization, has created a 'postnational'[62] citizenship that leads to the 'de-coupling of political identities from national membership'.[63] Secondly, with the emergence of de-territorialized citizenship, identity need not be tied to specific national residency, ethnicity, language, or other allegiance. The new disaggregated citizenship allows 'individuals to develop and sustain multiple allegiances and networks across state boundaries, in inter- as well as trans-national context' and cosmopolitanism based on multiple allegiances across borders can sustain different communities of language, culture, and so on.[64]

In contrast with the multiculturalist citizenship literature, Bosniak argues that the importance of the state is far from waning.[65] I assert that state-centric views in South Asian states were responsible for creating boundaries of belonging. While accepting Bosniak's argument, it can be contended that despite globalization, a rights-based understanding of citizenship in these states is well in place. Further, despite developments to incorporate facets of group or societal needs within it, the citizenship literature fails to address the key issue of the rights of refugees and aliens as non-citizens. Non-citizens are significantly disadvantaged by the current rights-based citizenship discourse as the citizenship literature has failed to accommodate the issue of 'alienage' for immigrants and refugees. While multiculturalists acknowledge the globalized views on universal citizenship, in reality, the conferral of such citizenship is limited to formal members of the state, which is implicit in the discussion of the quest for membership among non-citizens. When viewed from the perspective of refugees or other non-citizens, or aliens, the theoretical notion of a universal concept of citizenship seems questionable. Asylum states generally hold a state-centric approach to rights, which discriminates against non-citizens and exacerbates the unequal relationship between citizens and non-citizens. The lack of status in the asylum state is linked to the politics of belonging for refugees. Issues of identities of refugees are understated in the asylum state, but rights are defined based on belonging. As such, in the refugee experience, refugees eventually undertake acts of repatriation due to their prolonged stay in a given asylum state that denies them rights equal to those of citizens, coupled with their need to belong and to re-acquire lost identity.

Following Hannah Arendt's notion of 'the right to have rights', it is clear that among the refugee community or otherwise 'stateless' people, the need to belong is more significant since they lack status and rights. The state is not losing its significance; rather, the state has shifted its approach, advancing a rights-based membership status rather than status determined by one's location of stay. Drawing from the globalization literature on citizenship, a case for granting rights to non-citizens, especially refugees, can be proposed. I argue that the refugees' need for recognition or status (which need not be formal status) is quite acute. If state-based citizenship rights were to expand to accommodate other 'cross-border' dimensions, then non-citizens would have rights similar to those of citizens. However, it cannot be claimed that refugees seek 'national–formal' citizenship; rather they seek a status-based position in the hierarchy of belonging that would protect their interests from arbitrariness of state officials in interpreting status in exile. The states in developing countries have failed to attribute any status to non-citizens, as they are not nationals. However, the status of denizens would minimally protect the rights of non-citizens, rather than no status at all. If state-centric rights discourse were to accept different principles of inclusion, then providing rights of non-citizens would be addressed marginally. Thus, as per the globalization perspective the state-dominated citizenship rights need to accommodate other claims to rights and accommodate varied interests and differences.

CONSTRUCTION AND RECONSTRUCTION OF 'HOME' IN REFUGEE NARRATIVES

The concept of 'home' assumes a particular significance in refugee narratives. This chapter distinguishes between the concepts of 'home' and a 'homeland'[66] to which refugees may return. Displaced people or refugees during a period in exile (especially in camps) often stay together based on ties to the homeland. Refugees associate memories and a bond with 'home' and continue to strengthen such ties while living in exile. Such a spatial attachment occupies an important place in refugee narratives vis-à-vis home. For the displaced communities, place or land remains a crucial component of their identity; therefore, any 'loss of spatial attachment makes their identity incomplete'.[67]

The links between 'home' and a sense of 'belonging' by refugee communities in an asylum state can be studied from two different perspectives. Firstly, belonging is based on ties to home, which makes it possible for refugee communities to form distinct identities that aid in rallying refugee groups during their stay in exile: it has identity-forming capability. Secondly, belonging based on 'homeland' allows refugee communities to form a collective in an asylum state, which works well from the perspective of the asylum state, as refugee communities are encouraged to remain tied to the politics of their homeland.

In repatriation literature, scholars variously define 'home' as an analytical concept. Olwig, Berger and Kibreab have provided different perspectives on home.[68] Firstly, home is a personal space of identification; secondly, it is the 'nodal point of social relations';[69] and thirdly, 'home' can be the physical place existing within specific material and economic conditions. The idea of 'home' is a social-cultural construct that cannot be separated from its exact physical place. The possibility of constructing 'home' is affected by physical conditions of existence, material possibilities, and economic situations in one's country of origin. Refugees tend to come to terms with what, to them, constitutes 'home' while in exile or within the framework of repatriation; however, as they do so, the idea of 'home' influences refugees' decisions to repatriate.

There is a debate in the literature over how a perceived sense of ties to 'home' among displaced communities influences repatriation. The persistence among refugee communities to maintain feelings of attachment to their 'homeland' prevents them from forming 'new ties' while in exile. Coles and Karadawi argue that the basic need of human beings is to belong to a particular 'home' and community.[70] These scholars agree that 'home' remains a factor in refugees' decision to repatriate. However, Warner, Malkki and Hammond, and Allen and Turton disagree with this premise; they claim that 'the place attachment model' perceived 'home' as a fixed place capable of exerting considerable influence on refugees' decisions to repatriate.[71] The argument projected in this chapter is at par with scholars who argue against the validity of the notion of 'home' and its precise impact on refugee decision making. Allen and Turton contend that the 'idea that return represents the most desirable solution to refugee movement contains an implicit assumption that a given population has its own proper place, territory or homeland'.[72] Malkki asserts that the fixing of people in native places of origin is a reflection of the sedentary bias in dominant modes of imagining homes and homelands, identities, and nationalities.[73] Hammond and Allen and Turton[74] agree that home is a strong and valid concept, but they question its influence on refugees' decisions to return. To them, returnee-refugees can be involved in a process of emplacement: through stories and practices, they actively try to create relations to a place to belong, and they negotiate different concepts and notions of 'home'. Kibreab[75] appears critical of the nexus between the imaginary concept of 'home' as existing in the mind of refugees and the actual place of 'home' and argues that it may not be the sole factor in refugees' decisions to return.[76] Furthermore, the home that refugees have left behind may no longer exist, in physical form at least, because places, social relations, and culture can change in time, especially during conflict.[77] As such, there is an overemphasis on 'home' as a factor that motivates repatriation.

While scholars have different perspectives on what constitutes 'home' for refugees, they agree that the notion of 'home' affects refugees' decision making about repatriation. Despite varied notions of 'home', these notions have an impact upon the refugees' decisions of repatriation to 'home' and homeland.[78] The asylum state perceives refugee status as a temporary status and encourages repatriation to countries of origin.[79] Often, refugees repatriate with little or no information on the changes in the 'home' country.[80] Refugees tend to come to terms with what to them constitutes home while in exile or within the framework of repatriation; however, when they do so, the idea of 'home' influences refugees' decisions to repatriate. The concept of 'home' as envisioned by refugee communities is based on their ideas of belonging. The ideal image of 'home' evokes a strong bond to reclaim status lost in exile, which is accentuated by the absence of proper status in exile.

WHAT EXPLAINS BELONGING OF REFUGEES: A CASE OF SOUTH ASIA

There are a number of factors that influence the asylum state's decision to repatriate refugees. These include demographic imbalances due to an influx of refugees, the potential for political instability and political relations between countries. A few factors involved in the repatriation of refugees in South Asia is shown in Table 4.1. The first and second columns of Table 4.1 incorporate aspects of the first research question; the third column is more pertinent to the second research question. I present explanations based on state-centred constructions of citizenship in conjunction with these factors.

Table 4.1: Factors Determining Refugee Repatriation in South Asia

	Exile	Home country	Outcome(s) in repatriation
Refugees	claimants to status; physical protection, financial assistance	formal status; reinstatement of rights, especially on land; homestead	variation in Chakma returnee outcome; lack of state initiatives in implementation of CFA or PA; politics of exclusion
Country of refuge	ethnic affinity; adverse socio-demographic relation; security threat	inter-state relations; security concerns	no interference policies; return of twice-repatriated refugees or 'recyclers'
Country of origin	examine minority groups claims of marginalization; implement policies, peace initiatives, or accord	continuation of violence; devolution package; rehabilitation strategies to reintegrate returnees	strategies of accommodations; integration patterns of returnees

The ethnic affinity between the refugee group and the host population has an important role in determining the asylum state's management of refugees, as more refugee groups seek asylum in a society that shares a similar language, culture, and kinship structures. But shared ethnicity is also instrumental in determining whether refugee groups will be repatriated. The variation in refugee treatment and management cannot be solely attributed to the ethnic affinity factor. Good inter-state relations between the countries of origin and of asylum can lead to the improved treatment of refugees as the asylum state may choose to 'repatriate' to signal good relations between the countries of origin and of asylum. In either event, the lack of *defined* status or recognition creates instability and insecurity among refugee groups, which further enables asylum states to treat them as bargaining chips in bilateral relations.

This discussion problematizes refugee repatriation in the absence of political and formal recognition of refugees in the country of asylum and posits that as the primary cause of repatriation. Linkages between rights attributed to citizens and denial of rights to non-citizens as one of the effects of state-formation processes in postcolonial societies in India, Sri Lanka, and Bangladesh have been established on the basis of state-formation literature. I advocate that state-formation processes in South Asian countries have shaped state policies of accommodation as well as the marginalization of certain minority groups. In Sri Lanka, the unitary state was responsible in adopting policies that discriminated against the minority communities. These policies essentially failed to accept members of certain communities as full members. In Bangladesh, this is especially so with the indigenous communities. The relatively new states defined the boundaries of belonging based on citizenship rights and entitlements. Over a period of time, the sense of alienation and deprivation has led to conflicts, creating conditions of refugee flow into India. In India too, the state-centric view dominated citizenship rights, which was based on nationality. Nationality-based citizenship rights tend to draw legitimacy from the territorial boundaries of state, which by default exclude non-nationals.

While postcolonial societies have similar experiences, they have dissimilar outcomes. I do not claim that all postcolonial societies share or have similar outcomes; however, it is certainly true that South Asian countries share a similar history, heritage and past. The trajectories of state formation in these countries reflected the distinctive legacies of postcolonial societies. The state represented a set of institutions with extreme coercive power of domination and force, accompanied by a monopoly on the use of force,[81] with an aim to protect territorial integrity. Tilly defines states as 'coercion wielding organizations distinct from households and kinship groups and exercise clear priority in some respects over all other organizations within substantial territories'.[82] However, some would argue that state formation could evolve over a period of time and be transformed to accommodate different interests since policies may accommodate differences in alternative spheres. The state thus represents an institutionally complex body that provides a basis for the personal safety, rights, and entitlements of its citizens.

Most developing societies have adopted a model of state formation with a strong central state that may reduce external and internal threats. State formation was the means by which political entities acquired attributes of statehood, such as legitimacy,[83] which impacted the process of state building in decolonized societies. The assumption was that a strong state would ensure stability and survive conflicting tendencies that arise from the diverse needs of society. A strong state provides a strong institutional mechanism to diffuse or accommodate any divisive tendencies within predominantly pluralist societies. State formation involved the desire to have a strong state with an immense capacity and power both to accommodate and to balance the needs of every individual in society.

The postcolonial states in South Asia adopted a stringent centralized form of state. The centralized states in Bangladesh and Sri Lanka enforced policies of homogeneity over their diverse populace, which contributed to acute marginalization of minorities such as imposition of 'Islamization' in Bangladesh and 'Sinhala Only' in Sri Lanka; this marginalization paved the way to a discourse of majoritarianism. In

Bangladesh, these policies prevented the minority or indigenous people (Jumma) from being accepted and acknowledged within the structure of their formal constitutions. The new Bangladesh state defined boundaries of belonging based on citizenship rights and entitlements, which led to a direct confrontation between the Bangladeshi and Bengali identities. In Sri Lanka, the educated Tamil minority was forced to accept the Sinhalese dominance over language and religious practices. In both instances, the state processes were responsible for reversing the histories of these two countries. Recently, scholars have argued that interests in the study of state are a reflection of 'relationship of domination, politics and forms of state building'.[84] State formation involves an understanding of power, the authority to build states and to attribute meaning to categories through a process of construction and deconstruction. Krohn-Hansen and Nustad emphasize how the study of state formation has permitted a deeper understanding of cultural processes, institutional structure, and regimes of power.[85] Corrigan and Sayer identify the state as 'cultural forms' and state formation as 'cultural revolution', arguing that new identities are formed through constant categorization and re-creation of 'everyday state routines and rituals', which in turn produce 'individual and collective identities'.[86] The state can exert itself as a physical entity that imposes varied policies of either marginalization or, in some instances, accommodation, depending on the nature of state formation. The two-pronged process further demarcates boundaries between communities based on the shaping of rights and entitlement policies between the majority and the minority. The peculiarities in the study of state formation underscore the effect on minority communities, especially in relation to their strategies of accommodation. In reality, state building has imposed rigorous homogenization projects, especially in Sri Lanka and Bangladesh.

Earlier in the chapter, the literature on citizenship and

state formation has been discussed to assess why non-nationals remain outside the purview of a rights-based understanding of citizenship rights. Also, despite strides made in the globalized world, states have failed to acknowledge rights of non-nationals. This understanding in the South Asia case has been applied to understand rights of non-inclusion of certain categories of people and determine how postcolonial state formation shapes the rights of citizens. I contend that the refugees' desire to seek a 'home' in their homeland is a consequence of their lack of former status when they are in exile and the discrimination faced during that exile period. This is particularly relevant to two refugee groups: the Chakma and the Tamils in India. In India, the normative basis of membership was determined either through descent or residence; in reality it prefers nationality-based citizenship.

Postcolonial states in South Asia (India, Bangladesh, and Sri Lanka) favoured a state-centric view on citizenship with little scope beyond the territorial boundaries of the state in terms of rights, status and recognition. Postcolonial states failed to accord adequately status to certain categories of people during the process of state building and nation building, which led to the marginalization and alienation of ethnic minorities in countries like Bangladesh and Sri Lanka. Furthermore, the postcolonial policies of Bangladesh and Sri Lanka created conditions of refugee flow into India. Indeed, while seeking refuge in India as a country of asylum, few refugees were entitled to political status. From the perspective of the asylum state, the refugees were given low priority over citizens; hence, the less significant need to determine their status. The citizenship rules in India thus demarcated the boundaries of belonging to exclude refugees and other aliens.

Since the state provides legitimacy to members based on legal standing, it denies the same to non-members. Moreover, territoriality is the basis for rights and entitlements of members of a state. The notion of such membership or citizenship is based on the presumption of political belonging and positions derived from the placement within the state. In this manner, citizenship is a political tool to carve out principles of inclusion and exclusion based on formally established normative ties between the state and its subjects that may be characterized as contractual or legal. Herbst discusses the relationship between citizenship laws and their 'explicit tie to . . . unique territoriality defined politics'.[87] Citizenship can be seen as a contractual relation between the state and its inhabitant that also determines a particular trajectory of belonging.

The legitimacy of citizenship rights that are accorded on the basis of nationality determined at birth or marriage within a territorially demarcated state has been questioned in this chapter. The legality of refugees' belonging is based on their legal position within the asylum country. I argue that if refugees were to be accepted within a framework of partial recognition, the Indian state would find it difficult to repatriate, as exemplified by the Tibetans in India and some Afghan refugees in India. The political status of refugee communities in their countries of asylum has great significance for the determination of the future of such refugee communities. A very important connection should be drawn between 'belonging' based on membership or citizenship and the role of the asylum state with respect to refugees.

There is a need to discuss a lack of framework drawn from the citizenship literature to address the issue of alienage or formal recognition to non-citizens. There are many other reasons why an asylum state chooses to deny status to non-citizens. The rationale varies depending on the geographic location in which the refugees are staying. States with contiguous borders have little choice but to keep an 'open door' policy regarding refugees. Sharing ethnicity and a similar language with the asylum state can provide an incentive in the refugees' choice of a place of refuge.

Refugees are naturally inclined to seek refuge in areas where they share a similar ethnicity with the host population; this can be a cause of concern to the asylum state and affect domestic politics. However, a prolonged period of stay of a large number of refugee groups with similar cultures and languages can also be a deterrent for the asylum state. Ethnic affinity is thus a double-edged sword, since it influences asylum seekers to go to countries of asylum that offer a shared language, culture, and kinship, but the asylum state may also be threatened by the presence of a large number of refugees and the consequences for domestic policies. Another cause for concern can be the increasing burden on resources due to the presence of a large number of refugees that expedite the process of repatriation. Asylum states can provide minimum assistance and protection to refugees, but they appear reluctant to institutionalize the role in terms of formal charters of rights. The janus-face of the asylum state acts as a protector if need be, but it does not grant formal rights, which tilts the balance of power in favour of state bureaucrats, who have significant influence on the determination of the future of refugees. The overarching principle applied in the developing states is to refuse rights to refugees. Therefore, from the vantage point of the country of asylum, repatriation represents the 'end of refugee cycle'. While the refugees' lack of formal status should have limited application in determining the probability of repatriation, it nonetheless constitutes one of the predominant factors in the refugee narrative. The seemingly 'temporary' status of refugees warrants their lesser status in countries of asylum, which influences their decisions to repatriate.

Another reason refugees agree to repatriate is due to ties to 'home' or homeland. Homeland is one of the factors that influenced refugee repatriation to their countries of origin. These notions of home of refugees are also shaped by the asylum state's policies. In this case, the Indian state isolates refugees in campsites to prevent them from intermingling with the local populace. This segregated spatial arrangement reinforces refugees' imaginations of 'home'. Refugees residing in camp are a de-territorialized people[88] with deep associations with the physical location of campsite, which is an extension of the territory in the home country. These refugees seek to re-territorialize in exile in camp. Camp refugees consider the campsites as sites of mobilization and opportunities to create a new identity based on location-of-stay (that is, camped in enclosed areas with a bamboo structure and daily rations). The mobility and identity of refugees is drawn from 'camp sites', where the ultimate power lies with the state officials. Refugees residing in camps are engaged in an emotional construction and reconstruction of history as 'a people', which forms a part of the collective, influencing the return process. Refugees view themselves as a nation in exile often empowered to reclaim or create a new homeland upon return. The camp refugees constitute a different category of people residing in isolation and have the ability to retain the purity of their ethnicity protected through isolation in camps.

Examining the literature on state formation and citizenship, I have discussed notions of belonging held by states, the prioritization of rights-based approach on citizens, and the nexus between the state and those who can legally belong within the territory. The state-centric views of a rights-based approach tend to exclude 'mobile' communities on the criteria of belonging based on membership. I contend that refugee accommodation poses a challenge to the idea of citizenship based on notions of nationality. I have offered an analysis of the centrality of a rights-based approach and the manner in which it creates a hierarchy of belonging the literature on citizenship. The notions of 'home' in refugees' narratives has also been examined to discuss motivations of their repatriation, especially in the absence of status in exile. In this context, the nation-building projects of Sri Lanka and Bangladesh, especially how state formation demarcated boundaries of belonging between communities on lines of majority and minority, have been discussed.

NOTES

1 This chapter is a part of a larger article, 'Assessing "Belonging" and Claims of "Home" among Refugees: A Note on Repatriation in South Asia', *Peace Prints, South Asian Journal of Peacebuilding*. The copyright of the article rests with the author.
2 George Steinmetz, (ed), 'Introduction: Culture and the State', in *State/Culture State Formation after the Culture Turn* (Ithaca, NY: Cornell University Press, 1999), pp.1-51; state formation is defined as the 'creation of durable states . . . transformations of basic structural features of these states'.
3 S. W. Moore, *The Critque of Capitalist Democracy* (New York: A. M. Kelly, 1969).
4 L. I. Rudolph and S.H. Rudolph, *In Pursuit of Lakshmi: the Political Economy of the Indian State* (Chicago: University of Chicago Press, 1987).
5 Atul Kohli, *The Success of India's Democracy* (Cambridge: Cambridge University Press, 2001).
6 Pranab Bardhan, *The Political Economy of Development in India* (New Delhi: Oxford University Press, 1984).
7 Karen Barkey and Sunita Parikh, 'Comparative Perspectives on the State', *Annual Review of Sociology*, 17 (New York: Columbia University, 1991), pp.523–49.
8 'As a result of events occurring before January 1, 1951, and owing to *well-founded fear* of being persecuted for reasons of race, religion, nationality, membership of a particular social group or political opinion, outside the country of his nationality and is unable or, owing to such fear, is willing to avail himself of the protection of that country; or who, not having a nationality and being outside the country of his former habitual residence as a result of such events, is unable or; owing to such fear, is unwilling to return to it' (emphasis added).

9 The 1967 Protocol relating to the Status of Refugees removed the 'temporal and geographical limitations'contained in the 1951 Convention. The Protocol was intended to broaden the basis of the 'refugee-hood' criteria.
10 James C. Hathaway, *The Rights of Refugees under International Law* (Cambridge: Cambridge University Press, 2005).
11 M. Zieck, *UNHCR and Voluntary Repatriation of Refugees: A Legal Analysis* (The Hague: Martinus Nijhoff, 1999).
12 See Article V of the 1969 OAU Convention Governing the Specific Problems of Refugees in Africa; see also CM/Res. 399 (XXIV) Resolution on Voluntary Repatriation of African Refugees of the OAU Council of Ministers, Addis-Ababa, 1975.
13 See M. Zieck, *UNHCR and Voluntary Repatriation of Refugees: A Legal Analysis* (1999).
14 Art. 5 (4).
15 See UN Doc. A/Res/38/121 (1982).
16 UNHCR, *Handbook for Emergencies* (1983), p.231.
17 UN Doc. A/AC.96/815 (1993).
18 According to the cessation clause, refugee status can be withdrawn when 'situations have improved in the country of origin' and every other factor contributing to refugee's status ceases to exist. An interesting notion as in most situations, the timing of the withdrawal of status is crucial as it is meant to act as a deterrent, and refugees are encouraged to return with *slight* improvement in country of origin.
19 The cessation clause can be divided into two broad sets: the first set comprises of four clauses that relate to a change in personal circumstances of the refugee, brought about by the refugee's own act, and which results in the acquisition of national protection so that international protection is no longer necessary. The second set comprises of clauses that relate to the change in the objective circumstances in connection with which the refugee has been recognized, so that international protection is no longer justified (the ceased circumstances' cessation clause).
20 This was the case as asserted by refugee groups residing in open relief camps in Pessalai, located north of Sri Lanka, during the repatriation of Sri Lankan Tamil refugees in 1990-92 when the UNHCR was accused of working against the interest of refugees. Some local NGOs in Tamil Nadu questioned the role of the UNHCR

in ascertaining whether the refugees had voluntarily consented to go back. Most of the refugees were shown a video showing positive changes in Sri Lanka that encouraged refugees to consent; in reality, the returned refugees failed to notice any distinctive change in circumstances.

21 B. S. Chimni, 'Post-Conflict Peace Building and the Return of Refugees: Concepts, Practices and Institutions', in *Refugees and Forced Displacement International Security Human Vulnerability and the State,* Edward Newman and Joanne van Selm (eds) (New York: United Nation Press, 2003).

22 James C. Hathaway, 'The Meaning of Repatriation', *International Journal of Refugee Law (IJRL)* 9, 4, (1997), pp.551-58.

23 Ibid., p.553.

24 *The Refugee in International Law,* 2nd ed. (Oxford: Clarendon Press, 1997), p.276.

25 Article 1C (5) of the 1951 Convention.

26 Note that the following definition of 'facilitating' voluntary repatriation is categorically different from that used in the past when it characterized the UNHCR's role as regards voluntary repatriation at large (the time, moreover, when the major repatriation took place after clear-cut changes in the country of origin and the required assistance was of technical and financial nature).

27 UNHCR, *Handbook on Voluntary Repatriation: International Protection* (Geneva, 1996).

28 UNHCR Document *Protection Guidelines on Voluntary Repatriation* (1993) (emphasis original). Facilitated repatriation can take place on the basis of either bilateral or tripartite agreements. Thus there is a slight difference between facilitating and promoting repatriation. The difference is more in the nature of assistance and whether the UNHCR has been instrumental in providing that exact nature of assistance. A case in point may be the Guatemalan refugees in Mexico.

29 UNHCR Handbook. *Voluntary Repatriation* (1996) (emphasis original). The UNHCR seems to confine its role in situations in which it considers repatriation premature to provide guidance, making its position known.

30 Ibid.

31 UNHCR Document, *Protection Guidelines on Voluntary Repatria-*

tion (1993). Although there is no clear reference as to why the state has been given the responsibility and what the nature of the state is, it might be used in the context of liability and accountability for wrongful acts and their consequences, and it may be construed as such.

32 UNHCR Handbook, *Voluntary Repatriation* (1996). Similarly, in UNHCR Doc. 1993 these activities are discussed separately under the heading of 'encouraging' voluntary repatriation: a heading that serves to underline that encouragement of the solutions only takes place after its promotions have yielded the desired conditions 'conducive to return'. The Handbook retains a similar emphasis by distinguishing between the promotions of solutions on the one hand and the promotion of voluntary repatriation on the other.

33 In addition, the perception of the UNHCR speaking 'on behalf of the international community as a whole, representing a universal, non-political, humanitarian concern for refugees' could be adduced. Statement of the High Commissioner to the Third Committee of the General Assembly, 1992 (text printed in *IJRL*, 4, 541; 1992). Recognition of this perception was formulated as a prerequisite for the UNHCR's effectively extending international protection to refugees.

34 E. Kunz, 'The Refugee in Flight: Kinetic Models and Forms of Displacement', *International Migration Review* 7, 2 (1973); J. Rogge, 'A Geography of Refugees: Some Illustrations from Africa', *The Professional Geographer* 24, 2 (1977), pp.186-93.

35 B. Harrell-Bond, *Imposing Aid: Emergency Assistance to Refugees* (New York: Oxford University Press, 1986); J. Rogge, *Too Many Too Long: Sudan's Twenty-Year Refugee Dilemma* (Totowa, NJ: Rowman and Allenheld, 1985); J .Desbarats, 'Indochinese Resettlement in the United States', *Annals of the Association of American Geographers* (Routledge, 1985); Gaim Kibreab, 'How Durable Are the "Durable Solutions" to the Problem of African Refugees?' Overview paper for the Refugee Research Workshop, IDRC, Nairobi, 1987.

36 John Rogge and Joshua Akol. 'Repatriation: Its Role in Resolving Africa's Refugee Dilemma', *International Migration Review* 22, 2 (1989) pp.184-200.

37 See Nicholas Xenos, 'Refugees: The Modern Condition',

Challenging Boundaries: Global Flows, Territorial Identities, Michael J. Shapiro and Hayward R. Alker (eds) (Minneapolis: University of Minnesota Press, 1996), p.235. Xenos discusses how refugees can be used as pawns in struggles between states, for example, the Haitian boat people. He refers to them as 'strategic human flows'. The basis of these flows, Xenos maintains, 'is the development of the state in terms of national identity and the social construction of a people within specific territory, the hyphenating of state within borders'. Dillon, on the other hand, discusses 'the scandal of the refugees', which is a reaction to being outside, of being 'other' and part of 'otherness'. Dillon highlights the 'otherness' of the refugees as being outside the fundamental 'ontological determination of international politics and its exclusionary pressures'. See Michael Dillon, 'The Scandal of the Refugees: Some Reflection on the "Inter" of International Relations and Continental Thought', as cited in Daniel Warner, 'Refugee State and State Protection', *Refugee Rights and Realities*, Frances Nicholson and Patrick Twomey (eds) (Cambridge: Cambridge University Press, 1999); Michael Dillon, 'The Asylum Seeker and the Stranger: An Other Politics, Hospitality and Justice', paper presented in International Studies Association Conference, Chicago, 1995.

38 Jonathan Bascom, 'The Dynamics of Refugee Repatriation: The Case of Eritrean in Eastern Sudan', in *Population Migration and the Changing World Order*, W. T. Gould and A. M. Findlay, (eds) (New York: John Wiley and Sons, 1994), pp.225-48; J. Rogge, 'Repatriation of Refugee: Not So Simple "Optimum Solution"', in *When Refugees Go Home*, T. Allen and H. Morsink (eds) (Trenton: Africa World Press. 1994), pp.14-49.

39 Barbara Harrell-Bond, *Imposing Aid: Emergency Assistance to Refugees* (New York: Oxford University Press, 1986)and Allen and Morsink, *When Refugees Go Home* (1994) have argued that some international agencies encourage repatriation. Gervase Coles, 'Voluntary Repatriation: A Background Study', paper prepared for the Round Table on Voluntary Repatriation (San Remo, Italy: International Institute of Humanitarian Law, UNHCR, 1985) challenges his reader to re-think the 'exilic bias' of resolving refugee problems in contemporary refugee law (*also see* Coles 1987, 1989 and 1992a and 1992b).

40 With the exception of Laura Hammond. 'The Making of a Good Citizen in an Ethiopian Returnee Settlement, in *Coming Home? Refugees, Migrants and Those Who Stayed Behind*, Lynellyn D. Long and E. Oxfeld (eds) (Philadelphia: University of Pennsylvania Press, 2004), pp.206-25 and *This Place Will Become Home: Refugee Repatriation to Ethiopia* (Ithaca, NY: Cornell University Press, 2004).

41 Jonathan Bascom, 'The Dynamics of Refugee Repatriation', 1994.

42 John R. Rogge, 'Repatriation of Refugees: A Not-So-Simple 'Optimum' Solution', paper presented at the Symposium 'Social and Economic Aspects of Mass Voluntary Return of Refugees from One African Country to Another', Harare, Zimbabwe, 1991.

43 DaVanzo J., 1981, 'Microeconomic Approaches to Studying Migration Decisions', in *Migration Decision Making: Muliti-disciplinary Approaches to Microlevel Studies in Developed and Developing Countries*, G. F. De Jong and Gardner R. W. (eds) (New York: Pergamon Press; Pergamon Policy Studies on International Development, 1981), p.116.

44 E. Kunz, 'Exile and Resettlement: Refugee Theory', *International Migration Review* 15, 1 (1991).

45 Mary Ann Larkin, F.C. Cuny and S.N. Stein (eds), *Repatriation under Conflict in Central America* (Washington, DC: Georgetown University, Centre for Immigration Policy and Refugee Assistance, 1991); Allen and Morsink, *When Refugees Go Home* (1994).

46 G. Coles, 'Approaching the Refugee Problem Today', in *Refugees and International Relations*, Gil Loescher and Laila Monahan (eds) (New York: Oxford University Press, 1989); James C. Hathaway, *The Law of Refugee Status* (Toronto: Butterworths, 1991a); 'Reconceiving Refugee Law as Human Rights Protection', *Journal of Refugee Studies* 4, 2, 1991b.

47 Barry Stein, 'Voluntary Repatriation during Conflict: Contemporary Practice', in *Refugee Repatriation during Conflict: A New Conventional Wisdom*, Barry Stein, Fred Cuny and Pat Reed (eds) (Dallas: The Centre for the Study of Societies in Crisis), pp.1-28.

48 Nevzat Soguk, *States and Strangers: Refugees Displacement of Statecraft* (Minnesota: University of Minnesota Press, 1999).

49 T. H. Marshall, *Citizenship and Social Class* (Cambridge: Cambridge University Press, 1949). Marshall discusses progressive rights in civil, economic, and political spheres in capitalist

societies.

50 Cited by Linda Bosniak in 'Citizenship De-nationalized', *Indiana Journal of Global Legal Studies* 7 (2000a) that Black 'employs citizenship' as rights to have 'full and equal membership'.

51 Judith N. Shklar, *American Citizenship: The Quest for Inclusion* (Cambridge, Ma: Harvard University Press, 1991). Shklar refers to individual's standing in society.

52 Will Kymlicka and Wayne Norman, 'Return of the Citizen: A Survey of Recent Work on Citizenship Theory', *Ethics* 102, 2 (1994), pp. 352–81.

53 Saskia Sassen, *Guest and Aliens* (New York: The New Press, 1999).

54 I am grateful to Linda Bosniak for proposing the problem of alienage. In this paper I argue that state-centric views on citizenship rights determined issues of belonging. See Bosniak, 'Universal Citizenship and the Problem of Alienage', 2000b.

55 Linda Bosniak, Universal Citizenship and the Problem of Alienage', 2000b; Saskia Sassen, *Losing Control? Sovereignty in an Age of Globalization* (New York: Columbia University Press, 1996); *Guest and Aliens* (1999); Engin Fahri Isin, *Democracy, Citizenship and the Global City* (New York: Routledge, 2000).

56 A. R. Zolberg, 'The Dawn of Cosmopolitan Denizenship', *Indiana Journal of Global Legal Studies* 7, 2 (2000), Heinz Klug, 'Contextual Citizenship', *Indiana Journal of Global Legal Studies* 7, 2 (2000), and Kim Rubenstein and Daniel Alder, 'International Citizenship: The Future of Nationality in a Globalised World', *Indiana Journal of Global Legal Studies* 7, 2 (2000) in response to Bosniak's 'Citizenship De-nationalized', *Indiana Journal of Global Legal Studies* 7 (2000a), assert that there is a need to go beyond the notion of the state-dominated discourse on citizenship rights. The predominant position of state is challenged as a result of the movement of people across borders. Rubenstein and Alder (2000: 529) challenge the 'singular notion of citizenship or a single legal status linking directly to the state' and are a little cautious towards complete denationalized citizenship; instead they discuss trends away from a state-centred notion, in order to consider the impact of citizenship on the legal status of nationality.

57 Bosniak (2000a) asserts that the globalized literature tends to view claims of 'moving people' as postnational or 'transnational'

rather than denationalized. She tends to view these claims as the denationalized rights of people. But Sassen differentiates between denationalized and postnational. According to Sassen, 'The Need to Distinguish Denationalised and Postnational', *Indiana Journal of Global Legal Studies*, 7, 2 (2000), the foci of denationalized is 'national-state', whereas postnational is beyond 'national-state'. But Sassen tends also to differentiate between denationalized as conceptualized by Bosniak and as one put forward by her.

58 Yasemin N. Soysal, *Limits of Citizenship: Migrants and Post-national Membership in Europe* (Chicago: The University of Chicago Press, 1994).

59 Roger Brubaker, *Citizenship and Nationhood in France and Germany* (Cambridge, Ma: Harvard University Press, 1992), p.132.

60 Soysal, *Limits of Citizenship* (1994) and Sassen, *Losing Control?* (1996); E. Fahri Isin, *Democracy, Citizenship and the Global City* (2000).

61 Tomas Hammer, 'Citizenship: Membership of a Nation and of a State', *International Migration* 24 (1986), pp.735–47; *International Migration, Citizenship and Democracy* (Aldershot: Gower, 1990).

62 Y. N. Soysal, 'Citizenship and Identity, Living in Diasporas in Post-War Europe', *Ethnic and Racial Studies* 23, 1, (2000).

63 Saskia Sassen, *Guest and Aliens* (1999).

64 Seyla Benhabib, *Democratic Equality and Diversity: Political Identities in Global Era* (Princeton N.J: Princeton University Press, 2004), p.174.

65 Bosniak, 'Universal Citizenship and the Problem of Alienage', (2000b), pp.963-82.

66 By homeland, I mean an extension of refugees' idea of 'home'. Returnee-refugees do not hold similar views of homeland as that of rebel groups; rather, they view homeland as a safe place to be, within the country of origin.

67 See Stefan Wolff, 'German Expellee Organizations between "Homeland" and "at Home": A Case Study of the Politics of Belonging', *Refuge* 20, 1 (2001), pp.52-65.

68 Karen Fog Olwig, 'Cultural Sites: Sustaining a Home in a Deterritorialized World', in *Siting Culture: The Shifting Anthropology Object*, Karen Fog Olwig and Kristen Hastrup (eds) (New York: Routledge, 1997), pp.17-39; Gaim Kibreab, 'Revisiting

the Debate on People, Place Identity and Displacement', *Journal of Refugee Studies* 12 (1999), pp.384-411.

69 Olwig, 'Cultural Sites', 1997, p.236.

70 Gervase Coles, 'Voluntary Repatriation: A Background Study', paper prepared for the Round Table on Voluntary Repatriation (San Remo, Italy: International Institute of Humanitarian Law/ UNHCR, 1985); Ahmed Karadawi, 'The Problem of Urban Refugees in Sudan', in *Refugees: A Third World Dilemma*, John Rogge (ed.) (Totowa, NJ: Rowman and Littlefield, 1987), pp.115-29.

71 D. J. Warner. 'Voluntary Repatriation and the Meaning of Return to Home: A Critique of Liberal Mathematics', *Journal of Refugee Studies* 7, 2/3(1994), pp. 160–72. Also see Liisa Malkki, *Purity and Exile: Violence, Memory and National Cosmology among Hutu Refugees in Tanzania* (Chicago: University of Chicago Press, 1995) and her 'Refugees and Exile: from "Refugee Studies" to the National Order of Things', *Annual Review of Anthropology* 24 (1995), pp.495-523; Laura Hammond, 'The Making of a Good Citizen in an Ethiopian Returnee Settlement', in *Coming Home? Refugees, Migrants and Those Who Stayed Behind*, Lynellyn D. Long and E. Oxfeld (eds) (Philadelphia: University of Pennsylvania Press, 2004), pp.206-25; T. Allen and David Turton, 'Introduction', in *In Search of Cool Ground: War, Flight and Homecoming in Northeast Africa*, T. Allen (ed) (London: James Currey, 1996), pp.1-22.

72 Ibid, p. 10.

73 Malkki, *Purity and Exile* (1995), p.16.

74 D. Hammond, 'The Making of a Good Citizen', (1999) and Allen and Turton, 'Introduction' (1996).

75 Gaim Kibreab, 'Citizenship Rights and Repatriation of Refugees', *The International Migration Review*, 37 (Spring 2003), pp.24-74.

76 Ibid.

77 Warner, 'Voluntary Repatriation and the Meaning of Returning to Home', *Journal of Refugee Studies*, 2 and 3 (1994), pp.160-74.

78 Based on data collected on Tamils and Chakma/ Jumma refugee-returnees in Vavuniya, Mannar in Sri Lanka, and Khagracharri in Bangladesh, I assert the refugees' decision to belong 'home' is acute in the absence of status in asylum. But the idea of 'home' to refugees is dissimilar to insurgent views on homeland, such as Tamil Eelam, or Jummaland; rather, it means the possibility to

resume 'day-to-day activities'.

79 As stated in an interview in Chennai (India) July 2002, a higher official dealing with refugees stated, 'We don't understand the philosophy behind meanings of home, and so on, as long as refugees repatriate to country of origin we are alright with their decisions.'

80 The same official in Chennai stated in an interview in July 2002, 'These people need to go back to their "home".' In this instance 'home' was meant in the general sense of the term. Most of these officials were aware that the peace process in Sri Lanka was working well, which in the long run could facilitate the return of refugees as 'the killing etc., has stopped' in Sri Lanka.

81 Peter Evans, Dietrich Rueschemeyer and Theda Skocpol (eds.), *Bringing the State Back In* (Cambridge: Cambridge University Press, 1985); Joel Midgal, *Strong Societies and Weak States: State–Society Relations and State Capabilities in the Third World* (Princeton, NJ: Princeton University Press, 1988); Charles Tilly, *The Formation of National States in Western Europe* (Princeton, NJ: Princeton University Press, 1975).

82 Charles Tilly, 'War Making and State Making as Organized Crime', in *Bringing the State Back In*, Peter Evans, et al. (eds), (1985).

83 David Holloway and Stephan J. Stedman, 'Civil Wars and State-Building in Africa and Eurasia' in *Beyond State Crisis? Post-colonial Africa and Post-Soviet Eurasia in Comparative Perspective*, Mark R. Beissinger and Crawford Young (eds) (Washington DC: Woodrow Wilson Centre Press, 2002), pp.161-89.

84 George Steinmetz, (ed), 'Introduction: Culture and the State', in *State/Culture State Formation after the Culture Turn* (Ithaca, NY: Cornell University Press, 1999), pp.1-51; Thomas Blom Hansen and Finn Stepputat (eds), *States of Imagination: Ethnographic Explorations of the Postcolonial State* (Durham, NC: Duke University Press, 2001) and *Sovereign Bodies: Citizens, Migrants, and States in the Postcolonial World* (Princeton, NJ: Princeton University Press, 2005); Veena Das and Deborah Poole (eds), *Anthropology in the Margins of the State* (New Delhi: Oxford University Press, 2004)

85 Christian Krohn-Hansen and Knut G. Nustad (eds), *State Formation: Anthropological Perspectives* (London: Pluto Press, 2005).

86 Ibid.

87 Jeffery Herbst, *States and Power in Africa: Comparative Lessons in Authority and Control* (Princeton, NJ: Princeton University Press, 2000).

88 I follow Liisa Malkki's understanding on difference between camp refugees and non-camp refugees. See Malkki, 'Refugees and Exile' (1995).

Bibliography

Abrams, Philip. 'Notes on the Difficulty of Studying the State', *Journal of Historical Sociology* 1, 1 (March 1988).

Adhikari R.B. and N. P. Banskota. 'The Future of South Asian Regional Cooperation', in *Economic Institutions in India*, Parthasarathi Banerjee and Frank-Jurgen Richter (eds), New York: Palgrave Macmillan, 2003.

Agamben, Giorgio. *Homo Sacer: Sovereign Power and Bare Life*, Stanford: Stanford University Press, 1995.

Alam, Javeed. 'The Nation and the State in India: A Difficult Bond', in *India's Living Constitution Ideas, Practices and Controversies*, Zoya Hasan et al. (eds), London: Anthem Press, 2005.

Andrews, Geoff. *Citizenship*, London: Lawrence and Wishart Limited, 1991.

Appadurai, Arjun. 'Putting Hierarchy in Its Place', *Cultural Anthropology* 3, 1, 1988.

——. 'Disjuncture and Differences in the Global Cultural Economy', *Public Culture*, 2, 2, 1990.

Atul, Kohli. 'Introduction', in *The Success of India's Democracy*, Atul Kohli (ed), New Delhi: Cambridge University Press, 2002.

Austin, Granville. *Working a Democratic Constitution*, New York: Oxford University Press, 1999.

Bader, Veit (ed), *Citizenship and Exclusion*, New York: St. Martin's Press, 1997.

Basch, Linda, Nina Glick Schiller and Cristina Szanton Blanc. *Nations Unbound: Transnational Projects, Postcolonial Predicaments, and Deterritorialized Nation-States*, Luxembourg: Gordon and Breach, 1994.

Baubock, Rainer. 'Migration and Citizenship', *New Community*, 18, 1, 1991a.

——. 'Immigrations and the Boundaries of Citizenship', *Monographs in Ethnic Relations*, 4, Warwick: Centre for Research in Ethnic Relations, 1991b.
——. *Transnational Citizenship Membership and Rights in International Migration*, Vermont: Edward Elgar Publishing Company, 1994.
Benhabib, Seyla. *Democratic Equality and Diversity: Political Identities in Global Era*, Princeton N.J: Princeton University Press, 2002.
——. *The Rights of Others Aliens, Residents, and Citizens*, Cambridge: Cambridge University Press. 2004.
Berezin, Mabel and Martin Schain. *Europe without Borders: Remapping Territory, Citizenship and Identity in a Transnational Age*, Baltimore: John Hopkins University Press, 2003.
Bhabha, Homi K. (ed.), 'Introduction: Narrating the Nation', in *Nation and Narration*, New York: Routledge, 1990.
Bhargava, Rajeev. 'India's Secular Constitution', in *India's Living Constitution Ideas, Practices and Controversies*, Zoya Hasan (ed), London: Anthem Press, 2005.
Bosniak, Linda. 'Citizenship De-nationalized', *Indiana Journal of Global Legal Studies* 7, 2000a.
——. 2000b. 'Universal Citizenship and the Problem of Alienage', *Northwestern University Law Review* 94, 3, Spring.
Castles, Stephen. 'The Australian Model of Immigration and Multiculturalism: Is It Applicable in Europe?' *International Migration Review* 26, 2, 1992.
——. 'Multicultural Citizenship: the Australian Experience', in *Citizenship and Exclusion*, Veit Bader (ed) (1997).
Castles, Stephen and Alastair Davidson. *Citizenship and Migration: Globalization and the Politics of Belonging*, New York: Routledge, 2000.
Chatterjee, Partha. 'The Nation and Its Fragments: Colonial and Postcolonial Histories', Princeton, NJ: Princeton University Press, 1993.
—— (ed.). *State and Politics in India*, New Delhi: Oxford University Press, 1997.
——. *The Politics of the Governed: Reflections on Popular Politics in Most of the World*, New York: Columbia University Press, 2004.

Coles, G. 'The Human Rights Approach to the Solution of the Refugee Problem: A Theoretical and Practical Enquiry', in *Human Rights and the Protection of Refugees Under International Law*, Alan Nash (ed), Montreal: Canadian Human Rights Foundation/ The Institute for Research on Public Policy, 1987.

——. 'Approaching the Refugee Problem Today', in *Refugees and International Relations*, Gil Loescher and Laila Monahan (eds), New York: Oxford University Press, 1989.

——. *Appeal to Donor Governments*, Asmara: Commission for Eritrean Refugee Affairs, Provisional Government of Eritrea, 1992a.

——. *Approaches and Strategies in the Repatriation of Eritrean Refugees*, Asmara: Provisional Government of Eritrea, 1992b.

Das, Veena and D. Poole (eds), *Anthropology in the Margins of the State*, New Delhi: Oxford University Press, 2004.

Gellner, Ernest. *Nations and Nationalism*, Oxford: Blackwell, 1983.

Gould, Carol and Pasquale Pasquino, *Cultural Identity and the Nation-State*, New York: Rowman and Littlefield Publishers, 2001.

Hansen, Thomas Blom and Finn Stepputat Hansen (eds), *States of Imagination: Ethnographic Explorations of the Postcolonial State*, Durham NC: Duke University Press, 2001.

——. *Sovereign Bodies: Citizens, Migrants, and States in the Post-colonial World*, Princeton, NJ: Princeton University Press, 2005.

Hardgrave, Robert L. and Stanley A. Kochanek, *India: Government and Politics in a Developing Nation*, Fort Worth: Harcourt Brace Jovanovich, 1993.

Jaffrelot, Christopher. 'Hindu Nationalism and Democracy', in *Transforming India: Social and Political Dynamics of Democracy*, Francine Frankel, Zoya Hasan, Rajeev Bhargava and Balveer Arora (eds), London: Oxford University Press, 2000.

Jayal, Niraja Gopal (ed), *Democracy in India*, New Delhi: Oxford University Press, 2001.

Jayal, Niraja Gopal and Sudha Pai (eds), *Democratic Governance in India: Challenges of Poverty, Development, and Identity* New Delhi: Sage Publications. 2001.

Klug, Heinz. 'Contextual Citizenship', *Indiana Journal of Global Legal Studies*, 7, 2, 2000.

Kohli, Atul (ed.), *The Success of India's Democracy*, Cambridge: Cambridge University Press, 2001.

Kothari, Rajni. *Democratic Polity and Social Change in India: Crisis and Opportunities*, Bombay: Allied Publishers, 1976.

——. *Politics and the People: In Search of a Humane India*, vols. I and II. Delhi: Ajanta Publications International, 1989.

Rubenstein, Kim and Alder Daniel, 'International Citizenship: The Future of Nationality in a Globalised World', *Indiana Journal of Global Legal Studies*, 7, 2, 2000.

Sassen, Saskia, 'The Need to Distinguish Denationalised and Post-national', *Indiana Journal of Global Legal Studies* 7, 2, 2000.

—— (ed) *Global Networks, Linked Cities*, New York: Routledge, 2002.

Schmitter, Phillippe. 'The Scope of Citizenship in a Democratized European Union: from Economic to Social and Cultural', in *European Citizenship between National Legacies and Postnational Projects*, Klans Eder and Bernhard Giesen (eds), Oxford: Oxford University Press, 2001.

Schuck, Peter H. *Citizens, Strangers, and In-between: Essays on Immigration and Citizenship*, Oxford: Westview Press, 1988.

Schuck, Peter H. and Roger M. Smith. *Citizenship without Consent: Illegal Aliens in American Polity*, New Haven: Yale University Press, 1985.

Sieder, Rachel. 'Rethinking Citizenship: Reforming the Law in Postwar Guatemala', in *States of Imagination Ethnographic Explorations of the Postcolonial State*, Thomas Blom Hansen and Finn Stepputat (eds), Durham, NC: Duke University Press, 2001.

Silverman, M. 'Citizenship and the Nation-State in France', *Ethnic and Racial Studies* 14, 3, 1991.

——. *Deconstructing the Nation: Immigration, Racism and Citizenship in Modern France*, London: Routledge, 1992.

Skalnik, Peter. *Outwitting the State*, Piscataway, New Brunswick: Transaction, Publishers, 1989.

Smith, Anthony. *The Ethnic Origins of Nations*, Oxford: Blackwell Press, 1986.

Smith, A. D. 'The Problems of National Identity: Ancient, Medieval and Modern?' *Ethnic and Racial Studies* 18, 1995.

Soguk, Nevzat. 'Transnational/Transborder Bodies: Resistance, Accommodation, and Exile in Refugee and Migration Movements on the US-Mexican Border', in *Challenging Boundaries Global Flows, Territorial Identities*, Michael J. Shapiro and Hayward R. Adler (eds), Minneapolis: University of Minnesota Press, 1996.

——. *States and Strangers: Refugees Displacement of Statecraft*, Minnesota: University of Minnesota Press, 1999.

Zolberg, Aristide R. 'The Dawn of Cosmopolitan Denizenship', *Indiana Journal of Global Legal Studies* 7, 2 2000.

5

DO THE DISPLACED HAVE A RIGHT TO RETURN?

South Asian Experiences

BHAVANI FONSEKA

Displacement is not a new concept in South Asia. Throughout the centuries there has been displacement due to conflict, natural disasters, human rights violations, threats to human security and development. Because of threats and insecurities, there is an inability to remain in one's home, resulting in the movement within the community, village, region, or to other parts of the country, and in some cases, to other countries. Migration drives have been varied across the globe, but in most instances, it is in the search for safety and an improved quality of life.

Both external and internal displacement has wide-ranging consequences. The definition of a person who has fled his/her country is termed as a refugee (*see* Chapter 1). Persons displaced within their own countries are termed as IDPs. According to the Guiding Principles on internal displacement (hereinafter referred to as the Guiding Principles), Principle 1 terms IDPs as persons or groups of persons who have been forced or obliged to flee or to leave their homes or places of habitual residence, in particular as a result of or in order to avoid the effects of armed conflict, situations of generalized violence, violations of human rights or natural or human-made disasters, and who have not crossed an internationally recognized state border.

Throughout the years, there has been an increase in refugee and IDP numbers globally. Much of the displacement has been due to conflicts such as those seen in the Democratic Republic of Congo, Sudan, Rwanda, Burundi, Afghanistan, India and Sri Lanka. Natural disasters like the tsunami that hit Asia in 2004, earthquakes and floods too have had an impact. Since 2006 there has been an increase in refugee and IDP figures globally attributed largely to increasing conflicts and natural disasters across the globe. According to the UNHCR, there has been an increase of refugees in 2006 after a decline was witnessed between 2001-2005. At the end of 2007, there were 11.4 million refugees registered with the UNHCR compared to the 9.9 million who were registered in 2006. UNHCR has cited two patterns in the present refugee population: one, the majority of refugees are hosted by neighbouring countries and over 80 per cent remain within their region of origin; and two, there has been an increase in the number of urban refugees.[1]

Globally, it is reported that there are 51 million IDPs,[2] with 26 million conflict-affected IDPs[3] and 25 million displaced due to natural disasters, but these figures are not comprehensive because of limited access to areas and the dynamic nature of displacement. At the end of 2006, there was an estimated 24.5 million IDPs. The present increase is largely caused by numerous disasters and insecurities occurring globally.[4]

Displacement results in refugees and IDPs leaving their homes, land and property, and villages. Due to displacement the social systems and community networks are destroyed. Loved ones are lost, families are separated and livelihoods affected. Displacement not only brings with it security issues, it also creates other problems including social, economic and political. In such a context, it is imperative that a rights and policy framework is in place to address grievances, protect the rights of those affected and provide them assistance. These forms of assistance and protection can be for immediate and long-term needs. It is essential that durable solutions for IDPs are discussed and provided using principles such as equity, conflict sensitivity, participation and consultation. Special attention also needs to be given to special groups such as women, children and the differently able, taking on board their needs when formulating policies and programmes.

DISPLACEMENT IN SOUTH ASIA

South Asia has witnessed countless instances of displacement resulting in refugee and IDP populations. In Afghanistan, several thousands of people are displaced due to armed conflict, natural disasters and threats to human security (*see* Chapter 2). According to the Internal Displacement Monitoring Centre (hereinafter referred to as the IDMC) there are over 200,000 IDPs in Afghanistan but these figures are of those who were displaced prior to 2004. The UN and ICRC have recorded that there were 730,000 IDPs in Afghanistan due to conflict since 2006, amounting to an average of 400 a day. At the end of January 2011, 309,000 people remained internally displaced due to armed conflict, human rights abuses and other generalized violence.[5] As with many other countries, official figures are not comprehensive and merely indicate the magnitude of the problem. Similarly in Bangladesh, it is estimated that there are around 500,000 IDPs though these again are not inclusive.[6] Displacement in Bangladesh is mainly due to the conflict and persecution of religious minorities. The Chittagong Hill Tracts (CHTs) in Bangladesh is home to a large population of conflict IDPs (*see* Chapter 2). According to the IDMC, India is reported to have around 600,000 conflict-affected IDPs.[7] As of December 2011 at least 503,000 displaced persons have been displaced by armed conflict and violence.[8] Displacement in India is caused by threats to human security, attacks by militants groups and counter operations by security forces in Kashmir, the Northeast and other parts of India as well as natural disasters and development. In Nepal, approximately 50,000-70,000 people lived in displacement, mainly due to continued violence, threats to human security and lack of planning and proper assistance including inadequate land and property restitution and in June 2009, the IDP Working Group estimated that between 50,000 and 70,000 people displaced by the conflict, could not be returned, resettled or integrated locally.[9] Since April 2006, there are 281,698 IDPs in Sri Lanka.[10] As of 31 December 2011, more than 95,000 people (more than 54,000 'old' and more than 41,000 'new' IDPs) remained in displacement in Sri Lanka as a result of the armed conflict that ended in May 2009 (*see* Chapter 2).

A key issue that needs highlighting in South Asia is that not all IDPs own land and therefore are unable to return to one's 'own' land. Many live in displacement with nowhere to go and limited assistance including the government's inability to provide land to the landless. Another common factor in many situations of displacement is the inability to return to and access one's own land, house and property. This is evident in Afghanistan, Bangladesh and Sri Lanka. Land is a key issue in displacement and return processes. Without adequate attention and concrete steps taken to address land issues, large numbers remain in displacement. Policies and proposals on land not only need to be discussed and formulated, they also need to be implemented for the enjoyment of the affected communities. For example, a peace accord was signed in 1997 in Bangladesh to allow for return but thousands still live in displacement due to problems with land and property restitution.

In the South Asian context there have been multiple displacements. For example, Afghan IDPs who returned to their lands have been displaced after return, this happened in India and Sri Lanka too. As with other parts of the world, a problem that has been highlighted in several South Asian countries is that the emphasis placed on return is disproportionate to the sustainability of the return and that very limited attention is paid to conditions and assistance after return. More attention needs to be given to land and property restitution, compensation, livelihood assistance and development. The lack of reintegration assistance coupled with issues such as continued violence and threats can impact the sustainability and safety of return and in some instances can lead to renewed displacement.

This chapter will focus on the freedom of movement and right to return of IDPs. Though these rights apply to both refugees and IDPs globally, the focus will be specifically on conflict-affected IDPs in Sri Lanka. The right to return is firmly established in international law and in national frameworks. There have been developments in the field of international human rights law where conditions of return and restitution have been discussed and benchmarks established. As seen with the Sri Lankan case study, this is not always practiced at the national level. The Sri Lankan experience has been used to demonstrate that though national frameworks provide certain benchmarks and standards, there are violations and discrepancies on the return process. The benchmarks developed internationally and in other conflict settings need to be taken on board and the best practices be translated to suit the return processes. As set out internationally, return needs should be voluntary, safe, informed, dignified and sustainable. Any discussion of return, however, cannot exclusively focus on returning to one's land, but needs also to talk about restitution of land and property.

LEGAL AND POLICY FRAMEWORK

This section will examine the international legal and policy framework on the right to return and conditions of return. International human rights law and humanitarian law contain provisions to protect the rights of civilians, with international humanitarian law specifically focusing on the need to protect civilians in armed conflict. International humanitarian law applies to state actors and armed groups, and there is no derogation for humanitarian norms. The Geneva Conventions 1949 and the Additional Protocols 1977 provide general protection in relation to conflict, with the Additional Protocol II focusing on internal armed conflicts. According to international humanitarian law there needs to be distinction between civilian populations and combatants.

Furthermore, humanitarian law requires that persons who take no active part or have ceased to take an active part in the hostilities shall be treated humanely and without any adverse distinction. Article 3 in the four Geneva Conventions expressly prohibits acts of violence to life and person, taking of hostages, outrages upon personal dignity and passing of sentences without previous judgement pronounced by a regularly constituted court. Additional Protocol II provides further protection in internal armed conflicts. Article 17 of the Additional Protocol II provides that in situations of internal conflict it is expressly forbidden to compel civilians to leave their place of residence unless the security of the persons involved or imperative military reasons so demand it. The protection provided in the Geneva conventions and Additional Protocols have evolved into customary international law and become universal. Therefore, regardless of ratification, norms provided under the Conventions and Protocols apply to all conflict settings and these have increasingly become important in matters of civilian protection.

Freedom of movement and the right to return has reference in both the international framework and the national framework in Sri Lanka discussed below. In the Universal Declaration of Human Rights (UDHR), the right of movement was discussed in Article 13(1) stated that everyone has the right to freedom of movement and residence within the borders of each state. Though the UDHR sets out this right, there is no enforceability of rights provided within the UDHR.

Unlike the UDHR, the International Covenant of Civil and Political Rights (ICCPR) provides for enforceable rights. Article 12 of the ICCPR states that every citizen should have the 'liberty of movement and freedom to choose his residence'. But this right can be restricted on the grounds of national security, public order, public health or morals of the rights and freedoms of others.[11] According to General Comment No. 27 by the Human Rights Committee,[12] everyone lawfully within the state should enjoy the freedom to move and choose his residence and restrictions can only apply in accordance with paragraph 3.[13] The General Comment provides guidance on how restrictions can be introduced and limits the scope of the abuse of power. Further, the General Comments state that restrictions must be provided by national law and that conditions under which the rights may be limited must be established by national law. It goes on to state that restrictions must be consistent with all other rights provided in the ICCPR and that restrictions must not impair the essence of the rights. Accordingly, restrictions must conform to the principle of proportionality and the test of necessity. The General Comment also states that the principle of proportionality has to be respected not only in national laws but also in application through administrative and judicial arms. The General Comment is a useful tool in the national context, in the formulation and application of national laws and also in providing guidance in the proper use of restrictions so that rights enshrined within the ICCPR are not unduly abused.

There is no international law specifically governing IDP rights. While international human rights law and humanitarian law establish norms and standards that provide protection for civilians, there is no specific mention of IDPs in these documents. The Guiding Principles is the first international document which specifically deals with IDP rights though, not enforceable and can only be used as a guide in the protection of IDPs. The Guiding Principles which sets out a rights framework for the protection of IDPs, has specific mention under Principle 14 of an IDP's right to movement and choose his or her residence. It goes on to state that IDPs have the freedom to move freely in and out of welfare camps, which is directly violated by the Sri Lankan authorities in several instances as discussed below.

Right to return has specific mention in international law. Article 13(2) of the Universal Declaration of Human Rights sets out the right of return, but places no conditions on the quality of this return. The ICCPR in Article 13(4) also states that no person shall be arbitrarily deprived of the right to return to his country. None of these provides standards that can facilitate a safe and dignified return to a person's home.In the General Comment No 27: Freedom of Movement by the Human Rights Committee in 1999 there was specific discussion on the right of refugees and IDPs to return.[14] The General Comment states that 'no person should be arbitrarily deprived of the right to enter his or her country'. It goes on to add that restrictions by a state including national laws must be in accordance with the ICCPR and its objectives.

Further discussion on the conditions of return were held in the Sub-Commission on Prevention of Discrimination and Protection of Minorities, resolution 1998/26 on *housing and property restitution in the context of the return of refugees and IDPs* which held that basic standards need to be met for the return of refugees and IDPs. It goes on to state that the 'right of all returnees to the free exercise of their right to freedom of movement and to choose one's residence, including the right to be officially registered in their homes and places of habitual residence, their right to privacy and respect for the home, their right to reside peacefully in the security of their own home and their right to enjoy access to all necessary social and economic services, in an environment free of any form of discrimination' need to be met. Resolution 1998/26 states that returnees need to be treated as equal citizens and that there should be no discrimination upon return. It also provides basic benchmarks on property restitution which is essential on just and dignified return. In the General Recommendation No. 22, Article 5 and refugees and displaced persons (1996) by the Committee on the Elimination of Racial Discrimination, there was further discussion on conditions that need to be met for sustainable return. These conditions include safety, voluntariness, equality and property restitution.

As set out internationally, there are standards that need to be satisfied for return to take place and conditions that need to be met upon return to one's land. Dignity is closely connected to a voluntary and safe return and is a precondition for return. Article 1 of the UDHR stated that 'All human beings are born free and equal in dignity and in rights.' However, there is no commonly accepted definition of dignity in international law. Guaranteeing safety when returning and upon return are also key aspects that need to be given consideration. In country-specific cases too the right to return and conditions of return have been discussed. For example, in the case of Bosnia and Herzegovina, the Security Council Resolution 820 in 1993 stated that 'all displaced persons have the right to return in peace to their former *homes* and should be assisted to do so'. Subsequent Security Council Resolutions have reiterated this norm as seen with Kosovo.[15]

Standards and conditions for return are available internationally. What also needs attention is the situation after return. In 2005, a comprehensive set of standards on property restitution was introduced called the Principles on Housing and Property Restitution for Refugees and displaced persons (hereinafter referred to as the Pinheiro Principles).[16] The Pinheiro Principles recognized the importance of housing and property restitution, as well as a form of re-integration and rebuilding lives and livelihoods. The Pinheiro Principles are applicable to both refugees and IDPs and focuses on property restitution for all those who have been displaced from their properties. It also provides an operational approach on how property restitution can take place. The Pinheiro Principles came at a time when guidance was needed on the framework and application for housing and property restitution. These principles need to be used as a guide in the formulation of national laws and polices, and in the design of programmes and projects for restitution.

Return to one's home and land cannot be sustainable if conditions such as safety, dignity, voluntariness are not met. As already established by the international norms there is need to pay attention to restitution of homes and property. This is vital to ensure that the return is well planned and returnees are provided with assistance to rebuild their lives. Several peace agreements have also taken note of the importance of property restitution. For example in the Dayton Peace Agreement which ended the conflicts in the former Yugoslavia, individual property restitution rights were addressed through the setting up of formal institutions and claims procedures which saw the establishment of the Commission for Real Property Claims of Displaced Persons and Refugees. It is imperative that future peace agreements address this key component of land, property and housing restitution.

RIGHT TO RETURN: A BRIEF OVERVIEW

Right to return is generally perceived as return to one's own land and home. Under international norms and resolutions, as discussed above, it is treated as an IDP's right to return to his/her own home. In a broader sense, return to one's community and one's village can also be considered a form of return, though due to security and lack of infrastructure a person is unable to immediately return to his/her home.

Return to one's land and home needs to take place within a rights framework where IDPs and refugees are informed of their return and the return is voluntary. As previously stated, international law required basic conditions that need to be met prior to return and subsequent measures that need to be taken after return. Returns should be conducted in a manner where IDPs and refugees are empowered to make decisions and are provided with information on the status of their homes, lands, infrastructure, and security situation. There should be 'Go and See' visits arranged by the authorities which can be assisted by agencies with the lead taken by UNHCR, where IDPs are able to see for themselves whether returning to their homes is feasible. Such 'Go and See' should become an operational norm in situations of displacement, but such practices too need to be planned and informed. Such practices enable the IDPs to be involved in the process and to be informed of what the situation is at the places of origin.

In the process of informing IDPs of return, it is ideal if choices are provided to where IDPs can return. In many instances in Sri Lanka, IDPs have preferred to return to their own land and homes. But there are occasions when IDPs may prefer to relocate to a new area and community. In other cases, they may choose to remain in the places where they initially sort safety. There are also cases where IDPs may choose to remain near host communities and families, where they have integrated into society and established links with the community. Return programmes should also provide information on reintegration plans in one's own community and what forms of assistance will be available upon return. Those who choose to remain in the present place or relocate should also be provided with similar information and options.

In the context of refugees, the same principles of voluntary and informed return needs to apply. A sovereign state can restrict entry by non-citizens but many have forgone this in times of disasters and when refugees seek safety. However, when conditions in the refugee's country of asylum are stable and the reasons for the refugee's flight have been resolved, the host country can request the refugee to repatriate. Such repatriation should follow the same principles as seen with the return of IDPs.

If just conditions of return are in place, including basic security, respect for human rights and assistance with livelihoods and development, more IDPs and refugees are likely to make the choice to return voluntarily. This will reduce forced returns or repatriation. Return needs to be not only voluntary and informed; it also needs to be done in a way to safeguard the dignity of those returning. Authorities need to address the safety of those returning, and steps must be taken to focus on protection issues. Further, steps need to be taken to ensure that IDPs who return are not mistreated and no physical harm comes their way. Upon return, IDP families should be able to remain together as one unit rather than having to be separated. Sadly in the Sri Lankan context, there have been instances where IDPs who after returning to their homes have been threatened and attacked. Future returns need to treat safety and security as a key issue.

This chapter highlights that return should conform to certain principles including safety and dignity and that it should be done through a rights framework where the IDPs and refugees are informed and empowered in their return. Return that follows such measures ensures sustainable return where IDPs and refugees are able to reintegrate faster into their former social networks and communities. The onus is upon the national authorities and agencies such as UNHCR to ensure that return is in conformity to international and national laws, policies and principles. Further, restitution and compensation are closely linked to return and repatriation, and need also to be addressed sufficiently to ensure sustainable return. IDPs and refugees need to be provided information on assistance available and ways of obtaining such assistance. Information on restitution and compensation needs to be provided early on in the process, which can facilitate return and provide greater options for those returning.

SRI LANKAN FRAMEWORK

There is no specific legislation on IDPs presently in Sri Lanka but protection is guaranteed through the Constitution of Sri Lanka and other national laws which are discussed below. Case law also has broadened the scope of the rights of IDPs which are briefly discussed.

Sri Lanka has a legal framework starting with the Constitution of Sri Lanka which includes a fundamental rights chapter that protects the rights of all citizens including the right to equal protection, freedom of movement, right to choose one's residence, freedom of expression, freedom from cruel, inhuman treatment to name a few. Article 14(1)(h) states that every citizen is entitled to the freedom of movement and of choosing his residence within Sri Lanka.

Rights guaranteed under the Fundamental Rights chapter can be restricted in certain situations including in the interest of national security, public order and the protection of public health or morality by invoking the Public Security Ordinance (PSO), which empowers the president to declare a state of emergency and adopt emergency regulations if she/he believes they are necessary 'in the interests of public security and the preservation of public order'. A state of emergency was declared in Sri Lanka in August 2005 following the assassination of Foreign Minister Lakshman Kadirgamar. Emergency regulations were brought into force at that time and were renewed on a monthly basis for a long time. There are several emergency regulations that impact the rights of IDPs such as detention and arrests, and the setting up of a High Security Zone (HSZ) in Sampur in May 2007.[17]

Sri Lanka at present does not have specific legislation on IDPs, though a draft IDP Bill was in the process of being formulated by the IDP Unit of the National Human Rights Commission of Sri Lanka, however, it has been stalled since 2008.[18] Another important legislation in relation to return and resettlement is the Resettlement Authority Act of 2007. The act establishes the Resettlement Authority which has the primary function of the formulation of a national policy and the planning, implementation, monitoring and coordinating of the resettlement of IDPs and refugees. A notable inclusion in the legislation is that the Authority will formulate policies and programmes for resettlement and relocation of IDPs and refugees in safe and dignified manner—two principles that have previously not been included in any local legislation dealing with IDPs and refugees. Recognition by the authorities that return must be in accordance with basic principles and within a right framework is a positive step forward. It is to be seen how the Authority will deal with return and whether words will be translated into action. As discussed below, it is clear that there is much to be improved in return drives in the Sri Lankan context and that return should be voluntary, informed, safe, dignified and that development and restitution needs are addressed. Without addressing these areas, return is unlikely to be sustainable.

The ICCPR Act 2007 and Geneva Conventions Act 2006 are two pieces of legislation that were introduced as enabling national legislation to two key international instruments ratified by the Sri Lankan authorities, namely, the ICCPR and the Geneva Conventions, respectively. Though these pieces of legislations were introduced, the national law does not specify key rights as provided in international law. For example, the ICCPR Act contains only a few rights that are found in the ICCPR and leaves out important rights such as the right to life; the right to self-determination; freedom from negative discrimination on the basis of national or social origin; freedom from forced or compulsory labour; the security and liberty of persons deprived of liberty; right to require free consent to medical or scientific experimentation; right to leave the country; rights of minorities, including in respect of religion, language and culture and the right to privacy.[19]

Similarly, the Geneva Conventions Act has left out one of the most important components of the Conventions which is Common Article 3 that applies to internal conflicts and thereby to the Sri Lankan conflict.[20]

Further, case law has interpreted certain rights broadly and provided protection. In *Arumugam Peter Vadivelu* versus *the Defence Secretary*, the petitioner, a displaced person living in the Sithambarapuram camp in Vavuniya District claimed that the requirement to obtain a pass to travel from Vavuniya to Colombo was an infringement of his fundamental rights guaranteed in Articles 11, 12(1), 12(2) and 14(1)(h) of the Constitution. The respondents argued that the pass system restricting movement of persons was implemented in the interest of national security reasonable and necessary at the time. The court held with the petitioner stating that the travel pass system had violated the petitioners fundamental rights guaranteed in Article 14(1)(h) by executive action as restrictions of movement could only be imposed by law according to Article15(7) and the said restrictions were not authorized by law. Another case that broadened the scope of freedom of movement and provided protection from forcibly moved is the case of the evictions of Tamils from Colombo city in 2007 which is discussed below.

Though Sri Lanka has a legal framework in place to protect a person's freedom of movement and right to return, practice has shown that rights are not always protected and that much needs to be improved in the legal framework and its application. The Sri Lankan case study demonstrates that displacement and return is a continuous issue in Sri Lanka, though there are weaknesses and gaps in the protection aspect. The conflict and tsunami both witnessed restrictions in the freedom of movement and questions on sustainable and safe return. Therefore, while improvement is needed in the legal and policy framework, attention also needs to be given to resettlement and return drives. As established in the international framework, principles such as voluntariness, safety, equality and dignity need to be cornerstone in any resettlement and return drives South Asia including Sri Lanka.

Case study: displacement in Sri Lanka

There has been renewed displacement of civilians and communities in the north and east of Sri Lanka with the escalation of hostilities in December 2005 and threats to human security. With the escalation of violence, the peace process between the Government of Sri Lanka and the LTTE that was ushered in by the signing of the Ceasefire Agreement (CFA) in February 2002 was under threat. The government abrogated the CFA on 2 January 2008 and with it Sri Lanka returned to war. The Sri Lanka Monitoring Mission (SLMM) that was present to monitor the CFA left on 16 January 2008.

Sri Lanka experienced a humanitarian crisis in the north due to the situation of IDPs and affected communities and the shrinking space for engagement of humanitarian and relief agencies. The new displacement created with the renewed violence added to the already existing IDPs from the conflict and tsunami. Manmade and natural disasters in Sri Lanka created large numbers of IDPs. Reports stated that an estimated 800,000 civilians were displaced because of the conflict prior to the CFA.[21] With the December 2004 tsunami, around 1 million had already been displaced,[22] many among them experienced displacement multiple times. With the signing of the CFA many IDPs and refugees had been able to return to their homes and many relief, rehabilitation, resettlement and reconstruction projects were initiated by the government and international and national organizations (hereinafter referred to as the I/NGOs).

With the escalation in violence many who were previously settled in the north and east had either fled to the rest of the country or to South India and there were 281,689 new IDPs who are displaced since April 2006.[23] Such figures unfortunately only reflected IDPs who are registered with the government. Absent from the official figures were those who lived with family and friends and the civilians who sought shelter in common buildings and schools during the night, also known as the 'night time IDPs'.[24] Though there was increasing recognition of IDPs living outside of the welfare camp structures, with more donors and agencies looking at the plight of IDPs living outside the welfare camps, there was still no systematic process of addressing the needs of all IDPs. An added problem was that due to the dynamic and varied nature of displacement, and the fluidity of movement, it was challenging to register particular groups of IDPs. As research demonstrates, there were different levels of understanding of who constituted an IDP and what constituted a host family.[25] For example, many long-term IDPs who had now integrated into the local communities disliked being labelled as IDPs and therefore might not have been registered as IDPs. In contrast, there were particular long-term IDPs who were still dependant on assistance by the government and other actors and lived either in welfare camps or with host families. Therefore, such diversity in notions of displacement, and how IDPs perceived themselves further impacted numbers.

In the Sri Lankan context, ownership and access to one's land and property had a significant reflection of one's identity and status within the community. Return to one's land and property was, and is, crucial in re-establishing and maintaining such links. Return was also indicative of attempts of returning back to one's previous life prior to displacement. In such a light, return to one's land and home was in most cases welcome, though the final choice needed to be with the individual concerned. Resettlement drives needed to be in accordance with international and national framework and be informed and voluntary. It should not have been used as a political tool, where the return was encouraged and initiated due to other reasons. In other words, for effective and sustainable return, return drives had to be in accordance with a rights framework and the return needed to meet basic conditions. There were protection gaps including deliberate measures by authorities to limit responsibilities in relation to protection. These were because of economic pressures, security considerations and political reasons.

The Jaffna experience

One cannot understand the situation in Sri Lanka, without understanding or trying to feel the pulse of the Jaffna area (see Table 5.1), which remains as one of the most conflict-stricken areas in Sri Lanka. Again, the Sri Lankan experience is not that simple. While people were being displaced, there were also people who were making a return when there was a period of calm, which in most cases was of temporary nature. They would again get displaced when there was

Table 5.1 IDPs and Returnees in Sri Lanka's Northern Province as of 31 December 2011

	Total caseload	Returnees	in displacement		
			IDPs in camps	IDPs with host families***	Total no. of people still in displacement
"new" IDPs*	265,148	223,745	6,732	34,671	41,403
"old" IDPs**	251,442	197,311	7,518	46,613	54,131
Total	516,590	421,056	14,250	81,284	95,534

Source: UN OCHA, 22 November 2011, p.1 and UN OCHA, 24 January 2012, p.1

Notes:
* "New" IDPs : People displaced between early April 2008 and June 2009
** "Old IDPs : People displaced prior to April 2008
*** IDPs with : Information as of 31 October 2011; no updated information as of 31 December
host families : 2011 was available.

another outbreak of violence. The cycle of displacement and returning was an endless one. Like the Jaffna experience, the situation in Sri Lanka is also complex.

Freedom of movement and instances of abuse

Sri Lanka had witnessed several incidents where a citizen's movement had been restricted on the basis of security. Such restrictions had been evident throughout Sri Lanka but the violence and the security restrictions had made movement in and around the north and east, in particular, extremely difficult. Movement was affected at multiple levels and had a direct impact on lives and livelihoods, increasing the vulnerability of displaced and affected populations.

In the 1990s and early 2000, the movement of Sri Lankan citizen's movements from the north and east was curtailed through the practice of issuing a pass for civilians to move from the north and east to the south. Though this was established as a security measure, this created massive hardships to the affected communities. As discussed previously, in this case the Supreme Court held that the practice of the pass system was a violation of one's right of movement and ordered the authorities to do away with it.[26]

With the spate of hostilities in 2008, new restrictions on movement similar to those on vehicles were introduced. Severe restrictions on movement to LTTE-controlled areas and Jaffna were imposed. In August 2006, the A-9 was closed at Muhamalai and Omantahi. While the Omanthai checkpoint had been opened it was subject to severe restrictions and regular closures with limitations on the movement of civilians and vehicles. In addition, severe restrictions were imposed on the movement of civilians, humanitarian agencies and others at the Madawachchiya checkpoint, impacting the movement of civilians and items to areas in the north. There was no pass system but vehicles from the north and east had to obtain a vehicle pass and to undergo security checks. A new development in the north indicated that individuals who left the Madawachchiya checkpoint were provided a piece of paper which indicated the timeframe they were allowed to spend outside of the north. There was no law or regulation publicly available to indicate the rationale behind this new practice. Stringent security measures were also in place in Jaffna, where locals leaving the area needed to obtain security clearance and approval several weeks before departing the area. All the above not only restricted the movement of civilians and humanitarian actors, but created additional hardship in their lives.

A key issue that needed to be flagged with the military drives was the situation of IDPs and civilians living within the LTTE controlled Vanni area which covered parts of the Kilinochchi and Mullativu districts. According to reports, there were over 300,000 IDPs within the Vanni.[27] There were many more who were not displaced but had limited options with livelihoods due to security and restrictions in access. As a result, civilians who were not IDPs too faced severe hardships in getting sufficient food. This came at a time when military drives had increased and there were continuous shelling and aerial attacks. Added to this was the pass system imposed by the LTTE which inflicted restrictions on leaving the Vanni area. Those who wanted to leave needed to provide a 'guarantor' who acted as a surety. These restrictions in movement had trapped large numbers of civilians within the Vanni area and increased their vulnerability to the ongoing military attacks.

Restrictions had been imposed in other parts of the north and east. Roads entering Vaharai in Batticaloa district were shut in late 2006, and subsequently, entry point to Mannar West and Madhu, the Uliankulam point of entry in Mannar district was closed with the intensification in fighting in 2007. Many of the IDPs who had fled the Vanni area were presently in welfare centres in Mannar district such as the Kalimoddai and Sirukandal camps. These IDPs faced various restrictions on movement. Both the government and LTTE were to be blamed for the continued hostilities, restrictions on movement and resulting hardship on the civilians and communities in the area.

In conflict settings, security situations resulted in civilians being unable to move and were trapped. Such a situation increased their insecurity. Reports indicated civilians faced various restrictions on movement in the Vanni area and being trapped. Such reports had intensified calls for the establishment of humanitarian corridors for trapped civilians to be able to move to government-controlled areas. In August 2006, civilians from Allaipiddy, Jaffna Peninsula, were restricted from leaving their villages by the security forces.[28] On 22 September 2006, handbills were distributed by an unknown group demanding that the Muslim civilians flee the Mutur area. Fearing an attack by the LTTE, Muslim families attempted to flee Mutur but were stopped by the security forces who even imposed a ban on motor boats from taking any civilians across to Trincomalee town. These restrictions in movements were seen as an attempt at using civilians as human shields.

The restrictions on movement had an impact on day-to-day life. The restrictions had led to shortages of goods and price hikes. Even humanitarian agencies had faced a variety of restrictions limiting their ability to deliver goods effectively. It affected the effective functioning of essential services including that of the government, humanitarian and medical services.

Another instance of forced movement of civilians was the eviction of 376 Tamils from Colombo, who were taken to areas in the north and the east by the security forces on 7 June 2006. Several reported cases indicated that many who were evicted had fled the north and east due to increased hostility and insecurity. There were reported cases of women, children, elderly and the sick being forcibly taken and put in buses with no information provided as to the cause of the eviction or where they were being sent to. In a fundamental rights petition filed by the Centre for Policy Alternatives (hereinafter referred to as the CPA), the Supreme Court held that the eviction of 376 Tamils from Colombo was a possible violation of right to movement, right to residence, right to equality and freedom from inhuman and cruel treatment. The Supreme Court issued an interim order halting any future evictions taking place and ordering authorities not to stop anyone entering Colombo. A final order was issued by the Supreme Court in May 2008 holding that future evictions can only take place in accordance with the law and with a judicial order.

The establishment of the High Security Zones (HSZs) in Jaffna and in Sampur in the Trincomalee district are other extreme examples of restrictions on movement. Many thousands of Tamil people have lost their lands, homes and livelihoods due to the demarcation of particular areas as off limit to civilian access. HSZs account for some 18 per cent of the entire Jaffna Peninsula and are the primary cause for the non-return of the majority of persons in Jaffna's welfare centres.[29]

The HSZs have been challenged in court. Though the judiciary was positive and recognized the infringement of the right to movement in the two previous cases mentioned, there have been instances where national security has been held as paramount, even at the expense of fundamental rights. In 2003, the Jaffna HSZ was challenged in the Supreme Court by a petition filed by TNA MP Mavai Senathirajah and others. The case is still pending though the Chief Justice has requested that an arrangement has been made with the military commander of the area and the government agent in Jaffna to ensure that the HSZ is reduced and some of the land returned to the civilians.

A contrary position was taken when the HSZ in Sampur was challenged by two petitions in June 2007, one filed by CPA and the other by the four affected IDPs of the area. The Supreme Court held that this was a matter of national security and that resettlement will take place in due course. What is significant with the Sampur HSZ is that it was created under emergency regulations, making it extremely difficult for parties to challenge it and thereby providing the space for the authorities to continue maintaining it as a security measure. What is not well known is that while the HSZ in Sampur prohibits civilians of that area from entering their own land, a Special Economic Zone (SEZ) has been created by the authorities to open up economic activities in the area. There is clear evidence of the discriminatory nature of what is happening in Sampur, with civilians not being allowed to enter their land and homes, while potentially big businesses can establish their economic ventures.[30] Like many other instances, national security has been used as an excuse which cannot be questioned by either IDPs, affected communities or others in courts or other forums. In a recent development, the HSZ was reduced to include only the areas which have been identified as no return in a gazette dated October 30. The reduction is welcome but questions still remain on return processes and conditions in the areas. Questions also remain on the plight of IDPs whose lands and homes come within the newly gazetted HSZ and whether they would be provided alternate land and assistance. It is imperative that standards and benchmarks discussed above need to be taken on board with return and relocations.

Resettlement drives: A reality check

Displacement has resulted in subsequent resettlement drives in Sri Lanka. Migration of people and resettlement drives has raised concerns whether force has been used to move people. Since September 2006, the government has resettled displaced communities from Mutur, Vaharai, Western Batticaloa and Eachalampattu in their places of origin. While these initiatives have allowed the displaced to return to their homes and rebuild their lives, the manner in which the resettlement was carried out raised a number of concerns, including whether the resettlement process was voluntary. The Minister of Resettlement and Relief Services, Rishard Badurdeen, acknowledged that an element of force was used.[31] The voluntariness of return was further questioned by international and national agencies.[32]

With the so-called liberation of the eastern province in July 2007, resettlement drives continued. On September 30, according to UNHCR data, there were 21,549 IDPs remaining in the eastern province, compared to over 300,000 who were displaced in 2006/2007 during the peak of hostilities in the east. With the reduction of the HSZ in Trincomalee, many more IDPs were, it was thought, able to return to their land. Questions, however, remain on the voluntariness, safety and sustainability of such return. Later, there was a spate of violence including killings and abductions of civilians in the east, resulting in fear in remaining areas which were prone to violence. With the escalation of threats, it was reported that some civilians resorted to staying with family and friends during the night, thereby becoming night-time IDPs. Increased sign of violence in the area, no doubt resulted in repeated displacement.

It is also important to question the displacement in the north and future drives of resettlement and return. If any lessons are to be learnt from the past, with the more recent examples from the east as a good example, the future is bleak for voluntary return which conforms to international standards such as informed voluntary decision making, safety and dignity. If and when IDPs are allowed to return to areas in the north and to their own land and homes, what measures will be followed? It is vital that authorities reflect on past practices and use international and national framework as a guide to plan future return drives. Such return drives need to involve IDPs and affected communities, and ensure that their voices are heard in the planning processes. Authorities, with the assistance of humanitarian agencies, need to ensure that

'Go and See' visits are arranged and that IDPs are given the choice either to return to their homes or relocate elsewhere.

Upon return, the authorities need to ensure that restitution plans are in place to provide for the affected. Restitution of housing and property need to be a key component in return drives, with information provided to the returnees on their rights and assistance available. At present, there is limited discussion on this issue and the government must take the lead in having a comprehensive plan in place to address restitution in the future. Closely linked is providing returnees with assistance in obtaining lost documentation. At present a few actors such as UNHCR, NRC and Sarvodaya are involved in providing assistance. Such programmes need to be implemented in the entire country.

Compensation for lost and destroyed property and housing need to be part of a well-planned return process. Returnees need to be provided with assistance to rebuild their lives and homes and restart the livelihoods. Compensation schemes in Sri Lanka have been ad hoc and there is no consistency in provisions for affected communities. As seen with assistance to affected communities in parts of the east, compensation has become politicized. The government must take the initiative to have a comprehensive plan for the payment of compensation to affected communities and payment should not be dependent on undue influences and political affiliations.

TOWARDS CONSOLIDATION OF RIGHTS TO RETURN

I have set out the legal and policy framework available for the freedom of movement and the right to return. Using the example of IDPs in Sri Lanka, the chapter has highlighted the international norms in place including the UDHR, ICCPR, Refugee Convention and Guiding Principles and goes on to discuss resolutions and General Comments on the right to free movement and the right to return. Right to return is enshrined in international human rights law and includes benchmarks, such as safety, voluntariness, dignity and equality for a sustainable return. International norms and standards and best practices from other conflict settings have established that return needs to be within a rights framework. But it needs to go further. Return needs to be closely connected to development and restitution. Yet again, there are standards available to ensure that restitution can be implemented to assist the affected communities and help rebuild their lives.

In return and resettlement drives, national governments must take the lead. Governments must ensure that national laws and policies provide for and protect the freedom of movement and the right to return. Government must also take the lead in implementing these laws and policies and ensure that return drives adhere to established benchmarks and standards. Protecting the rights of its citizens is the primary responsibility of the government and they need to fulfil this responsibility. UN agencies and I/NGOs can work in partnership and provide assistance, but the primary responsibility remains with the national government.

Finally, return to one's land and home is paramount for effective and sustainable reintegration and rebuilding. But return which does not conform to basic standards is futile since the problems and vulnerabilities will continue to remain. Return to areas which are not safe or do not have basic infrastructure will result in insecurities and possible future displacement. The vicious cycle of displacement and return will continue if proper care and planning does not take place at the initial stages with the involvement of all relevant actors including the affected communities. Local communities and IDPs need to be part of the process of planning and thereby empowering these communities to decide what is best for themselves. The right to return not only means returning one's land and home, it also means that conditions are met for a sustainable and safe return, reintegration, development of the area and helping with rebuilding efforts.

NOTES

1 See http://www.UNHCR.org/cgi-bin/texis/vtx/home/opendoc PDFViewer.html?docid=4852366f2&query=november% 202008% 20two%20patterns; last accessed on 13.11.11.
2 www.UNHCR.org as at November 2008.
3 http://worldsavvy.org/monitor/index.php?option=com_ content&view=article; last accessed on 18.11.12.
4 According to UNHCR, it is providing protection or assistance either directly or indirectly to 13.7 million of them of the IDPs. See www.UNHCR.org.
5 http://www.internal-displacement.org; last accessed on 19.1.12.
6 www.internal-dispalcement.org as at November 2008.
7. Ibid.
8 www.internal-displacent.org; last accessed on 12.2.12.
9 Ibid.
10 www.UNHCR.lk as at October 2008.
11 Article 12(3) ICCPR.
12 UN doc. CCPR/C/21/Rev.1/Add.9 (1999).
13 Paragraph 3 deals with 'restrictions'. So, though freedom of movement is an important right, restrictions can only be imposed in certain cases. Paragraph 3 talks of those instances; for details see: http://www.unhchr.ch/tbs/doc.nsf/0/6c76e1b 8ee1710e38\02568240005a10a9?Opendocument.
14 UN doc. CCPR/C/21/Rev.1/Add.9 (1999).
15 Security Council Resolution 1244 in 1999 on Kosovo stated 'Reaffirming the right of all refugees and displaced persons to return to their homes in safety'.
16 UN doc. E/CN.4/Sub.2/2005/17 (2005).
17 *Centre for Policy Alternatives* v. *H.E Mahinda Rajapakse and others*.
18 There is no information available when the IDP bill will be enacted into legislation.
19 CPA press release on the draft bill purporting to enact the International Covenant on Civil and Political Rights (ICCPR), 3 October 2007 found on www.cpalanka.org .
20 CPA Policy Brief on Humanitarian Issues, December 2007.
21 Land and Property Rights of Internally Displaced Persons, CPA, 2003.

22 'Post-Tsunami Recovery and Reconstruction', Joint Report of the Government of Sri Lanka and Development Partners, December 2005.

23 Bhavani Fonseka, 'A Profile on Internally Displaced Persons Living with Host Families'; for details see http://www.nrc.no/arch/_img/9293518.pdf), last accessed on 18.11.12.

24 Night Time IDPs are generally civilians who stay the night in common building and religious buildings and return to their homes during the day.

25 Bhavani Fonseka, 'A Profile on Internally Displaced Persons Living with Host Families', at www.cpalanka.org

26 http://www.internaldisplacement.org/idmc/website/countries.nsf/(httpEnvelopes)/D19BC2605A15FBF2C12578160004B8C9D?OpenDocument#45.2.1, accessed on 15.2.12.

27 For more information—www.cpalanka.org .

28 Joint UN Rapid Assessment Mission, October 2008.

29 IASC, 'Conflict Related Displacement in Sri Lanka', July 2007, p.20.

30 HRW, 'Return to war – Human Rights under Siege', August 2007, pp.34-37.

31 CPA and IMADR, 'Fact Finding Mission to Trincomalee', 23-27 April 2007, p.10.

32 'IDPs Moved against Their Will', *Daily Mirror* , March 20 2007.

PART II

Issues

6

PAKISTAN
Displacement Puts Thousands at Risk

HINA SHAHID

Stories of developmental projects, which were considered economic miracles for developing countries, have gained ground in recent times. Why is it that these miracles begin to evaporate overnight during the implementation processes? There is a strong lobby of people, planners and engineers who think that the loss of few for the benefit of others is an acceptable norm, as in the conclusion of cost-benefit analysis, but the ratio between the multiple losses incurred and the benefits accrued are way below what had been calculated originally.

Displacement is becoming a notorious issue as states take the road to fast economic growth. Development planners always initiated capital-intensive, foreign loan-funded projects, without internalizing social and environmental costs. Unfortunately, for a long time what have not changed are development planning and implementation patterns. We have learnt very little from past failures in developmental projects, and we do not even dare to accept what we have learnt as the truth. Development-induced displacement[1] poses as one of the most critical challenges to deprived communities. Several developmental projects either failed or were unable to deliver as the design promised, and had massive consequences on social and environmental structures. These costs are never included in traditional cost–benefit analysis at the planning and screening stages of the projects. In addition to one-time losses, some projects by design have a feature to damage and devastate the natural ecology permanently.

Developmental projects happen to focus on poor communities in rural areas, especially herders, landless people and smallholders. Increasingly, it is said that such developmental programmes and projects target the most disadvantaged regions, particularly tribal areas and semi-arid, mountainous and environmentally sensitive areas. It attempts to introduce technological improvements in livestock, agriculture and irrigation to reduce rural poverty by boosting productivity and raising incomes. It supports efforts of mechanization and help communities to organize groups to manage finances and disseminate training and knowledge. At the policy and institutional levels, these projects are bound to work to secure long-term access to land and water resources for the rural poor. The strategies of such developmental projects theoretically include empowerment of women, agricultural and rural development, food security and diversification of production, decentralization and access to natural resources.

There are millions of IDPs in developing countries such as Pakistan, India, Sri Lanka, Bangladesh, Nepal, and so on. Available reports indicate that development projects in India have created 21 million IDPs,[2] apart from 250,000 people displaced from Kashmir,[3] 45,000 people who are still displaced along the Indian side of the LoC between India and Pakistan and cannot return despite the ceasefire, 230,000 displaced in Assam due to the conflict between Santhals and Bodos, 31,000 Reangs displaced from Mizoram to Tripura and 45,000 displaced in the state of Chhattisgarh due to insurgency.[4]

The number of IDPs are increasing continuously and there does not seem to be an end to the plight of these people. In this chapter, the context of internal displacement in Pakistan has been discussed and issues of displacement, wheat crisis, sugar crisis, foreign exchange crisis or power crisis are put in a single framework, rather than analysed individually, to understand if there is a common denominator to all that is happening in Pakistan.

COMMITMENT TOWARDS DEVELOPMENT

The analysis begins from 1947 (*see* Chapter 2). The governments that came from 1947 onwards were committed to development. Being aware of the lack of industry, food production, schools, hospitals, electricity, roads, and so on, development was a major objective for the government. The whole effort of the government should have been to provide these economic assets. In conceptual terms, Pakistan was a development state. Since 1977, however, Pakistan ceased to be a development state, and till today, it is a national security state, where the main objective of the state is to ensure national security. Development is no longer the main objective of the state, and 'national' is being increasingly defined narrowly from the perspective of the military.

After obtaining Independence, Pakistan imported just about everything—toothpaste, toothbrushes, shoes, matchboxes—because it produced practically nothing. Even most food items were imported because it grew little. But by the end of the 1960s, Pakistan was producing a large variety of agricultural, industrial and consumer goods. Political capital was invested into development. During this time the British government had offered assistance to former colonies, and a meeting was held in Colombo, where India, Pakistan and Sri Lanka were invited to come with a list of development projects which the British government would finance. In 1947, there were no government offices in Karachi, but by the 1950s, there were several of them, built in various cities of Pakistan, and the industrial and agricultural outputs had risen; in fact, most of the basic consumer goods were already being produced in the country like match boxes, toothpaste and shoes.

The first military dictator of Pakistan, President Ayub Khan, promoted development by expanding the economic infrastructure. In fact, out of the eight Five Year Plans that Pakistan created, only the second, implemented during the 1960s under Ayub Khan, was wholly successful. It was successful in the sense that most infrastructure targets were achieved. In fact, in some cases, when it was said that 500 MW of electricity would be produced, the output had been 550 MW. An agreement was made with India—the Indus Water Treaty (1960)—owing to which Tarbela and Mangla dams came into being. The whole objective of coming to an agreement with India on water was driven by economics, not by military considerations. Without the supply of water, agriculture would have died in Pakistan. New canals were dug out of the dams.

The report of the World Commission on Dams has taken up the case study of Tarbela Dam, and found that out of the total of 96,000 displaced, two-thirds qualified for replacement of lands in Punjab and Sindh. Of these some 2000 families or 20,000 people, approximately, did not receive land.[5] With more development projects, such as National Motorways, Layari Expressway, Left Bank Outfall Drainage, Right Bank Outfall Drainage I and II, Salinity Control and Reclamation Project, National Drainage Programme, and so on, being commenced, displacement augmented further. Ghazi Barotha Hydropower Project affected 52 villages and displaced around 21,653 people.[6]

While no country, rich or poor, has escaped the impact of neoliberal structural adjustments in the age of globalization, I focus in particular on Pakistan's dilemma of development. For the technocratic development elite of Pakistan, long used to complying with the conditions laid down by World Bank/

IMF loans, the implementation of structural reforms was simply the next step to be followed in the process of development planning. Perhaps they did not have much of an option as the country was brought to heavy dependence on foreign economic assistance. By 1980, Pakistan had become the tenth largest recipient of the World Bank/IMF loans.[7] Initially the loans under the Structural Adjustment Programme (SAP) was approved in 1982, when General Zia had established his military rule. But after receiving the first tranche of the SAP loan, the general's economic managers decided not to proceed with the rest, perhaps anticipating with some foresight that the enforcement of required adjustments would hurt the common people, making the general more unpopular than he already was.

DEVELOPMENT YIELDING DISPLACEMENT AND MARGINALIZATION

Prior to Independence, the British rulers had commissioned the Sukkur Barrage, in 1932, thereby introducing one of the major irrigation systems of the world in Sindh. The irrigation system launched by the British rulers had been brought to its zenith during the green revolution of Ayub Khan, which gave a boost to the agricultural sector. However, dearth of indigenous expertise in the implementation of this irrigation system soon started eating away short-term agricultural benefits. Non-availability of the drainage system started playing havoc with the fertile lands, inviting the menace of waterlogging and salinity. Government authorities awoke to the problem in the 1970s. The absence of resettlement policies and laws, or the use of laws promulgated during the colonial period, had left a large population marginalized. At the time of the commencement of a development project, all public eyes focus on the 'development', not on the cost. More remarkably, issues like cost towards compensation, rehabilitation and resettlement become a game between the government and the investors of the project.

A number of drainage schemes in Sindh were introduced to minimize the degradation of the fertile lands. The Left Bank Outfall Drain (LBOD) was launched with the aim of providing a long-term solution to the drainage issue of Sindh, disposing the saline drainage water for the first time into the sea. Around eight donors financed the project: World Bank, Asian Development Bank, Saudi Fund for Development, Overseas Development Administration, Canadian International Development, Islamic Development Bank, OPEC Fund and the Swiss Development Corporation, contributing millions of US dollars. Since its inception, LBOD is very controversial, as its faulty design proves, and it backs its ambitious technical structure without any proper outfall results. Pakistani professionals have been trained in a way to conceive, design and build the hardware without consulting with the locals, who were going to be the ultimate users. This is very typical of technocrats, who are educated and trained in foreign lands. Later, in the late 1990s a cyclone hit the project area. At this point, the project became counterproductive, and destroyed agricultural lands, groundwater quality, biodiversity, and other livelihood resources of the coastal communities of the Sindh province. Because of several technical problems, which were largely unseen, the drainage effluents, instead of going into the sea, started destroying lands and internationally recognized wetlands. What was worse was that more than 300 people were killed and more than 5000 people were displaced as a result of the LBOD since it was launched. Some 10,000 fishermen lost their livelihood, becoming victims of development-led displacement, and about 52 species in the area suffered harm.[8] Both the government and international financial institutions (IFIs) do not even identify the importance of wetlands, and the risks involved in implementing such developmental projects.

A breach in LBOD had led to the submergence of hundreds

of villages. Newspaper reports mention about thousands of affected villagers squatting alongside the roads at temporarily relief camps without government help.[9] At some camps set up by the government in Badin district, people had no food and water facilities. However, while talking to the media at an Iftar party given in honour of the mediamen, Sindh's minister for rehabilitation, Muzaffar Ali Shujra, announced that only around 300,000 to 400,000 people had been affected.[10] He said 25 people including 12 in Mirpurkhas district, lost their lives while 140 sustained injuries.[11]

After the failure of LBOD, another mega drainage project RBOD-II in Sindh is coming up. The ongoing project with the length of 273 km could jeopardize hundreds of villages from Dadu to Gharo. The estimated loss due to RBOD in 18 districts has been calculated by a survey carried out by community groups.[12] Hundreds of small farmers will lose their sources of livelihood, and thousands will be displaced.

Several mega development projects have caused, and are causing environmental degradation, perpetuating inequality and generating poverty. The focus on the poverty–environmental linkage has emerged from two different camps. Those concerned with poverty studies have increasingly realized the importance of environment in determining the magnitude of poverty. The poor depend on the income derived from the use of the natural resource base. The role of poverty in resource degradation has become a major concern for environmentalists. Whereas environmental NGOs previously were preoccupied with pure conservation projects, they have become increasingly engaged in integrated conservation development projects (ICDP). The poverty-environment nexus has been well elaborated in the National Environmental Action Plan (NEAP).

Presently, more than one dozen multinational oil and gas companies are engaged in the exploration and production of oil and gas in Sindh. Besides onshore oil and gas exploration, the Government of Pakistan has also issued licenses to multinational companies for offshore exploration in the coastal waters of the Indus delta. For Pakistan, the province of Sindh produces 56 per cent gas and 70 per cent oil. These multinational companies, however, are violating international and national laws, rules and regulations, including Corporate Social Responsibilities (CSR), Petroleum Concession Agreement (PCA), Petroleum Exploration and Production Policy 2007, Pakistan Environmental Protection Act 1997, and other such laws. These laws are meant to protect the environment, which would in effect empower the poor people who depend highly on common property resources. If the environment is not taken care of, then the poor will be disempowered and their source of livelihood jeopardized. As a result, the local communities will be deprived of social and community development programmes, as well as non-technical and technical jobs.

Nature has created and sustained a balance between riverine forest, flora fauna, grazing areas and hill torrents for several centuries. Many small and large hill torrents annually bring water, silt and nutrients maintaining the ecological balance. Such developmental projects that are being induced have already reduced freshwater flow in the river Indus. Riverine forests and rangeland are a second major source of livelihood for thousands of families engaged in agriculture. Alteration in the ecosystem has created joblessness, with hundreds of kilometres being destroyed by saline water.

Besides development projects, there are other factors like natural disasters such as drought, earthquake and floods which result in displacement. So far, floods have displaced millions of people in Pakistan. The British-ruled Sindh witnessed heavy floods in 1882, 1897, 1903, 1914, 1917, 1921, 1924, 1930 and 1942. The 1973 floods affected approximately 166,000 people of eight districts of Sindh during the era of Zulfiqar Ali Bhutto. Some 5000 cattle were lost in Larkana district alone. The people experienced flood disasters in 1975 and 1976 subsequently. Around 314,039 people were affected by floods in 1975, while approximately 2,67,995 people were displaced and 23,360 houses damaged in Nawabshah district alone. The floods in 1976 are considered to be the worst. The flood affected some 28,260 villages, with 3,276 people displaced. Acres of cultivated land were damaged and 9,087 cattle were lost.[13]

The drought spell in 2000 in the province of Sindh created *mandis* (markets) of women and young girls, where they were sold like animals. These women were kept in private prisons or taken to other parts of Pakistan and abroad for resale and prostitution, drug smuggling and slave labour. Around 200,000 trafficked women and children from Bangladesh to Pakistan were either sold into prostitution or were thrown into bonded labour. Most of them are still living as slum dwellers. By bulldozing their colonies or by claiming that they have not given their *bhatta* (share), law officials compel these women to succumb to displacement from time to time. Generations have grown up with the same violation of human rights, yet, women are still persecuted because of their status of 'illegal' migrants.

In 2001, Musharraf launched a number of mega projects in Balochistan, including Mirani Dam, a 633 km Gwadar-Pasni-Makran Coastal Highway and a 97 km Turbat-Mand road. Socially and economically, Balochistan is the most backward province in Pakistan. It has been at the bottom of the list in terms of social conditions compared to the rest of the country; 85 per cent of the population is without drinking water, 80 per cent without electricity and 60 per cent are living below the poverty line. It has the highest infant mortality rate and lowest literacy rate where 70 per cent children are deprived of modern school amenities.

In 2005, the army stationed 35,000 paramilitary troops in Balochistan to suppress armed protests by tribal militias. Thousands of people have been displaced. At least 84,000 people, mostly from the Marri and Bugti tribes, were displaced in the districts of Dera Bugti and Kohlu alone. According to a humanitarian assessment, the displaced people, including 26,000 women and 33,000 children, lived in makeshift camps without adequate shelter in Jafarabad, Naseerabad, Quetta, Sibi and Bolan districts. Over 80 per cent of the deaths among those surveyed in 2007 were of children under five.[14]

Thousands of Baloch reportedly remained displaced and lived in miserable conditions in June 2007. Displaced families had to live without clean drinking water and medicines. Women died during childbirth and dozens of children died due to malnutrition and diseases such as typhoid and hepatitis. There have been rocket attacks on gas pipelines, railway tracks, power transmission lines, bridges and communications infrastructure, as well as on military establishments and government facilities. The tribal militias continued with their acts of sabotage on a daily basis across the province, with no political solution to the conflict in sight. Displacement occurred in Balochistan not only as a result of conflict, but also because of floods in June and July 2007 that affected 2.5 million people and displaced 300,000.

The National Resettlement Policy, 2002, has been formulated not only to include the affected persons in the existing system, but also to ensure an equitable and uniform treatment of resettlement issues all over Pakistan. The policy applies to all developmental projects involving adverse social impacts, including land acquisition, loss of assets, income, business, and so on.

DISPLACEMENT OWING TO MILITARY OPERATIONS

An estimated 17,000 displaced Kashmiris remain in refugee-like conditions on the Pakistani side of the LoC. It was reported that the Government of Pakistan was considering issuing identity cards similar to those issued to Afghan refugees to individuals who had fled Indian-controlled Kashmir after 1990. The rate of displacements has picked up in mid-August 2008 in Pakistan, when the Pakistani authorities launched a military operation against pro-Taliban militants in Bazaar Agency bordering Afghanistan. Around 190,000 people have been displaced and are sheltering in Pakistan's North West Frontier Province (NWFP), while 20,000 Pakistanis and Afghans, approximately, have fled into eastern Afghanistan's Kunar province. Authorities in Pakistan say there are 168,463 IDPs in NWFP. The UN refugee agency cannot verify this figure as population movements are fluid, and registration is continuing in official IDP camps. The UNHCR has signed an agreement in October 2008 with the NWFP government to extend registration to IDPs living with host families.[15]

The displaced people complain about the overcrowded makeshift camps, erratic food supplies, and limited water. Most of the families at Kacha Garhi camp have come from Charmang, Loy Sam and Khar areas of Bajaur. As a contingency step, the government has closed down all schools and colleges to accommodate refugees in these buildings.

The largest displacement due to military operations in Pakistan in 2007 occurred in Swat Valley in NWFP. The Valley, with a population of 1.5 million people, was seized by pro-Taliban fighters. In 1992, the fundamentalist cleric Maulana Sufi Muhammad launched the movement, *Tehrik-e-Nifaz-e-Shariat-e-Muhammadi* (TNSM), for the Enforcement of Islamic Law in the Malakand region of NWFP. Maulana Fazlullah rose to power as a preacher, broadcasting fundamentalist sermons over private radio stations. By May 2007, he had attracted a core group of 5,000 militants. Following the army's storming of the Red Mosque in Islamabad, Maulana Fazlullah ordered his supporters to take up arms against the government. In Swat Valley, the militants attacked security forces and police stations. The TNSM also began to send threatening messages and bombs to pro-government tribal leaders, government officials, music and video shops, internet cafes, aid agency offices and girls' schools.

Hundreds of displaced families, mostly women, children

and the elderly, fled to the neighbouring Tank district and North Waziristan. Some had to walk for two days to reach Tank over the rough terrain, with little food and water along the way. There are reports of children dying due to the cold weather. The condition of young girls has turned grim. Maulana Fazlullah launched an aggressive campaign against girls' education through his illegal FM channel from a small village of Imam Dheri close to Mingora town of Swat district, North West Pakistan, owing to which girls were stopped from attending schools. Every night after the Isha (Night) prayers, he delivered special speeches on the topic, terming girls' education against Islamic commands and as a source of vulgarity. Sources say that followers of Maulana Fazlullah have started wall chalking to communicate their fundamentalist religious views on girls' education[16] and against administration of polio drops to children. According to one report, about 1100 children were deprived of polio drops during the previous anti-polio campaign.[17] The exact figures of the girls withdrawn from schools were not found. However, the majority of the parents in the rural areas of Mingora are avowed followers of the extremist views of the Maulana, and forbid their girls from attending schools. The number is increasing day by day. There are around 11 illegal FM radio stations in Charsadda, 4 in Mardan, 28 in Swabi, 13 in Buner, 4 in Hangu, 1 in Karak, 2 in Mansehra and Batagram, respectively. Apart from these, 8 FM illegal stations are in lower Dir, 3 in upper Dir, around 14 in Malakand and 6 in Swat. One could imagine the height of exploitation perpetrated by these religious extremists, who are targeting women and young girls using a strong media tool of having their own radio stations.

Angry protests broke out in Mingora, around 150km northeast of the capital of NWFP, Peshawar, as thousands of people protested against the suspension of power, gas and water mainly due to militant attacks on installations. Severe food shortages were reported in the area due to disruption in transport amid intensified conflict. Security forces opened fire on the protesters, killing at least six people, and this has led to a fresh wave of anger. As of May 2009, almost 2.4 million people have fled the fighting that for several weeks opposed Pakistan's army and the Taliban in the Swat Valley in north-west Pakistan. This has made conditions for people with disabilities or in vulnerable situations even more precarious. The displaced continue to flee the Swat Valley where fighting between Pakistan's army and the Taliban continues. During the recent fighting, almost 2.4 million people have left the combat zone, heading towards Peshawar, abandoning their homes on the spot. Some of these displaced persons have found shelter in camps, whose population may reach up to 100,000 people, and are living in extremely precarious situations.[18] Though few have returned, many are still housed in camps in the adjacent district of Lower Dir or in other parts of the NWFP.

The Government of Pakistan has no national policy on addressing conflict-induced displacement, and there is no systematic government assistance to these types of IDPs in the country, the majority of whom are displaced as a result of combat between the army and insurgent forces. Government agencies have not only failed in arresting displacement caused by armed opposition groups, their operation against them has itself displaced hundreds of thousands of innocent people. In Balochistan, efforts by international and national aid agencies to assist the IDPs have been rejected by authorities. Due to the unstable security situation in Waziristan, the ICRC has not been able to travel to areas most directly affected by the armed conflict.

A more urgent humanitarian response is needed in the current conflict situation in Pakistan. As of July 2010, more than 300,000 people were displaced from South Waziristan, around 40,000 from Frontier Region Peshawar, up to 80,000 from Khyber and at least 150,000 from Bajaur. Swat recorded displacement of 360,000 people. Advocacy is needed to advance the international human rights agenda and to disseminate important instruments such as the Guiding Principles on Internal Displacement, so that these are well understood by UN agencies, NGOs and government. It is unlikely that adequate humanitarian support will reach populations displaced by the conflicts in Pakistan unless international agencies continue to urge the government to increase access. The Government of Pakistan must promote initiatives to get aid to displaced people and protect civilians during military operations.

NOTES

1 My ability to speak on the issue of development-led displacement in rather simple language, like the language of ordinary people, developed when I started to work with the deprived communities of Sindh and Balochistan. This is because I had to explain the right to livelihood to people who were either primary school dropouts or uneducated. Like many of us in the human rights community, I thought I must work with people and it is working that gave me the ability to speak the language of the people.
2 Bjorn Petterson, 'Development-Induced Displacement: Internal Affair or International Human Rights Issue?'. For details see: http://www.fmreview.org/sites/fmr/files/FMRdownloads/en/FMRpdfs/FMR12/fmr12.6.pdf; last accessed on 19.11.12.
3 http://www.internal-displacement.org/idmc/website/countries.nsf/(httpEnvelopes)/90E174CA3D9CF14CC125779-0002402F2? OpenDocument#22.2.1; last accessed on 19.11.12.
4 The last three figures are cited in http://www2.ohchr.org/english/bodies/cescr/docs/info-ngos/IDMC2India40.pdf; last accessed on 19.11.12.
5 Atta ur Rehman Sheikh, 'Pakistan: Development and Disaster', *Internal Displacement in South Asia,* Paula Banerjee, Sabyasachi Basu Ray Chaudhuri and Samir Das (eds), (New Delhi: Sage, 2005), pp.62–109.
6 For details see: http://www.mcrg.ac.in/tmd06.htm; last accessed on 19.11.12.
7 Hassan N. Gardezi, 'Globalisation and Pakistan's Dilemma of

Development', *The Pakistan Development Review*, 43, 4: 1 (Winter 2004), pp.423–40. For further details see: http://www.pide.org.pk/pdf/PDR/2004/4/PartI/Gardezi.pdf; last accessed on 19.11.12.

8 'Revisiting the LBOD Issue', Dawn.com. For details see: http://dawn.com/2011/10/06/revisiting-the-lbod-issue; last accessed on 19.11.12.

9 'Floods Uproot 0.4million', *The Nation*, 16 August 2011. For details see: http://www.nation.com.pk/p; last accessed on 19.11.12.

10 Ibid.

11 Earth Changes and the Pole Shift: Information and Discussion about the Earth Changes and the Pending Pole Shift, 16 August 2011. For details see: http://poleshift.ning.com/profiles/blogs/pakistan-badin-sinking; last accessed on 12.3.12.

12 'Joint Rapid Assessment of the Cyclones and Flood Affected Areas of Balochistan and Sindh', Inter Agency Standing Committee 9-15 july, 2007. For more details see: www.filter-systems.com/upload/file199.pdf.

13 Mansoor Raza, '*Disasters and Sindh*' as cited in 'The Disaster Waiting in Sindh's Wings', *The Express Tribune Blogs*. For more details see: http://blogs.tribune.com.pk/story/941/the-disaster-waiting-in-sindh%E2%80%99s-wings/; last accessed on 19.11.12.

14 'Complete Text of Hayrbyar Marri's Speech at the House of Lords'. For more details see: http://balochhomeland.weebly.com/facts-article6.html.

15 'Nearly 190,000 People Displaced by Fighting in Pakistan's Bajaur Area', *Briefing Notes*, 14 October 2008. For details see: http://www.unhcr.org/48f474e52.html); last accessed on 19.11.12.

16 'Attack on Girls' Education in Northwest Pakistan', *Oh My News International World*; for details see: http://english.ohmynews.com/articleview/article_view.asp?no=355932&rel_no=1; last accessed on 19.11.12.

17 Many people project polio vaccine to be anti-Islam.

18 'Pakistan: Millions of IDPs and Returnees Face Continuing Crisis. A Profile of the Internal Displacement Situation', IDMC, 2 December 2009; for details see: http://www.internal-displacement.org/8025708F004BE3B1/(httpInfoFiles)/824D103A25A742E4C1257680005872C3/$file/Pakistan%20-%20December%202009.pdf; last accessed on 19.11.12.

7

HUMANITARIAN ASPECTS OF BORDERS IN THE EAST AND THE NORTHEAST

PAULA BANERJEE

The present state system in South Asia, in particular the state system of the sub-continent, is a result largely of the partitions in the eastern and western parts of the erstwhile united India, giving birth to three states—India, Pakistan and Bangladesh. The borders dividing these countries are markers of past bitter history, underlining their current separate, distinct and independent existence. The bitterness of the past, lack of mutual confidence at present, security concerns of all these states, at the same time, their inter-linkages, make the South Asian borders unique. These represent lines of hatred, disunity, informal connections and voluminous informal trade, securitized and militarized lines, heavy paramilitary presence, communal discord, humanitarian crisis, human rights abuses and enormous suspicion, yet informal cooperation.

While the Indo-Pakistan border and the LoC are in the eye of world attention, therefore closely monitored, the borders in the east—Indo-Bangladesh border and Indo-Nepal open border—remain neglected in terms of attention. Security concerns overwhelm all other equally legitimate concerns and values. Regarding the Indo-Bangladesh border, military security dominates over human security. As a result, states often forget that borders are not only lines to be guarded, they are also lines of humanitarian management, because borders are not lines but borderlands—that is to say, these are areas where people live, pursue economic activities, and lead civilian lives attuned to the realities of the borders. Human security in the borderlands would first mean security of the civilian population along the borderlines. But that never happens. Both sides of the Indo-Nepal border have security concerns as they feel that unwanted elements, including migrating hordes, are encroaching through these borders.

Two of the most important threats faced by these borderlands are human trafficking and AIDS. Newspaper reports from the borderlands are rife with news of human trafficking along the border, and one of them stated, 'India was among the seven Asian nations put by US on its "watch list" of countries involved in human trafficking'.[1] This is not isolated news but such statements from the West keep recurring. It was also stated, 'not only India is facing this huge problem but also has become a transit point for prostitution from nearby countries like Bangladesh, Myanmar and Nepal'.[2] India was also marked as the destination for sex tourism from Europe and United States. These reports portray that human trafficking is a thriving proposition and there are a number of routes through which women and children are trafficked into and out of this region. For a while the Assam–Siliguri route was identified as the main trafficking route through which the victims of the flesh trade were transported across Northeast India.[3] But routes change, and when one route is identified traffickers begin using another. Through these routes in the Northeast, women from Nepal, Burma, Bangladesh, the Northeast itself and Bengal are seduced, coerced or forced into flesh trade and trafficked. This is both a procurement area and a transit area. Any report on migration in this region would remain incomplete without a stocktaking of trafficking that goes on in this region because it leaves enormous consequences not just for the victims but also for the security of the region. Here the security of the state is not at stake but of the people who are affected by trafficking.

INCREASING MARGINALIZATION OF WOMEN: HUMAN TRAFFICKING

To find out why this whole region is vulnerable to traffickers, one needs to realize that this is a region of endemic poverty, social imbalance and political violence particularly against vulnerable groups, of whom women form a large part. Each part of this region is undergoing certain social and political turmoil where more and more women are getting marginalized. In Bangladesh, for example, globalization, growth of fundamentalism, modernization policies such as building of dams, and so on, have all contributed to violence against ethnic and religious minorities and against women. The minority women are in a double bind—they are attacked both as minorities and as women. The fundamentalists who have increased their control in the political arena strive to maintain a predominantly male-dominant status quo. This strategy puts both minorities and women in general at the receiving end. Religion has come to be used by fundamentalist groups as one of the primary means by which male-dominant values and existing gender-oppressive ideology are imposed and perpetuated.

There are cases where women who are brought from Bangladesh to the metropolitan towns in India face tremendous brutality. One such case is that of Hamida, a young Bangladeshi girl, who was brought to India at the age of ten. She 'suffered a series of brutal rapes at the hands of the man who brought her to New Delhi, along with some of his friends who were Delhi policemen . . . Only one of the accused men has served jail time'.[4] That this is a region of extreme insecurity for men and women crossing the border has been dramatically portrayed by the case of Jayanti Bala Das of Bangladesh.[5] In January 2003, five Bangladeshi nationals, of whom two were minor children crossed the Indo-Bangladesh border and entered India. The Border Security Force (BSF) arrested them from Baro Bridge across the Ichhamati River. The area in which the incident took place is under the jurisdiction of the Basirhat Police Station in North 24-Parganas. The Bangladeshi nationals including Jayanti Bala Das were all taken to the Soladana BSF camp at around 5 pm. On the same night (10 January 2003), a BSF personnel allegedly raped Jayanti Bala. Thereafter these 'infiltrators' were put in a small boat with holes and efforts were made to push them back. Allegedly when the boatman refused to go he was threatened on the point of gun. The boat capsized in the middle of the river and only Jayanti Bala and her one-year-old son could save themselves. On 13 January the villagers of Bagundi, who had given her shelter, handed her over to the police of Basirhat. She was charged under Section 14 of the Foreigners Act, 1946. On 21 January a dead body was found in the Brickkiln Canal in south Basirhat. The man was identified as Jayanti's husband Basudev. When a case was lodged against five BSF personnel, the BSF men were unwilling to hand over their personnel to the Basirhat police. Although the BSF disagreed that Jayanti was raped, the officer in charge of this case stated that initial examinations proved that she was molested.[6] On 27 January, the Sub-Divisional Judicial Magistrate (SDJM) of Basirhat issued warrants against five BSF men. In July Jayanti was handed over to the Sromojibi Mahila Samity for safe custody and on 15 September 2003 a writ petition was filed on her behalf. The cases are still pending.[7]

Jayanti's case reflects the situation of women who are trying to cross the border. Their status of being foreign-born women increases their vulnerability. No one is willing to shoulder any responsibility for these women. The state that they leave is glad to get rid of them and the state that they enter finds them unwanted. This has been proved in February 2008, when 213 gypsy snake charmers, who have always led a life of seasonal mobility crossing borders at certain times of the year, were stopped at zero point in Satgachi, Cooch Behar. They had to remain there for days as both India and Bangladesh were unwilling to take them back until one night they just disappeared. No one knows what happened to them and few people care about them. From the Indian side, we were told that they were pushed inside Bangladesh. No one even asked for evidence of what happened because this is a grey area. In such a situation woman can be exploited by anyone, and are, therefore, particularly vulnerable to traffickers.

The border itself is a place of endemic poverty, substantial illiteracy among women and children and enormous violence against women. In a survey undertaken in three border villages, namely, Shikarpur, Charmeghna and Nasirerpara, it was found out that most women in this area are illiterate. In Shikarpur out of 515 women only 190 have some forms of literacy, in Charmeghna out of 590 only 100 women are literate and in Nasirerpara out of 470 women only 85 are literate.[8] These women have very few options to improve their situations. Their problems are compounded by increased militarization and criminalization of the area. Here every other day women and children are molested or killed. On visiting one such border near Charmeghna two chroniclers poignantly write:

> To assert that the control of the border still belongs to them, the border security on both ends sporadically do a well-orchestrated show of national safety through aggression. It is then that one witnesses the elaborate, flexing of muscles and the violent exchange of fire and mortar. On such occasions the border sky is lit up by man-made conflagrations and the air swells with the sound of brutal human games. At the end of it all, what are lost on both sides are the expendable lives of

> common people like Baba-Hasim and Kanakchampa and the eyesight of six-year-old Sonia, who paid the price for playing, foolishly enough, in her own front yard.[9]

Women in these borders live a life of extreme hardship. They are the quickest targets for both the security personnel and the criminals. 'The robbers demand women during their raids and when they get none they leave threatening dire consequences: "You can hide your livestock in the camp. You can hide your money in the bank. But where will you hide your women?"'[10] Any study on traditional security pays no attention to such insecurities, which has become a part of their everyday lives.

Not just from Bangladesh but women from Nepal also cross the border and move to India. There are many reasons why these women migrate. Political instability in Nepal has compounded the problem. Conflict between the Maoists and the state has contributed to increasing instability. Now with the end of the conflict things would probably be better but even recently people faced great instability. A report from Nepal stated that the People's War in Nepal has resulted in death and displacement of people from conflict areas and that 'people living in the remote places of Taplejung District are leaving their houses behind and moving to the headquarters, Kathmandu or India'.[11] Such reports also mention that both the Maoists and the state have been responsible for the harassment and displacement of people in the past. Newspaper reports also reveal how women are particularly vulnerable to such harassments, particularly one stated that a woman of 'Tehrathum fled to Kathmandu after Maoists coerced her to join their militia. Her pursuit for a secure life in the valley was wrecked after her colleagues sold her to a brothel in Mumbai'.[12] Although she was rescued with five other Nepali girls no one knew whether she would be rehabilitated in her own society. The future will tell what happens but the past remains problematic.

When women are trafficked across borders such as from Nepal to India it makes them even more insecure. After crossing a border these women can become stateless if they are without any papers or proof of citizenship. Often they are coerced to do so to repay their family loan. It has been stated 'about 153,000 Nepali girls were in Indian brothels in 1990 and the number has been steadily increasing at a rate of 5,000 every year'.[13] Nepal is considered as the most significant source of girl-child commercial sex workers to India. The average age of Nepali girls entering into Indian brothels ranges from 10 to 14. 'Economic stress and historical oppression coupled with immense profits which accrue to the trafficker lead to the rapid flow of girl children from Nepal to India'.[14] In this era of globalization, tourism has become another occasion for child trafficking from Nepal. Although Nepal has passed the Human Trafficking (Control) Act of 1986, such acts are hardly ever implemented. Trafficking of Nepali women to India continue unabated. A very disturbing phenomena within this process is that young Nepali 'virgins' are trafficked because people not only prefer their fairer complexions but also there is a ridiculous but common belief among some communities that having intercourse with a young virgin can cure many sexually transmitted diseases as well as AIDS. So the price for these girl children has gone up, but the moment they contract the illness they are thrown out of the brothel and they come back to their homes where their families are often loathe to taking them back.[15] These children, in most cases, are oblivious of the risk they are in. According to one social worker in J. J. Hospital in Bombay 'one 15-bedded women ward was occupied with 13 patients with HIV infection, out of this 11 were Nepali'.[16] What people in the sex trade do not realize is that trafficking is not merely violence against women but against humanity. These young girls living in brothels are so powerless that they can hardly insist that their clients use safety measures. Once they contract the disease they inadvertently infect many more and contribute to destabilization and insecurity of the whole region. Once their disease is discovered they are treated like pariahs. They are punished for something over which they had hardly any control and yet the process continues. Trafficking finds little space in traditional security discourse yet it is one mode of migration that actually leads to physical insecurity of a region.

Disempowering women: AIDS

The border area is looked upon as a site of pervasive threats. If it is not the threat of security, migration or terrorism then there is AIDS, a seemingly insurmountable threat to collective health. And the site of that threat remains the border, whether it is with Bangladesh or with Nepal or even with Myanmar. A newspaper report from eastern India encapsulates this threat well: 'AIDS, the most feared of modern day diseases, is stealthily spreading from villages along the Indo-Bangladesh border to other parts of the country. Its progress has so far been unhindered, thanks to the large migrant population . . . West Bengal has the longest border-sharing zone with Bangladesh, and there is a constant flow of infiltrators from Bangladesh to West Bengal'.[17]

Thus, attached to this threat of migration is the threat of AIDS. One workshop on AIDS received special coverage because it was designed for migrant workers. The participants were '35 migrant workers, most of who hailed from Bihar and Bangladesh'.[18] The attendance of the workers was meant to seem almost as an admission of guilt. There are other news items that blame the porous border instead of only the migrants for the growing number of AIDS cases in Northeast India. One such coverage stated: 'The Northeast, which borders the heroin producing "golden triangle" of Thailand, Laos and Myanmar, has a major problem with intravenous drug use and that is the most common cause for the spread of AIDS in the region'.[19] In another report on Manipur, a state with one of the highest prevalence of HIV-positive people, it was stated that 'Manipur's proximity to the notorious "Golden Triangle" of South East Asia, a major narcotics centre, has led to the easy availability of intravenous drugs among the youth'.[20] Another report on the same lines stated the following: 'The first group that spread the dread disease like HIV/AIDS includes the injecting drug users. As this region is nearer to the Golden Triangle, drug trafficking is continuously going on through Manipur, Nagaland and Mizoram. The young people in these states have easy access to injecting drugs. The second group includes the heterosexual promiscuity mainly through travellers and migrants.'[21] The main purpose of the news becomes clear a few sentences down the line when the commentator states the 'problem arises from the fact that the society has to be made responsible for the problem which has evolved due to its own act of omission and/or commission'.[22] It is this question of responsibility that concerns the media in Northeast India and often there is an effort to place responsibility on marginal groups such as the migrants, injecting drug users (IDUs) or sex workers who are easy targets.

That the female sex workers are one of the easiest targets is clear from a number of media reports. There is a plethora of reports that clearly blames female sex workers for the spread of HIV/AIDS in Northeast India. One such report mentions:

> The flesh trade is fast spreading its net in Arunachal Pradesh. So are HIV-positive cases. The impact of this double trend has made people of the state to sit up . . . The mission to check sex trade—which is more prevalent in Itanagar—was triggered by the detection of HIV virus in 38 blood samples out of 22,000 during a survey . . . With flesh trade expanding its base the situation can only become worse.[23]

Almost every month there are such reports in the media of East and Northeast. A similar report stated:

> An alarming rise to the HIV-infected patients in the Barak Valley of South Assam and a spurt in prostitution in Silchar town have set the alarm bells ringing.
>
> Several NGOs engaged in AIDS awareness campaigns in the region said the spread of the disease in Cachar district was highly alarming because it never been an HIV prone area. However the district recorded more than a thousand HIV-positive cases in the past couple of years.[24]

Sex workers are one of the most disempowered groups who are easy targets for anyone trying to ascribe blame. One report on interventions stated that 'special awareness programme should be undertaken among the women, especially those engaged in the sex trade'.[25] Female Sex Workers (FSW) are already deviant figures and by casting blame on their presence the media is able to maintain the myth that AIDS is a disease of the deviant. There is little understanding that the groups that are seen as threatening are all marginalized. This is a common phenomenon the world over. It is believed that HIV has the potential of becoming an explosive epidemic in places where there are highly mobile populations and gender inequality.[26] Migrant workers or sex workers are easy target groups. It is easy to spread a facile belief that by controlling such groups AIDS can be curbed. But there is little effort to either find out or address the efficacy of such arguments.

In recent years there is a new threat perception arising out of the flesh trade. This relates to the security forces and their vulnerability to AIDS. Hitherto these security forces were considered invincible and they were the instrument for controlling the malaise of the borders but now they are themselves falling prey to AIDS. From different parts of the Northeast there is a recurring concern that AIDS is the most important threat to security as it is affecting security forces themselves. In Tripura, cases of AIDS are on the rise among the forces. It was stated that out of the 79 AIDS patients, 43 are jawans from the security force.[27] In a more recent report the CRPF was the cause for concern. The report stated: 'Forty CRPF personnel posted in Manipur and Nagaland have tested HIV-positive, according to findings of a voluntary testing drive that the paramilitary force conducted among 11,000 of its men recently.'[28] Worse still there are reports that 'The Assam Rifles has received threats from militant organizations of this region that they would let loose HIV-infected women to spread the disease among jawans posted in Meghalaya, Manipur, Naga-land and Tripura'.[29] So it seems that AIDS is winning the battle against security forces. Hence, the fear is centring more on unreported AIDS cases. There is a witch hunt for AIDS patient. At the receiving end of this witch hunt are gay men, women sex workers or migrant workers.[30] Even though the more knowledgeable people are aware that woman with single partners are getting infected in large numbers and from urban areas HIV is spreading to rural areas, yet for interventions the easy targets are sought out. However, what remains constant is the perception of AIDS as a phenomenon of the borders.

TACKLING THREAT

People living in the borders, whether they be migrants or settled communities, face multiple threats, few of which are listed below:

- many immigrants are prima facie accused of illegal entry and do not get due recourse to law;
- the BSFs on both sides engage in forcible push-backs—extreme harsh methods of deportation resulting in loss of limbs, lives, money and dignity;

- daily economic activities of segments of population, eg, like fishermen fishing in river borders are hampered;
- long and undue detention at jails and sub-jails;
- rampant sexual abuses;
- threat to public health;
- harassment of immigrants allegedly terrorists;
- extortion of money by people allegedly working as part of smuggling;
- distress of the inhabitants of border enclaves;
- boundaries running through villages and consequent harassment of villagers;
- fencing and electrifying the fence with high voltage;
- people forcibly stranded on the no-man's land as security forces on both sides refuse to accept them;
- communalization of border villages and subsequent killings of apprehended immigrants;
- shifting of river borders;
- different types of boundaries in different terrains, including river, village, train line, hills, and so on, as well as places having no natural demarcation lines;
- existence of stateless population;
- trafficking in labour, sex, animals and goods.

If the situation of the borders are to be improved these threats need to be addressed.

NOTES

1 'Human Trafficking Cases in Meghalaya Draw US Attention,' *Shillong Times*, 16 June 2004.
2 Ibid.
3 'Assam, Siliguri Main Trafficking Routes in NE', *Shillong Times*, 5 June 2004.
4 Upala Devi Banerjee, 'Sexual Exploitation and Trafficking of the

Girl Child: The Indian Scenario', *Migrant Labour and Trafficking of Women: Workshop Report* (Nepal: National Network Against Girl Trafficking, 1999) p.64.

5 The case was registered at the Basirhat Police Station on 13 January 2003, under Section 376 (B)/280 of the Indian Penal Code.

6 *Ananda Bazar Patrika,* 14 January 2003.

7 'News from The Indo-Bangladesh Border', *Refugee Watch,* 19 August 2003, p.2.

8 Survey undertaken by Subharati Banerjee under my supervision for her unpublished M.Phil thesis, 'Bharat Bangladesh Simanta Samasya: Charmeghna, Shikarpur o Nasirerparar Porjalochona' (Problems in Bengal Bangladesh Border: A Discussion of the Three Villages of Charmeghna, Shikarpur and Nasirerpara), (Department of South and Southeast Asian Studies, University of Calcutta, 2000–2001), p.73.

9 Krishna Banerjee and Purna Banerjee, 'Lives Delimited by Barbed Wires', *Refugee Watch,* 13 April 2003.

10 Ibid.

11 'People Displaced from Village', *Human Rights Situation Report (INSEC),* 10, 2 (1 August 2002), p.23.

12 'Rural Women Caught in Rebels, Traffickers', *Kathmandu Post,* 18 May 2004.

13 Quoted in Upala Devi Banerjee, 'Sexual Exploitation and Trafficking of the Girl Child', p.68.

14 Ibid.

15 Pushpa Bhatt, 'Trafficking of Nepali Girls in India and AIDS', *Women's Voice* (Report published by National Network against Girl Trafficking, Kathmandu; n.d.), p.27.

16 Ibid.

17 'AIDS: The Enemy at the Frontier', *The Statesman,* 15 October 2006.

18 'Advocacy Prog on HIV/AIDS for Migrant Workers', *Nagaland Post,* 28 March 2004.

19 'Rebels Threaten Death to Drug Addicts, Peddlers', *The Shillong Times,* 2 July 2004.

20 'Fighting AIDS', *Assam Tribune,* 24 April 2004.

21 'Perspective of Drug Abuse and HIV/AIDS in NE', *Meghalaya,* 1 December 2005.

22 Ibid.

23 'Arunachal Wakes Up to Flesh Trade and HIV Risks', *Hindustan Times*, 13 May 2005.
24 'Flesh Trade Sets Off Barak AIDS Alarm', *Times of India*, 1 October 2005.
25 'Rising AIDS Graph Threatens Tripura', *North East Reporter*, 12 April 2004.
26 Tony Barnett and Alan Whiteside, *AIDS in the Twenty-First Century: Disease and Globalization* (New York: Palgrave Macmillan, 2002).
27 'Aids: Threat to the Army in the Northeast', *Nagaland Post*, 25 September 2005.
28 'CRPF Men in AIDS Grip', *The Times of India*, 18 November 2006.
29 'AIDS Threat to Army in NE', *Nagaland Post*, 25 September 2005.
30 A report in a newspaper well portrays this fear by stating that, 'As the world hunts for preventive measures against the deadly HIV/AIDS Guwahati continues to contribute to the number of HIV positive patients with the detection of 11 more cases among the homosexuals in the city'; *The Sentinel*, 10 August 2006.

8

VICTIMS OF VIOLENCE IN THE BORDERS AND HUMANITARIAN TASKS: The Jammu and Kashmir Case

ANURADHA BHASIN JAMWAL

Borders are defined as geographic boundaries of political entities or legal jurisdictions. Borders, however, are not just demarcation of territories, simply lines drawn on the maps. They are also places inhabited by people and in many parts of the globe, areas where the ugly manifestations of violent conflicts including wars are staged. Borders, thus, not only become zones of ambiguity, vulnerable to challenges, especially during times of war but also areas where residents bear the brunt of violence often from both sides or face the threat of displacement. Even in times of peace, borderlands frequently suffer from violence, insecurity and lawlessness, when neighbouring countries are drawn into conflicts or where the state's authority and control are constantly challenged and subverted by transnational forces. However, in most conflict areas, victimhood at the borders is something that the majority are in total denial of; in fact, it may even be unheard of. The inaccessibility and lack of development of the hostile borderlands make its people totally invisible and unheard.

Passi, a geographer, suggests that 'a boundary does not exist in the border area, but manifests itself in many institutions'.[1] These are effective expressions of narratives linked with boundaries and border conflicts and serve as reference to the other. These institutions that Passi talks about are decisive forces in determining, defining and reinforcing nationality and territoriality, as perceived by the state, as also about who qualifies to be a victim of violence. The border people are powerless against such manifestations and discourses from an essentially statist viewpoint that chooses to negate not just their competing claims but their very existence. Borders are thus deemed to be just lines on the map, areas that are demarcated and those that demarcate boundaries, inhabited by valorous army personnel who protect the 'nation's' territorial integrity. From a state's perspective, protecting borders means to protect the territory, not the people. And, often in pursuit of this aim, killings, harassment and forced displacement of the civilian population residing there, and not just the 'enemy' across the dividing line, become signs of moral appropriation, often also purification of territory. In popular knowledge they are not deemed to be areas that belong to its people, a civilian population that lives there and owns land, or should have belonged to them.

It has been argued by several political thinkers that violence and victimhood at the borders does not stop at the borders. It percolates further into the interior affecting the lives of millions of people on either side of the border, often even those miles away from these lines on the map. While what happens at the borders affect lives in the interiors and even decision making at the highest seats of power, the policies and decisions determined at the power centres impact the lives of the people at the borders. This correlation is well understood in situations of heightened hostilities; tit-for-tat policies followed by hostile neighbours, especially so in times of a full-fledged war. What happens at the level of high politics clearly impacts those living at the borders, not only adversely affecting their day-to-day life but also controlling their lives.

As such, geographical boundaries come to define and delimit the spatial extent of state sovereignty through which the agents of control are able to exercise their power over a given area and its constituent inhabitants effectively. Chaturvedi, while arguing that much of the political thoughts, institutions and practices travelled from the West to the East, explains that 'while the Western principle of territoriality endowed borders with institutional value and tangible quality, nationalism became a specific, strategic form of territoriality and an expression of the struggle for control over land and socio-spatial consciousness'.[2] In fact, the notion of nationalism qualified by territorial security and purity, drawing distinct lines between patriot and traitor, us and them (The 'Enemy') is sacred and unquestionable; hence, the territory, seen to be as something uncomplicated, demarcated by lines on the map, is always held supreme. Many believe that by focusing on the threat to the borders, which in most cases are 'perceived' and not 'real', the states divert attention from the continued violence that produces and sustains the borders.

Conflict with the separated other becomes an organizing principle on which a variety of exclusions and inclusions are based. In the case of the Indian sub-continent, the 1947 Partition shaped the destiny of not just politics but also of the people divided by the line that separated a single geographical unit into not only two countries but two entities pitted against each other, with constant rhetoric of binaries of 'us and them'. The brunt was borne by not just the divided families or the divided land of Punjab and Jammu and Kashmir but more so by the people living on the borders, who had no say while the lines were being demarcated, running at places through villages and slicing them into two halves with different nationalities.

The powerlessness of the people is best demonstrated by the people of Turtuk, a village on the LoC close to the glacial heights of Siachen. In 1947–48, the village became part of the territory ceded to Pakistan and later carved into what is known as Pakistan's Northern Areas. The people automatically became citizens of Pakistan. In the 1971 war, the village, along with its people was occupied by the Indian army and, shortly after, granted Indian citizenship rights. Interestingly, owing to their 'Pakistani' history, they are not looked upon with much trust by the Indian army manning the borders. But did they get to choose their nationality at any given point of time?

Not much different is the fate of the people in border areas, both on the International Border (IB) and the disputed LoC , even though many of them have not gone through the ordeal of identities being changed by force. Yet, the unnatural line that demarcates boundaries between India and Pakistan, especially the bloody LoC, cuts through mountains, often slicing a village into two halves with people living side by side, sharing the same address in terms of the name of village but different nationalities. The forced division and partition that came about in 1947, is just one part of the problem. Through much of the sub-continent, especially Bengal and Punjab, the partition of 1947 created a violent uprooting, stemming from communalization, pushing millions into carving survival strategies in new surroundings. The tragedy of the people living at the borders (see Table 8.1) is far greater because of the continuum of violence they are caught in through the past six decades. Unlike the people who migrated from this side to that or vice versa, settling in the interiors to carve their new destinies, the people living on the fringes do not even enjoy that luxury. For them, there is only the choice of accepting violence and its repercussions as their fate. The worst is the plight of the border people in Jammu and Kashmir, especially those living right on the LoC.

On both sides of the dividing line, people in these border

Table 8.1: IDPS in and from the Bordering Areas of Jammu and Kashmir

Reason for displacement	Date of displacement	Number of people	Number of families	Number of people	Situation	Sources
Conflict between the Government of India and separatist militants in Jammu and Kashmir; fear of targeted killings and abductions	From 1990 onwards	250,000	57,863		37,285 families in Jammu; 19,338 families (100,000 people) in Delhi; 1,240 families in other states and Union Territories	ICG, 3 June 2010 p.5, GoI-MHA, 2 March 2010, p.9, Reuters Alert Net, June 2010
		450,000				*IANS*, 20 June 2010
Border fence erected in Poonch district, 5 km away from the LoC inside Indian-controlled territory	2009	15,000			People cut off from their agricultural land, livelihoods, educational opportunities	*The Hindu*, 20 December 2009
IDPs in and from Jammu and Kashmir				265,000		*IANS*, 20 June 2010, *The Hindu*, 20 December 2009

Source: 'India: National and State Authorities to Protect IDPs, a profile of the Internal Displacement Situation'; IDMC, 2 September 2010.[3]

areas have borne the brunt of the hostility between the armies of India and Pakistan, during wars and so-called peace times. These border areas are too heavily militarized for any semblance of normalcy and normal life. Accumulated displacement in the Azad Kashmir region is 40,000 and the total number of IDPs as of July 2010 was less than 5000.[4]

BORDER VIOLENCE: VARIED MANIFESTATIONS

The levels of violence are not always visible; they are often not reported but only felt psychologically. The impact of continuous violence need not be physical but psychological. The continuous presence of troops, excessive restrictions, fenced and mined areas add to the psychological suffering of the people. There need not be constant gunfire and artillery shelling alone to make life perilous and uncomfortable for the people at the borders. Violence and victimhood at the borders manifest in several ways.

Firing and shelling

The people at the borders often become victims of cross-firing between armies on both sides, shelling and explosions. In Jammu and Kashmir, according to Anand,[5] the people on the Pakistani side bear the worst brunt because their villages are right on the IB or the LoC. She narrates several incidents of farmers who lost their agricultural lands because constant shelling had turned them barren. She gives the instance of Saleen village, where 40 families have been deprived of their agricultural lands, either due to shelling or mining. She also maintains that there is a high number of casualties on the borders and quoted Pakistani Rangers, who maintain that whenever Indian forces fire, civilians become the target. According to her, this is done to maintain pressure on the Pakistani forces, which in turn use the civilians as shields, failing to relocate them to safer zones. The people in these villages on the Pakistan side of the LoC maintain that they have been uprooted thrice in 1965, 1971 and 1986. Anand explains that there were occasions when Indian forces entered these villages, heavily mined them and left; most of these areas have not been de-mined since then. Similar stories abound on the Indian side, as would the stories from hostile border areas, around the globe. Take for instance, the Palestinian experience where Israeli forces have engaged in human rights violations against Palestinian civilians, including extra-judicial killings, collective punishment, shelling of and incursions into Palestinian areas, house demolitions, agricultural land levelling and arbitrary arrest and detention. As in Palestine, in several border areas, attacks on the civilians are often inter-ethnic or communal in nature. So is the Turkish engagement with Syria based on the Kurd revivalism on the Syrian borders. On the Chad-Sudan borders, the Sudanese Janjaweed militia attacks have singularly targeted the Chad civilians in eastern Chad. *Human Rights Watch* reports that it appears that some Chadian Arab groups became involved in Janjaweed atrocities in Chad, forcing 50,000 to migrate. Though the partition of the sub-continent took place on communal lines, border clashes do not target a particular communal/ethnic group but civilians in general. For instance, in Poonch, where most of the border villages comprise essentially Muslim population, with mixed population only in three villages, people maintained that whenever the Pakistani forces attacked, they deliberately targeted the civilian population, each time triggering displacements. However, though targeting people on ethno-religious lines is not the norm, there might be aberrations.

Landmines

As a matter of policy, both India and Pakistan, have heavily mined their respective territories on the borders, especially during the wars, ever since 1948. Landmines that were laid in 1948 continue to exist. The numbers have simply multiplied over the years. At least 25,000 acres were affected by the 2002 mine-laying operation in Jammu and Kashmir alone. This meant several people were rendered homeless and several acres of agricultural lands barren and fallow. Besides, the landmines that were being treated as military wisdom, also took a heavy toll of the people, leaving several killed and many permanently disabled. Indian army officials admitted in July 2002 that mines had been laid over 70,000 hectares along the frontier that divides Kashmir between India and Pakistan. Thousands of acres along the Indo-Pak border have been mined by the army, with no markers to serve as warnings. In some places, a narrow ribbon with a faintly written 'Danger' sign is the only indicator for the largely illiterate village population not to stray into these heavily mined fields. The effect of landmines is likely to be more prolonged than the hostility between the two countries. Even army officers on conditions of anonymity admit that most of the mines are never de-activated. Firstly, clearance is a difficult job that claims several lives and takes many years to complete in striking contrast to the emplacement of mines. Secondly, as a policy, no mine-fields are cleared along the LoC. Thirdly, and more importantly, the army was rushed into the job of laying landmines and much of the operation was carried out in haste without relying on proper maps, thus making detection and defusing them a difficult task. When the army maintains that 98 per cent of mine-fields have been cleared, it is misleading because it does not include the LoC. Percentages are meaningless in such cases because even one or two per cent of left-out mines would mean that thousand or more mines are still existing.

The economy is severely affected as many persons have been deprived of their agricultural land due to mining and fencing. Villagers at Akhnoor, where the IB with Pakistan ends and the LoC begins, is one of the worst affected areas because, as mentioned earlier, mined areas are never cleared. The villagers were supposedly paid some regular compensation till 1999 for their fields that were mined in the 1971 India-Pakistan war. But after their flight in 1999, they are being paid no compensation either for the previous lands that were turned into mine-fields or those that became ticking time-bombs in 1999 and 2002. Ninety per cent of the fields are either under landmines or fenced out, providing little access to the farmers.

In Kerni alone, 35 people are maimed by landmines. An unknown number of cattle have also perished due to landmines. In villages along the LoC, the Mendhar sector of Poonch district, the locals maintain that 10 per cent people have been maimed by landmines. No authentic documentation on this, however, is available. There is high incidence of cattle casualties due to landmine blasts at both the IB and the LoC but these cases go unreported and the owners get no monetary compensation for the death or injury of the cattle. For human casualties, the compensation is a pittance; Rs 75,000 for deaths, which are rare. India uses light-weight plastic MM16 landmines which are targeted to blow off the limbs of the victims. For injuries, the government pays only Rs 5,000–Rs 10,000. Further, Persons with Disabilities (Equal Opportunities, Protection of Rights and Full Participation) Act, 1995, which can ensure jobs for the physically challenged, is not applicable to Jammu and Kashmir.[6]

Landmines seem to be a universal military strategy employed by governments the world over, not only to defend the territories but also control the people living on the fringes. The heavily mined Afghan-Pakistan borders ever since the Soviet war in the 1980s, have taken a high toll of civilians on both sides of the borders. Kyrgyzstan is believed to have placed landmines along its border with Tajikistan and has no immediate plans to sign the Ottawa Convention banning landmines. According to Ramazan Dyryldaev, chair of the Kyrgyz Committee for Human Rights, landmines in that area have killed 20 people but this has not been confirmed.[7] Members of the Kyrgyz Parliament have publicly charged that Uzbekistan has been laying mines on the Kyrgyz side of the undetermined Kyrgyz–Uzbek border to demarcate it in a way that is more favourable to Uzbekistan. The Kyrgyz Parliament has also criticized Uzbekistan for breaking international law by not marking its minefields. Despite reports of increasing casualties and landmine use in the region, the landmines issue was not raised by either side. This is similar to the India–Pakistan situation where, too, the issue has never been raised at the official level in the last six decades. The only time, one heard of the existence of landmines officially was when minefields were cleared to pave way for the opening of the Srinagar-Muzaffarabad Road in 2005 and the Poonch-Rawalakote and other three routes a year later. Denial to admit the existence of mines also stems from the fact that neither country is signatory to the Landmine Ban Treaty.[8] India, however, is signatory to 1996 amendment of Protocol II of the Convention on Conventional Weapons (CCW), which forbids use of landmines in civilian areas. The Jammu and Kashmir situation, however, proves that this is not being adhered to.

This may be quite unlike the Kurdish situation. According to Armin Köhli,[9] all the countries where the Kurds live (Iraq, Iran, Syria and Turkey) are heavily mined, mainly along state borders, with mines generally imported from Western countries. The Kurdish region lies in one of the centres of ongoing global conflicts and has its own, home-grown disputes. Conflicts both with 'global players' and internally are still 'hot'—or at least latent—and far from being resolved. Ongoing conflicts, varying state legislation, and the differing interests and agendas of the involved states and non-state actors define the condition of mine action for the Kurdish region. Of the states with Kurdish populations, only Turkey and Iraq have signed the Anti-Personnel Mine Ban Convention. Since parts of the territories are controlled by armed NSAs,[10] who have signed the Deed of Commitment, banning anti-personnel mines (AP), territories of Turkey and Iraq, unlike other Kurd-inhabited countries, are not mined. In the late 1990s, the Kurdish Parliament passed a law unifying the two existing mine action centres into the Iraqi Kurdistan Mine Action Agency, something it had done even before Iraq joined the Ottawa Convention. A unified mine-action agency for the whole region is a big step towards further strengthening of mine action and a mine-free Kurdistan.

BORDER FENCING

Fencing at the borders may be justified by the army, quoting strategic reasons but it has seriously impacts on the life of the people at the borders. Significantly, fencing usurps agricultural lands of the people and deprives them of their livelihood; besides it imposes several restrictions. While border fencing had started in 1999, by 2002, 45 villages in the twin districts of Rajouri and Poonch of Jammu and Kashmir were fenced out totally, though the exact number of villages for which cluster colonies have come up, marking the finality of partial dislocation, is not known. The idea was first mooted after the Kargil War, when India began re-planning its strategies in civilian areas and decided to shift the villages on the fringes more to the interiors. The plan could not be wholly expedited probably in view of the lesser availability of land. So on an experimental basis, 14 villages were first selected for the construction of cluster colonies. (In Mendhar alone there are 10 cluster colonies.) Kerni and Birhuti in Balakote (an area of 10 border villages) are two such villages. In both these villages situated on the LoC, cluster colonies have been created 4 km–6 km away from the original homes and fields (most villages in this area sprawl across the hills and the fields are adjacent to each home, making the nearest neighbour a good kilometre or so away) for the people to put up at night. The idea behind setting up cluster colonies is not really known but it was deemed strategically important for the Indian defence forces, who offer no rationale behind the scheme. But it was done with the coordination of the civil administration, which had located the alternate space for cluster colonies close to the villages and released money for the construction of the same. Whatever had been the purpose behind the exercise, it has become a nightmare for the villagers, who are expected to vacate their village before dusk and shift to the cluster colonies. Every morning they return to their homes and fields, work there and the children go to schools, but at night no one is allowed to stay back, thus dislocating them, pushing them into the congested rooms of the cluster colonies. This also means a daily trek of 4 km–6 km for everyone, including children, the aged and the infirm. It also causes economic constraints because as they say, they are unable to look after their fields at night when wild animals destroy their crop or devour their cattle.

Kerni was apparently the first village where this exercise began. In both the villages, five marlas of land were allotted to each family, irrespective of the number of its members, and the administration also promised a sum of Rs 100,000 for the construction of one-room tenements. In most cases, half the payment has been made and the rest is still awaited. In several other cases, people alleged discrepancies. In instances where several joint families had broken up into nuclear families, they were clubbed together as one family while allotting land or disbursing money for construction, leaving some of them to fend for themselves. In Kerni, the land allotted to the villagers for the construction of the colony is located on a steep hill and is a landslide-prone area, where people have already faced difficulties during the 2005 snowstorms. People complained that several representations made to the government have fallen on deaf ears. The defence authorities had sanctioned Rs 500,000 for erecting crates to check slides in 2002. For the past two years, 109 crates are lying unused, as the callous civil administration has not bothered to do the needful. In turn, a proposal of plantation was mooted in which the inhabitants were involved. Plantation was done, but as promised, no payment was made to the villagers. A District Forest Officer (DFO) misappropriated the entire amount earmarked for the purpose. Inquiry has been ordered against him, but no action has been taken so far against the culprit, while the villagers await justice.

These areas have always lacked on the development front. With the cluster colonies, their economy, agricultural fields and development are further threatened. Kerni appears to be the worst hit because the cluster colonies have been created outside the fenced border. In fact, the village has been divided into two parts by the border fencing, isolating 16 families out of a total of 106 families in this hamlet. One portion of the village was sliced away in 1947 and is now a part of the Pakistan administered Kashmir. The fencing has further trifurcated the village (because the fence is also erected on the gorge between the two hills over which the Kerni village is spread over). Communication between the two Indian administered parts of the village is obstructed by this fencing where timings for crossing over have to be strictly adhered to. Movement is not an easy task. It is further restrained by the presence of landmines.

In Kerni, the local army unit further restricted the timings. In summer the gate shuts at 4 pm and opens at 9 am when villagers can move from the cluster colonies to work in their fields and tend to their homes. But they must all return by 4 pm. This time, the villagers feel, is inadequate for their daily chores. The army was earlier keeping the gates open till 6 pm. The change of timing came about after the discovery of a packet hung on a tree just close to the LoC by a villager, sometime in March 2005, who brought it to the notice of the army men. The packet found in a polythene bag contained some grenades and explosives. Villagers are unwilling to talk about the kind of interrogation they faced following this incident by the army and the latter's repressive measure. The army monitors their movement and actions closely and talking freely inside the village or in the cluster colonies may be fraught with dangers. It was in Poonch town that some people were able to narrate the incident of finding the ill-fated packet of explosives and many more episodes of this kind. About 15,000 people in the Poonch district of Jammu and Kashmir state were cut off from their land and livelihoods by border fencing in 2009.[11]

Repression

Close monitoring by the army on the day-to-day lives of civilians is obvious. The army personnel's presence in local traditional dress is very conspicuous. During the author's first visit,[12] three of them apparently followed her team wherever they went and would either hide behind bushes or begin chatting to each other. When approached, they were unwilling to talk. On the team's second visit, two months later, one army man dressed in traditional dress escorted them around the village and talked about the strategic importance of wearing a local dress to fool the other side, a rationale one finds amusing and absurd after learning about the awareness of even local lads. Every villager can point out at the Pakistani army bunkers just over the hill overlooking the village and say, 'that's a Pakistani soldier in uniform, there is another in a civil dress'. But the presence of the army men inside the village also visibly sparks off a fear psychosis. It is common to find villagers talking something and then deviating from the topic after spotting an army man or even a local. It is practically impossible to get them to say anything in group discussions without being superfluously sycophantic about the service being rendered by the army for civilians in their village. The same has been true of the other villages along the LoC. One can find the tones changing, once in a while, when the number of people talked to are fewer. The use of locals as army informers is almost a well-known fact, though not many would talk about it. If one queries, the answer is: 'Yes, it happens in other villages—not in ours.' But if one talks to individuals, some of them do admit this fact. During the author's second visit to Degwar, after the 8 October 2005 quake, the army soldier accompanying us in civil dress was overheard talking to sixty-year-old Feroz Din: 'You haven't gone across?' 'When the commander wills', Feroz Din replied, flashing his toothless smile. A person from the village whispered to us: 'He works for the army, if they give him the orders right now, he'll be ready to go in an hour.'

But everyone becomes tongue-tied when asked if any Pakistani informers or militants cross over to this side. They plead ignorance. In fact, nobody wants to publicly acknowledge that he or she has a relative across the LoC (barring the exception of mothers and fathers talking about their sons or daughters on the other side). Probably the silence stems from a history of repression. It may not be a regular feature but the slightest of untoward incident can provoke repression from the army. In Kerni, the timings of closing down the fence gates were preponed because of this reason. Some men from Kerni, whom the author had met in Poonch town, also narrated a recent incident about a family forced to flee to the Pakistani side because the head of the family, who was working for the army, refused to carry on with the work. He and his family were locked up in their house for two days. The family managed to give the army men a slip and ran for safety. Such, incidents, they say, are common. The army's repression can be provoked at the slightest of suspicion, sometimes quite baseless.

On the other side of the story, speaking against the army is not considered a crime by the villagers only because of the repression. The army is their sole provider for basic needs too.

There is practically complete absence of civil administration. The only link is the tehsildar's office which apparently is not well equipped to deal with their day-to-day grievances. Though army occupation, in its literal sense, cannot be defined as the direct reason for displacement, yet in the wake of armed conflicts, it is the rule of the army which prevails over their lives in all terms. The idea of setting up cluster colonies too was mooted by defence authorities to 'rehabilitate' the villagers away from their houses. But the villagers believe that their villages have been fenced out because the army or more specifically India does not trust them. They maintain this belief on the basis of their experiences. Majority families, in both Kerni and Birhuti like elsewhere in the border areas, have suffered multiple displacements, that is, in 1947, 1965, 1971, and in 2002. Their experiences have made them believe that their religion and their proximity with the people across the border, who are their blood relations, make them 'untrustworthy' in the eyes of the army.

In 1965, when trained guerillas entered Poonch and Rajouri and sought shelter from local population, the repression by the army began. In the absence of the local administration, the army got a free hand to deal with the people. The perpetration of human rights abuse by the army, including torching of homes and beating or killing several people, sharpened the communal divides and led to large-scale migration of Muslims towards the Pakistani side. In Darhal, a pro-Indian Zaildar Choudhary Karamat Ullah was shot dead publicly. Many of those who migrated to the other side returned within a year or two. Repression of the army continued in some areas even after the 1965 war. In 1966 when a batch of 25 people from Mendhar, who had migrated to the Pakistani side, returned, the army men opened fire at Saghra nallah, following a tip off by some locals who wanted to settle their scores with them, and killed them. Such incidents are deeply embedded in the psyche of the people of Rajouri and

Poonch districts, causing deep-rooted alienation. Army repression after the 1965 war lasted for a longer time.

The inhabitants in the borders also face harassment at the hands of the army, during the wars and after militancy. In Uri and Baramulla borders, in the Kashmir Valley, while the army's repression was comparatively less till 1989 when militancy began, the people have been victims of political repression right from 1947. After 1947, the local National Conference leaders who were made administrators of these areas started a reign of terror, torturing political opponents and supporters and forcing people to flee. Non-cooperation with one of the most vulnerable section of the population is equivalent to any form of repression. Not enlisting IDPs in official documents means shying away from responsibilities. The National Database and Registration Authority (NADRA), a federal body, is responsible for issuing National Identity Cards (NICs) to Pakistani citizens, which usually verifies the registration of IDPs according to criteria established by the army (Special Support Group) in consultation with provincial and national authorities.[13] To qualify for registration (and through that, humanitarian assistance), the displaced had to prove that they were residents of areas notified by the security forces as being in conflict. Registration was thus tied to geography and time rather than needs.[14]

Political interests can sometimes influence data. The inability to assist all IDPs, combined with public resentment over army operations, might sometimes induce local political administrations into minimizing the figures. For example, a week after a military operation started in Orakzai in November 2009, only 7,700 people were displaced according to the local government. However, independent sources insisted that the actual numbers exceeded 70,000.[15] On the other hand, there might be another problem—NGOs, other agencies and local authorities may also have incentives to exaggerate the number of IDPs so as to attract more funding and assistance.[16]

Spies and human shields

The massive presence of security forces in the bordering towns or villages makes the women in such areas vulnerable. Besides performing household chores, women, comprising both young and old, tend the fields and cattle. Intriguingly, for the males here, the security of the women, who in most cases act as a shield for their husbands, brothers and sons and do better part of the household as well as the field work, is not a major concern. Since these civilians, particularly the male population, are looked upon with an eye of suspicion by the security personnel for, what they allege, 'helping or harbouring' the militants from across the border and are targeted from the other side as 'informers', the women bear the brunt on all the fronts as the 'shield'. Whether they are spared by the two sides cannot be said with certainty because they evade the issue seemingly for fear of something 'hidden'. Since 1947, when raiders from the NWFP of Pakistan attacked the territories of Jammu and Kashmir and the Indian army landed, people have been sandwiched, exploited and compelled to aide this side or that, often for paltry monetary benefits. This is similar to the Afghan-Pakistan borders where people from the NWFP, bordering Afghanistan, have liberally been used as spies and mujahideens in war-torn Afghanistan.

MIGRATIONS

Migrations from the border areas or across the borders are an abiding reality rooted in the division of India in 1947. The more the borders and the LoC are fenced or militarized by increasing presence of troops, ironically the greater is the insecurity and war threats, causing frightening displacements internally or across the dividing line.

One of the biggest migrations on the Indian side, since 1947, took place in 1971 during Indo-Pak war when the entire

Chhamb area in Jammu division went into Pakistan. Interestingly, Chhamb was also home to several thousand Hindus dislocated from Mirpur, Bhimber and other parts of Pakistani side of Kashmir in 1947. When they were dislocated again, several of them were rehabilitated and resettled in villages along the IB to the south of the state in villages that were totally abandoned in 1947. Most of the villages in RS Pura and some areas of Samba tehsils had over 90 per cent Muslims and these were totally abandoned between 1947 and 1971, where the Chhamb refugees settled. The displaced families were first kept in tented camps at Manwal, about 60 km from Jammu. The government did provide them with some land and cash doles in 1976 but their demands of adequate rehabilitation are still pending.

Birhuti, in Balakote area of the tehsil of Mendhar, lying within the Poonch district, is one such village that is divided into two and straddles the delicate line demarcating the boundary between India and Pakistan.[17] The Indian side of this village along with some adjoining villages was occupied by the Pakistani army in 1965, and thereafter, the Pakistani forces retreated within a year. Administratively, however, this area continued to be a no-man's land with neither Pakistan nor India willing to accept the responsibility of the people in this area. Till 1970, it was a forgotten strip of land and its people did not exist or belong to anyone. There are several areas that come under the occupation of the other side during wars for long periods ranging from a few days to six months, forcing people to flee and making their fate uncertain. There are temporary alterations and some that become permanent. The cessation of Chhamb in 1971 by the Pakistani army may be another case that altered boundaries and left several thousands homeless. But stranger still is the case of the people of Turtuk in Ladakh, who did not lose their land but lost their enforced nationality in 1971, when this piece of land was ceded by Indian forces along with its people.

The prolonged border dispute has visibly shattered the

economy of the border districts and the villages. Despite being agriculturally rich and possessing rich natural resources, wars and hostilities on the borders render several people jobless and fail to provide new avenues for work. Even the agricultural and pastoral lands are turned into wastelands due to mining and fencing. There are unused natural water resources at the borders. Several restrictions are imposed on the people denying them better opportunities. The conflict also causes large-scale economic migrations with young men moving out of their villages for jobs and petty labour in various parts of the state, country and even to the Gulf countries.

Migrations across LoC

Coerced either by economic conditions, deprivation or extreme militarization of borders on this side, a large number of the displaced persons include those who crossed the borders since 1947. A large chunk of people were said to have crossed the LoC after every war, the largest migration having taken place in 1965, many of whom returned a year later. There is no documented record of the exact number of such displaced. However, these displaced persons have been registered as refugees in Pakistan after 1990 and many of them are putting up in camps set up by Pakistan's Azad Jammu and Kashmir (AJK) government. Since 1990, there are 35,000 unregistered refugees. According to statistics of Rehabilitation Department of AJK, this mass migration includes 1236 families (11,018) persons.[18]

Rubina Ishaque, who has done an extensive study on the patterns of migrations across the LoC in her thesis, provides an insight into the causes behind crossing the boundaries and the impact. Included among these refugees are also a few families who migrated between 1985 and 1989.[19] All these displaced persons get a paltry relief of Rs 600 per person and settlement. Those who were displaced before this period got no aid from AJK or the Pakistan government. Rubina has also maintained that in 1965 and 1971, 50,000 persons (9800 families) were displaced to AJK from the Indian side of the state. She points out that there were no mass migrations past 1990, reasoning that this was owing to what she terms as 'the "sealed borders" by India and Pak'. Though there is no knowledge of sealed borders, there is a common perception among the displaced across the LoC that the borders were heavily mined thereafter, making both mass migrations or their return impossible.

Those displaced live in 14 refugee camps in AJK—Muzaffarabad, Bagh, Kotli, Mirpur and Rawalakot. Atrocities by Indian security forces against Muslim Kashmiris are only one of the reasons of Muslim Kashmiris' migration. It is a multi-causative phenomenon. Rubina, who met several groups of migrants mentions of the displaced people at AJK from a village called Keran.

> Almost everyone in the camp told me that Islamic freedom fighters forced them to move to AJK or any other safe place, saying that, in coming days they wanted to attack Indian troops and in reaction to these attacks, Indian army will suspect them and be harsh to Muslims. Haneef Lone, an old man in the camp told me that Freedom Fighters told us to move to Azad Kashmir border, only for one week. They were sure that in one week, they will free Kashmir by attacking Indian army and then we can come back to our areas.'

In many cases, the militants misled the people, asking them to join the struggle and cross the LoC, or telling them that Pakistan was going to launch an attack on the districts of Kupwara and Baramulla, which would make their lives vulnerable.

Stories of repression by Indian army also abound. Younger boys were fed up of interrogation, checking and patrolling of Indian troops in their villages and outside. News of crackdowns and rapes from elsewhere added to the fear psychosis. Refugees maintained that in October 1990, the crisis became worse for them. They had no other option, but to migrate. The Indian army atrocities compelled them to change direction and cross the dreaded LoC. There were also political reasons for intimidation, especially in villages where people had supported a particular party or individual or aided militants. If a few individuals felt threatened and decided to leave, the others followed in a panic reaction. For example, a woman followed her brother. Later, her husband and children followed. Crossing the boundaries was not easy. Some displaced from Kupwara maintained that when a huge crowd decided to move, the Indian army started firing on them. In return, the Pakistan army also used firing to save these refugees and provided them a way to cross the borderline.

The displaced, who crossed the LoC, find themselves in a situation worse than before. Added to their vulnerability owing to involvement in crime or because of being pushed by agencies within Pakistan to work as spies, are also the economic and social problems. They are deprived of their land, property, culture and even their identity. They have no legal national identity as citizens of the host country and no ownership of land.

ATTEMPTS AT HUMANITARIAN TASKS

There are enough humanitarian tasks that can be taken up on both sides of the borders for the people. But the major problem in the India–Pakistan case is the denial of absolute inaccessibility of the border areas for the common masses. It is very difficult for NGOs to penetrate. The only time that a few organizations began working on the displaced persons at the IB in Jammu was during the mass mobilization of troops in 2001–2002 and the large-scale mine-laying operations that displaced people in huge numbers. The only time that the

NGOs ever reached the areas close to the LoC was after the October 2005 earthquake but the movement remained restricted on both sides. Several organizations who operated in these areas maintain that their performance had limitations since they could not do without the army's strategic support, rather their permission, every time that they had to visit these areas. Interestingly, even the civil administration is not very active in these areas because of the restrictions that the army imposes due to security reasons. A naib-tehsildar in Mendhar maintained that he has to deposit his identity card to cross the border fence and visit villages that have been fenced out. Restrictions and remoteness of these villages are the major reasons why education and health facilities are so meagre.

To project its 'humane face', the army has embarked upon 'Sadbhavna (goodwill) Projects' offering educational facilities at some places and vocational training at some other places, thus replacing the civil administration, in border areas. The army provides basic health care and have opened some schools. Besides, it is also running some vocational training centres for women to train them in the skill of handicrafts but neither the civil administration nor the army provides them a market or organizes the skilled women to form a SHG or something of the kind. In fact, some villagers say, it all depends on which unit and officer is posted. They have seen such centres and schools open for two or three years and then gradually close down. In the total absence of civil administration, this of course, comes as a little relief for the people at the border areas but the lack of consistency or continuity generally turns much-hyped projects into mere rhetoric.

A serious impediment is that agencies including international agencies step in only when there are displacements. The UN or the ICRC is unable to perform. The only working regional groups in Asia are sub-regional organizations:

Association of South-East Asian Countries (ASEAN) and the South Asian Association for Regional Co-operation (SAARC). While the former primarily discusses refugee issue, the SAARC has not involved itself in either issues of the displaced or those of the border people. This in fact is a problem worldwide in border areas where people bear the brunt of hostilities. There is precious little done till the people are displaced. Many humanitarian organizations have been unable to abide by the Guiding Principles[20] of internal displacement, as finalized at the 1998 meeting in Vienna of legal experts and represen-tatives of the UN agencies. This has only exposed the victims to more abuse and lack of protection.

While displacements cannot be avoided totally, the basic reasons of victimization need to be dealt with. Pertinent issues need to be addressed. While there is need to recognize people living at the borders as not just vulnerable but also international victims, there is also need to grapple with the question whether these people can be relocated to safer areas with dignity, not in shabby cluster camps for the displaced but by providing reasonable land for rehabilitation, resources for housing, and so on. More crucially, since their very victimization stems from political conflicts with communities across the borders or because governments on both sides of the borders are engaged in a dispute that assumes violent proportions, the very conflict needs to be addressed. Neocleous[21] stated that founding violence and the continuous creation by violent means are the hallmarks of the state. The states have to become more conscious and responsible of their role vis-à-vis the civilians who bear the brunt of their politics and their poor tackling of foreign relations. At least, the existence of these victimized people and their rights need to be recognized. Their humanitarian and security needs should be treated with as much importance, if not more, as the territorial security of the boundaries they inhabit.

NOTES

1 A. Passi, 'The Role of Identities and Boundaries in the Contemporary World'; for more details see: http://www.geo.ut.ee/nbc/paper/paasi.htm.
2 Sanjay Chaturvedi, 'The Mental Borders in South Asia', Ranabir Sammadar and Helmut Reifeld (eds), *Peace as a Process* (New Delhi: Manohar Publishers, 2001).
3 For details see: http://www.internal-displacement.org/8025708F004BE3B1/(httpInfoFiles)/58CE50923D581936C12577920056 95C3/$file/India+-+September+2010.pdf); last accessed on 21.11.12.
4 'Pakistan: Flooding Worsens Situation for People Displaced by Conflict in North-west, A Profile of the Internal Displacement Situation', IDMC, 6 September 2010. For more details see: http://www.internal-displacement.org/8025708F004BE3B1/(httpInfoFiles)/719B7634A7238264C12577960032832C/$file/Pak) last accessed on 21.11.12.
5 Jyoti Anand writes for Vinayak Features, a news service agency.
6 It extends to the whole of India except the state of Jammu and Kashmir. However, its application to the state of Jammu and Kashmir can be specified by the President of India only after the government of Jammu and Kashmir concurs on the application of this law to that state. For more details see: http://socialjustice.nic.in/pwdact1995.php.
7 Ramazan Dyryldaev, 'Citizen of Kyrgyzstan Perished from the Mine Explosion at the Border', press release by the Kyrgyz Committee for Human Rights in Exile, 26 April 2001, available at: www.eurasianet.org/resource/kyrgyzstan/hypermail/200104/0074.html. For more details see: Landmine and Cluster Munition Monitor; http://www.the-monitor.org/index.php/publications/display?url=lm/2002/kyrgyzstan.html, last accessed on 21.11.12.
8 The treaty was signed on 3 December 1997. The Mine Ban Treaty or the Ottawa Treaty is the international agreement that bans antipersonnel landmines. Officially entitled *The Convention on the Prohibition, Use, Stockpiling, Production and Transfer of Antipersonnel Mines and on their Destruction*, the treaty is sometimes also referred to as the Ottawa Convention.
9 'Kurdish Landmine Plight across and along the Borders', *The*

Journal of Mine Action, April 2008; for details see http://maic.jmu.edu/journal/11.2/focus/kohli/kohli.htm, last accessed on 12.10.11.

10 NSAs refer to armed non-state actors. 42 NSAs from Burundi, India, Iran, Iraq, Myanmar/Burma, the Philippines, Somalia, Sudan, Turkey, and Western Sahara. The *Deed of Commitment* banning AP mines was signed by 42 NSAs. Overall, signatory NSAs are abiding to the core prohibitions on the use, production, acquisition and transfer of AP mines. Most signatories are also undertaking humanitarian mine action activities such as demining, stockpile destruction, mine risk education and victim assistance, often collaborating with humanitarian organizations. In addition and as a result of Geneva Call's efforts, several NSAs that have not signed the *Deed of Commitment* banning AP mines have nevertheless pledged to prohibit or limit the use of AP mines. They have done so either unilaterally or through a ceasefire agreement with the government, while some have undertaken mine clearance and victim assistance in areas under their control. For details see: 'Anti-personnel Mines and Armed Non-State Actors', *Geneva Call*, 2009; http://www.genevacall.org/Themes/Landmines/landmines.htm), last accessed on 21.11.12.

11 After March 2005, when in Kerni village a bag of explosives were found, the author paid visit to Poonch town. For further details see: *The Hindu*, 20 December 2009.

12 My observations as an activist working with the displaced people of this region. As part of the *Kashmir Times* team, I visited Poonch sometime in August–September 2005 and again in October–November 2005. The first time was to address the problems of the people at the borders; the second visit was post October 2005 earthquake which had badly affected some of the border villages in Poonch. The border fencing started sometime in 1999 and by 2002, the villagers were totally cut off by the border fencing at the LoC.

13 As reported by *The News*, December 2009.

14 http://www.internal-displacement.org/idmc/website/countries.nsf/(httpEnvelopes)/944667B8E6F38FDFC12577 8C00711DD9?OpenDocument

15 *Dawn*, December 2009; *The News*, December 2009.

16 *Dawn*, May 2009 and January 2010; for details see: http://

www.internaldisplacement.org/idmc/website/countries.nsf/%28httpEnvelopes%29/944667B8E6F38FDFC125778C00711DD9?OpenDocument, last accessed on 6.1.12.

17 Poonch is bounded by the LoC (boundary between Indian and Pakistan-administered Kashmir) on three sides (north, west and south). The 1947–48 war between India and Pakistan divided it into two parts. One went to Pakistan and the other became part of the Indian state of Jammu and Kashmir.

18 AJK statistics as cited by Rubina Ishaque, 'Migration, Acculturation and Criminality: An Anthropological Inquiry into the Effects of Forced Migration in Azad Kashmir', thesis paper, Jinnah University, Islamabad. Also see, 'Kashmiri Refugees: Facts, Issues and Future Ahead', Institute of Policy Studies, Islamabad. For more details see: http://www.ips.org.pk/pakistan-and-its-neighbours/1117-kashmiri-refugees-facts-issues-and-the-future-ahead.html.

19 Ishaque, 'Migration, Acculturation and Criminality: An Anthropological Inquiry into the Effects of Forced Migration in Azad Kashmir'.

20 The Commission on Human Rights and the General Assembly had requested Francis Deng to draft a legal framework addressing the issues of the internally displaced. This led to the drafting of the Guiding Principles, which sought to address the grey areas. After the draft was placed in 1998, the Commission had adopted a resolution, taking note of the Guiding Principles.

21 M. Neocleous, 'Off the Map on Violence and Cartography', *European Journal of Social Theory* 6, 4 (November 2003), pp.409-25, deals with the importance of cartographic violence: the way the state and its violent constitution of territory have been sanctified through the project of the map.

9

MEDIA AND DISPLACEMENT:
Erasure, Aggravated Focus, Identity Building

PAMELA PHILIPOSE

The twentieth century has been characterized as the 'century of displacement' and the first decade of the twenty-first century has produced little evidence of a reversal of this trend. An estimated 40 million people worldwide has been uprooted and forced to flee violence and persecution.[1] Every year, hundreds of millions of persons are persuaded to leave or are forcibly evicted from regions they have regarded as their homes. Despite the greatness of their numbers and the magnitude of their personal trauma, they have remained in the periphery, not just in terms of spatial location but in terms of mainstream consciousness.

The media has played a central role in the othering of the displaced. Newspapers and television channels, through a combination of sophisticated communications technology and resources, have improved their accessibility. They can bring incidents, played out in anonymous corners of the world, right into the living room in almost real time. They have, thus, the potential of tearing through the screens and masks used by the powerful to exercise the politics of repression with impunity. In the process, the media, with its ability to interpret current events, can help to deepen the general understanding of human rights violations, further the articulation of outrage and resistance to them, and ensure important corrective action through the delivery of justice.

It is, therefore, essential to recognize the unique power that the media has to defend the common good in times of great human suffering. Many newspapers and television channels have on occasion achieved this. The question is, why is such an outcome so rare. Two broad reasons can be cited: one, the nature of media content in present times; two, the manner in which the media has come to be used and deployed by the power elites within countries.

Few social philosophers have attempted to understand the unique nature of modern media content, especially television content; eminent French sociologist, the late Pierre Bourdieu being most prominent among them. He systematically analysed why 'real information', analysis, in-depth interviews, expert discussions and serious documentaries lose out to pure entertainment and staged 'exchanges' in the talk show format.[2] This may be more true of television, but in India, as in most parts of the world, mainstream newspapers are competing not with other newspapers, but with television for attention and mindspace. Television has become the dominant media model and this has a knockdown effect on print media coverage. The media, Bourdieu said, tries to avoid the 'quagmire of intellectual complexity': the less one knows, the better one feels. In the process, 'current events' become 'an impassioned recital of entertaining events', which tend to lie about halfway between the human interest story and the variety show. The result 'is a litany of events with no beginning and no real end, thrown together only because they occurred at the same time'. In other words, media practitioners are ruled not by an anxiety to make sense of the day's events meticulously, in a way that informs the viewer or reader, but by an anxiety not to bore their readers and viewers. There is a tendency to shut out anything that requires detailed comment or investigation, and instead go with the formula that 'less is better', the 'newer is better', 'the more dramatic is better'.

Besides, the market-driven focus of the media in present times seeks to erase the distinction between reader/viewer, on the one hand, and the consumer, on the other. The pressure to attain higher profit levels leads to a conscious blending of news with entertainment as a strategy to gain higher readership/viewership ratings. Indeed, the new emphasis on ratings is comment enough. Perhaps the most debilitating consequence of these developments—as Daya Kishan Thussu,[3] a media and communications academic, pointed out—is the general homogenization of news. Thussu cites a major study conducted by the Project for Excellence in Journalism, which examined the US mass media over a span of 25 years. According to the study, there has been a distinct shift towards lifestyle, celebrity, entertainment and celebrity crime/scandal in the news.

Such a media vision is 'dehistorisized and dehistorisizing, fragmented and fragmenting', as Bourdieu put it, and has a decided impact on society. The world is represented in terms of a philosophy that sees history as an 'absurd series' of disaster which the ordinary person can neither fully under-stand nor influence. This worldview, Bordieu argued, fosters fatalism and disengagement which obviously favours the status quo. This 'fatalism and disengagement' of the viewer/reader[4] assist the process; hence, power elites are allowed to use and deploy the media for their own purposes without let or hindrance.

The media has become strategic assets of powerful politico-corporate interests and are used to further their influence and achieve their objectives. This is a mutually rewarding relationship, driven by the neo-liberal ideology that both the state and the media have come to share. Given the huge investments and privileges required to keep newspaper houses and television channels running, being patronized by the ruling elite ensures access to both capital and decision making. Therefore, despite the media gaining their credibility from the fact that they represent the fourth estate and are meant to play an independent watchdog role in order to protect the interests of society, the reality is that the media ends up becoming both publicists/apologists and advisors to those who control the state.

This melding of objectives and interests is evident at its most heightened form during situations of conflict. A US military spokesman once explained: 'If we keep them (the American people) informed, if we keep them educated, they stay with us'. The Pentagon went on to show what it means by being 'educated' by coming up with the convergence of military operations and media coverage, which threw up the new model of 'embedded journalism', officially inaugurated in the Iraq War of 2003. Reporters were allowed to cover the war from the very scene of the fighting, subject to two conditions—they were never to jeopardize troops or the mission. What then US Defence Secretary Donald Rumsfeld desired was 'total immersion' on the part of the reporters.[5] The strategy seemed to work: the Pentagon was pleased with the results, the media not displeased, and many ordinary Americans believed that they were getting the best media coverage that their money could buy, a coverage that was up-close and personal. It should surprise no one that for many years the great majority of Americans believed that the Iraq war had a humanitarian motive, and that the Saddam Hussein government was in cahoots with the al Qaeda.

The 'immersion' Rumsfeld talked of is evident closer home. After the attack on the Indian Parliament in December 2001, the amazing 11-month eyeball-to-eyeball confrontation between two nuclear powers across the India–Pakistan border was evident. If war did not break out at that point it was not because of the innumerable media commentators on both sides of the divide who shrilly advocated 'direct action'. This is where the media acts as spokesperson for the nation state which, as peace activists have pointed out, seeks to transform borderlands into markers of identity and 'zones of anxiety and conflict'.[6] The movement of people across the border is regarded as extremely destabilizing for the nation state, feeding into local insurgencies and terrorist networks. The media's routine use of the military term 'infiltrator' to characterize everybody from environmental refugee and distress migrant to a person who actually intends to commit acts of terrorism, is an indicator of the distorting nature of this discourse.

Given the nature of the media today it should, therefore, be no surprise that the coverage of displacement and of people who are essentially marginalized, has been shabby, disconnected, superficial and negative for the most part. This chapter highlights three broad mainstream media narratives about displaced populations, both from within the country and from outside its borders. One, they are erased from the public gaze and their status is consciously trivialized; two, they are occasionally subjected to an aggravated focus, especially in the wake of disturbances like bomb blasts, and so on; and three, they are used in the construction of national or regional identities through the politics of inclusion/exclusion.

TRIVIALIZING DISPLACEMENT

One reason for the trivialization of the displacement of populations through forced evictions—described as the 'removal of individuals, families or communities from their homes, land or neighbourhoods, against their will, directly or indirectly attributable to the state'—is because it is viewed by both the state and the media as a simple consequence of development[7]—for urban renewal or for economic progress and foreign investment, or for energy generation—which is constructed as imperative for the 'good' of the nation. The fact that it dismantles assets of those who are powerless and voiceless is airbrushed out of the frame.

This country saw the issue dramatized in the struggle against the Narmada Dam. The mainstream media went along completely with the view that the entire multi-million-rupee project was highly desirable in the 'national interest'. But the question as to what constitutes 'national interest' and the 'public good' was never raised, or indeed who constitutes this 'public' and who benefits from this 'good'.[8] The essential cost-benefit assessment considering not only direct economic costs but also the social costs of the project, exploring the least-displacing alternatives and ensuring that over-acquisition of land or the change in the declared use of land did not occur, were not carried forth in a comprehensive manner.

Instead, the benefits of 'rehabilitation' of the ousted—unsatisfactory at best—were played up by the media. A Supreme Court judgement on Sardar Sarovar expressed the hope that 'a properly drafted R&R plan would improve living standards of displaced persons. For example, the residents of villages near the Bhakra Nangal Dam, Nagarjun Sagar Dam, Tehri, Bhilai Steel Plant . . . are better off than people living in villages in whose vicinity no development project came in'. This was taken as having been translated into reality. What little came to these displaced communities by way of rehabilitation happened not because of media coverage but because of the activism of NBA and allied groups. In fact, mainstream media went the extra mile to vilify the Andolan, and its leader, Medha Patkar, sometimes even portraying her as anti-national, retrogressive and excessively dogmatic.

UNCALLED SENSATIONALIZATION

If trivialization and erasure is the treatment accorded to IDPs, those characterized as 'Bangladeshi infiltrators' are perpetually on the radar of suspicion. The lines of separation between those who come to India in search of livelihoods or to escape an environmental catastrophe and those entering with the express purpose of creating instability through targeted attacks of violence are consciously blurred. This means that large numbers of innocent people come periodically under aggravated media scrutiny in the wake of terrorist attacks.

Two instances demonstrate this effect. After the serial bomb blasts that Jaipur experienced on 13 May 2008, a large numbers of Muslims were rounded up by the Rajasthan police, often in clear violation of the norms laid down in the Criminal Procedure Code. The first community to be targeted in this way were the miserably poor Bengali-speaking migrants living in colonies on the outskirts of Jaipur. The adult men in the community were indiscriminately arrested after saffron outfits campaigned on the need to push 'Bangladeshis' back into Bangladesh. The media discourse at this juncture revolved largely around information from 'privileged intelligence sources' about how illegal Bangladeshi migrant communities have become 'terrorist recruitment grounds'. There was little independent attempt to find out more about these Bengali-speaking communities, some of whom—as civil rights activists pointed out—were from the Indian side of the border and had settled in this area a good forty to fifty years earlier.

Directly after the serial blasts of 30 October 2008, which struck Guwahati, Barpeta, Kokrajhar and Bongaigaon, the media immediately concluded that they were planted by jihadi outfits in the state. The sites of the blasts were also regions where the ULFA had a decided presence, but there was a general effort either to completely discount ULFA involvement, or see the outfit as having acted in concert with jihadi groups. The day after the blasts one of the news reports ended with the comment seeking to meld the latest strikes with an old concern:

> The rise of Islamic outfits mostly comprising Bangladeshi immigrants as their cadre, have essentially to do with the 'indulgent' attitude of the Congress government in the state towards illegal migrants due to alleged votebank considera-

> tions. This despite former Assam governor, Lt Gen S. K. Sinha's earlier warning that illegal immigration from Bangladesh was changing the demographic structure of several districts of Assam and could ultimately lead to disintegration of Assam and its severing from the mainland.[9]

Another report went back to an earlier interview given by A. K. Mitra, the earlier chief of the BSF, on the eve of his retirement. It went on to say: 'Throughout last year the BSF had intercepted 807 Bangladeshis trying to illegally cross over to India—the actual infiltration is roughly estimated to be double the number intercepted—the BSF said the figure was almost 10–12,000 till a few years back. In other words, at least 24,000 Bangladeshis have been infiltrating every year.' Notice how the figure 807 becomes 24,000 in the course of a single sentence with no evidence to back the final figure. Interestingly, the report goes on to quote Mr. Mitra's answer to a question whether investigative agencies feed the BSF with credible information on Bangladeshi infiltration. Mr. Mitra said, 'We do not get authentic information from investigating agencies on time. Whatever action we have taken so far against militant outfits like Huji and LeT along the border were based on media reports'.[10]

Here then is the classic 'circular circulation of information' that communications experts speak about, with the media making little attempt to disentangle the truth from surmise through painstaking investigation. The tendency is to either invisibilize Bangladeshis as people who have no entitlements, or visibilize them as aliens, Muslims, bearers of trouble, disease, insecurity, who are out to ruin the economy, inundate the neighbourhoods, and plant grenades in public spaces.[11]

ADDING REGIONAL OR NATIONAL DIMENSION

The third media narrative is to use the displaced or 'the outsider', to construct a national or regional identity through the politics of inclusion/exclusion. The Muslim Bangladeshi has been used by BJP and its cohorts in election rhetoric to shore up the construct of a Hindu India under siege from its Muslim neighbours. But a recent example of ethnic profiling for political purposes is the campaign launched by Raj Thackeray's Maharashtra Nav Nirman in Maharashtra, a virtual repeat of the Shiv Sena campaign launched by his uncle, Balasaheb Thackeray, earlier. The idea was to shore up the identity of the '*Marathi Manoos*' by targeting 'outsiders', primarily from UP and Bihar, who travelled to Mumbai to appear for the Railway Recruitment Board's (RRB) examination for the posts of gangmen, helpers and *khalasis* (unskilled labourers). This editorial in the Shiv Sena-run *Saamna*, written by Bal Thackeray in 2003, ushering in the Party's '*Bihari ani bhaiyya bahar kada mohim* (the movement to drive away all Biharis and *bhaiyyas*)' provides the clear game plan. Thackeray talked about the 'unimaginable' dangers posed by 'outsiders' taking away jobs that are due to Maharashtrians. He then asked: 'If Biharis are as hardworking as Lalu Prasad Yadav says they are, why don't they work hard in Bihar? . . . Why is that North Indians are getting a better deal and local Maharashtrians are victimized in their own land? The rules have to change and the Maharashtrian youth is willing to shed his blood for that.'

What happens invariably is that sectarian agendas are begun by interested groups like the MNS and Shiv Sena, but once they begin to hold public attention, they quickly become mainstream discourse with very few media agencies willing to buck the trend, especially given the ubiquitous threat of violence from lumpenized political cadres. It was only in the wake of the recent MNS campaign this time, for instance, that the Marathi press in general began to raise questions like: Why did the youth have to travel 2,000 km to take this exam? Why was the RRB examination not publicized in local newspapers? and so on. This dogmatic assertion of ethnic identity at the expense of people constructed as the 'Other' ends up actually making outsiders out of insiders. The media plays an important role in this assertion.

This leads to the question: is it possible for the media to stop viewing migrants through the prism of 'national or regional security', and perceive it through the prism of the 'security of people'? For instance, in the case of IDPs, displacement comes with a great human cost which is usually invisibilized because the human rights of those who suffer it remain invisibilized. People who are evicted lose not only their homes and neighbourhoods, but also the entire social network of reciprocal ties which have been a source of their support thus far. They are generally forced to move to places where they cannot earn, where their families do not have access to healthcare and their children, proper education. The costs of this dislocation is of course borne most by the people who suffer it, but society too has to pay a price in terms of alienation, social tensions, health epidemics, disruptions in schooling and criminalization. The media, by projecting these, could help society arrive at a rational cost-benefit assessment that takes into consideration not just the direct economic costs of a particular project, but its social costs. This would contribute immeasurably to the exploration of the least displacing alternatives and ensure that the routine miscarriages of administration, for instance, over-acquisition of land, is avoided.

Conversely, in expanding on the social and economic costs of the narrowcast politics of irredentist forces which targets the 'outsider', the media can play a powerful role in upholding the fundamental right of every Indian to move freely throughout the territory of India. Indeed, during the recent fracas caused by the disruptive violence of Raj Thackeray's Nav Nirman Movement, there were persuasive articulations of this position in the national media as a counter to the chauvinism exhibited by the regional press in Maharashtra.

The case of the migrant from outside the country is more complex given the fact that the national media is one of the prime sites for the construction of the ideology of national identity, the creation of the great imaginary 'We, The People' against 'Them, The Aliens'. But even here we see variations depending on political and social circumstances. The refugee flow from East Pakistan in 1971 which reached about 10 million by December 1971, was met with a rare national consensus, created in part by the Western media's extended coverage of the tragic events in East Pakistan, including the massacres in Dacca, and in part by the stance of the Indian political leadership. In her statement in the Lok Sabha, made on 27 May 1971, widely endorsed by the media of the day, Mrs. Indira Gandhi said, 'I hope that this Parliament, our country and the people will be ready to accept the necessary hardships so that we can discharge our responsibilities to our own people as well as to the millions, who have fled from a region of terror to take temporary refuge here'.[12] Again, the Tamil refugees during the early 1980s were welcomed and given staunch support in local press coverage.

The present political exigencies are, of course, radically different, but the lack of a law or cogent policy on refugees based on a rights approach[13] has only added to the great confusion marking the national discourse on displaced people from across the country's borders. The great majority of Bangladeshis are migrant workers. Many of them have lived in this country for decades and have got integrated into the local economy, either as agricultural labour, petty traders or unorganized workers. According to Article 2 of the Migrant Workers' Convention, the term 'migrant worker' refers to a person who is to be engaged, is engaged or has been engaged in a remunerated activity in a state of which he or she is not a national. The Convention also provides for various categories of such workers, such as seasonal worker, self-employed worker, frontier worker, and so on. A media coverage that is better informed would make these distinctions. This, in turn, would help persuade the government into evolving an ethical and legal framework to deal with what are essentially human crises. Such a framework would also address concerns of national security in a far more effective and useful manner than the sledgehammer approach of demonizing an entire community.

NOTES

1 Statement of UNHCR chief, António Guterres, on World Refugee Day, 2007.
2 Pierre Bourdieu, *On Television and Journalism* (Pluto Press, 1998).
3 Daya Kishan Thussu and Des Freedman (eds), *War and Media: Reporting Conflict 24x7* (Sage Publications, 2003).
4 Bourdieu, *On Television and Journalism*.
5 Stephen Hess and Marvin Kalb, *The Media and the War on Terrorism* (Pakistan: Oxford University Press, 2005).
6 R. Manchanda (ed.), *Media Crossing Borders* (South Asia Forum for Human Rights, 2004).
7 Fact Sheet No. 25, 'Forced Evictions and Human Rights' (United Nations Centre for Human Rights, 1996).
8 P. Philipose, 'The Forgotten and the Damned', *The Indian Express*, 2000.
9 'Death Toll in Assam Blasts Rises to 77', *The Economic Times*, 31 October 2008.
10 'Bangladeshi Migrants Crux of Problem, Ex-BSF Chief Had Warned', *The Economic Times*, 31 October 2008.
11 P. Philipose, 'Borders in the Mind: Bangladeshis, a Nowhere Policy for a Nowhere People', *The Indian Express*, 2003.
12 *Lok Sabha Debates*, 2.
13 R. Samaddar, *Refugees and the State: Practices of Asylum and Care in India* (Sage Publications, 2003).

10

CLIMATE CHANGE, ENVIRONMENTAL REFUGEES AND FUTURE CONFLICT PATTERNS IN SOUTH ASIA:
Ominous Portents

SUBIR BAUMIK

In the foreseeable future the world faces a huge threat from increasing global warming, rising population levels and fast rising energy demand in the wake of speedy industrialization. Schwartz and Randall argue that the adverse climate change scenario could potentially de-stabilize geo-political environments, leading to skirmishes, battles, and even war due to resource constraints.[1] Byers and Dragojlovic stated that 'in the future, as climate change progresses, conflicts over natural resources could increasingly take centre stage'.[2] They argued that the 'Darfur conflict was likely to be linked to climate change.' More than 30 years ago, Mesarovic and Pestel said that during acute resource crisis and shortage of essentials caused by climate change, 'there will be a thousand desperadoes terrorizing those who are now "rich" and eventually nuclear blackmail and terror will paralyse further orderly development'.[3] Nuclear blackmail or not, there's no doubt that unless the adverse climate change is effectively checked, it will cause acute pressure on scarce resources and lead to a sharp rise in conflicts across the world.

Adverse climate change has often caused severe catastrophes before. Davies in his seminal work,[4] detailed the linkage between global climate patterns and political economy, particularly the meteorological phenomenon called El Niño-Southern Oscillation (ENSO). It described how colonial policies aggravated the impact of ENSO-triggered famines in 1876-1879, 1896-1897 and 1899–1902 that ravaged India, China, Brazil, Ethiopia, Korea, Vietnam, the Philippines and New Caledonia, and in which 30–60 million people died. But the global warming-induced climate change that is beginning to unfold could cause much worse catastrophes.

This chapter examines projections of adverse climate change as a result of global warming and the way it would impact migration patterns and future conflicts of South Asia, which is one of the world's heavily populated region with a high level of poverty. The chapter postulates the following arguments: *(a)* illegal migration would increase from Bangladesh to India—and within India from coastal to inland regions and within inland areas depending on resource scarcity and availability—due to the impact of climate change; *(b)* the increase in migration would not only exacerbate existing ethnic and religious conflicts, like the one already witnessed in Assam, but the conflicts will also spread to other regions of South Asia; *(c)* the conflicts will focus more directly on resources such as control of fertile lands and water resources; *(d)* they will seriously undermine government control and weaken governance in large parts of the region.

CLIMATE CHANGES: LOOMING DANGER

The Intergovernmental Panel on Climate Change (IPCC) in their Third Assessment Report (TAR) 2001[5] emphasized on the linkages between global environmental issues and the challenge of meeting key human needs such as adequate food, clean water, clean air and adequate and affordable energy services. The IPCC Fourth Annual Report (FAR), 2007,[6] stated that it is 90 per cent certain that mankind is responsible for rising global temperatures. At continental, regional and ocean basin scales, numerous long-term changes in climate have been observed. These include changes in Arctic temperatures, widespread changes in precipitation amounts, ocean salinity, wind patterns and aspects of extreme weather including droughts, heavy precipitation, heat waves and the intensity of tropical cyclones. Listed below are some of the effects that may be forthcoming, according to the IPCC.

- Average Arctic temperatures have increased at almost twice the global average rate in the past 100 years. Arctic temperatures have high decadal variability, and a warm period was also observed from 1925–45.
- Satellite data since 1978 showed that the annual average Arctic sea ice extent has shrunk by 2.7 [2.1–3.3] per cent per decade, with larger decreases in the summer of 7.4 [5–9.8] per cent per decade. These values were consistent with those reported in the FAR.
- Temperatures at the top of the permafrost layer have generally increased since the 1980s in the Arctic (by up to 3°C). The maximum area covered by seasonally frozen ground has decreased by about 7 per cent in the Northern Hemisphere since 1900, with a decrease in spring of up to 15 per cent.
- Long-term trends from 1900 to 2005 have been observed in precipitation amount over many large regions. Significantly, there is increased precipitation in eastern parts of North and South America, northern Europe and northern and central Asia. Drying has been observed in the Sahel, the Mediterranean, southern Africa and parts of southern Asia. Precipitation was highly variable spatially and temporally, and data have been limited in some regions. Long-term trends have not been observed for the

other large regions assessed.

- Changes in precipitation and evaporation over the oceans were caused by freshening of mid- and high-latitude waters with increased salinity in low-latitude waters.
- Mid-latitude westerly winds have strengthened in both hemispheres since the 1960s.
- More intense and longer droughts have been observed over wider areas since the 1970s, particularly in the tropics and subtropics. Increased drying linked with higher temperatures and decreased precipitation had contributed to changes in drought.
- Changes in sea surface temperatures (SST), wind patterns, and decreased snow pack and snow cover had also been linked to droughts.
- The frequency of heavy precipitation events has increased over most land areas, consistent with warming and observed increases of atmospheric water vapour.
- Widespread changes in extreme temperatures have been observed over the last 50 years. Cold days, cold nights and frost have become less frequent, while hot days, hot nights and heat waves have become more frequent.
- There has been observational evidence for an increase in intense tropical cyclone activity in the North Atlantic since about 1970, correlated with increases of tropical sea surface temperatures. There have been suggestions of increased intense tropical cyclone activity in some other regions as well.

Given the possibilities for conflict created by the above changes in the global climate, whether it is over petroleum, uranium, refugee flows, fresh water or food, it becomes apparent that in South Asia, given its high population levels and endemic poverty, the possibilities for conflict are overwhelming. Glaciers in the Himalayas from which much of South Asia obtains its water supplies are retreating, the Gangotri Glacier is retreating at 23 m per year. The Khumbu

Glacier on Mount Everest has retreated more than 5 km from the time when Sir Edmund Hillary and Tensing Norgay first conquered the world's highest peak in 1953. The Himalayan glaciers supply water to the Ganges, Indus, Brahmaputra, Mekong, Yangtze and Yellow rivers. Any disruption of water supply in these rivers can have serious consequences for the region.[7] The predicted increase in extreme weather including higher temperatures, changing patterns of precipitation, coupled with increasing domestic and agricultural use of water, is a recipe for disaster.

The IPCC, in its provisional 2007 report, detailed a frightening future scenario for South Asia. It stated that sea levels will rise by at least 40 cm by 2100, inundating vast areas on the coastline; the Ganga, Brahmaputra and Indus will become seasonal rivers; and crop productivity will fall with rise in temperatures. In some parts of South Asia, like the Sundarbans delta, the impact of climate change has been felt by residents much before the world started talking about it in a big way. Presently, the ghost of climate change haunts the delta residents much more than the lurking tiger or the crocodile. This is one area—like the Arctic up north where the ice cap melt is visibly upsetting—where the impact of climate change is beginning to be felt in daily lives. I have been a regular visitor to the Sundarbans since 1995. In 2003, I first reported the disappearance of four Sundarbans islands for the BBC. I was there during the 2008 monsoon for news coverage and once later, in connection with a BBC. World Service Trust-sponsored disaster management course for the media and the government officials. That gave me the opportunity to compare the impact of climate change and speak to residents about how they proposed to handle it. The feedback I got was straight and unambiguous: 'We cannot live here for long.' And that was followed by the eternal question of choice that potential refugees have to handle: 'where do we go now?'

Kabita Patra and her fellow villagers at Madangunj on

the Namkhana Island in the Indian side of the Sunderbans delta go to sleep every night with lurking fears of being swept away into the sea as the dykes are ringing the islands. They fear that one day, they might succumb to the force of the high tides. These are the people who will be hit the hardest by global warming and consequent rise in sea levels that is expected to submerge much of the human habitations in the Sunderbans, the largest deltaic region in the world, by the turn of the century—if not by the middle of it. 'The dykes were con-structed a century ago by the British to settle people in the islands and prevent submergence. But now the sea waters flow over the dykes during the high tides and the islands are flooded, at times, twice a day,' says Badal Mallick, 65, at Madangunj. 'We may not be able to live in such conditions for long.'

Kabita Patra echoes similar sentiments. 'Our people are very tough and we don't give up easily, we have fought with tigers and crocodiles but can we fight nature and survive? 'Either we leave this place or the sea devours us with our islands.' She and her folk are part of South Asia's fast-growing brigade of 'environment refugees', the first obvious victims of climate change in the region's Low Elevation Coastal Zone (LECZ) that may displace up to 125 million people or more by the turn of the century, as projected by a 2008 report released by Greenpeace. It said: 'Looking at India and Bangladesh alone, approximately 125 million migrants, comprising about 75 million from Bangladesh and remaining 50 million from densely populated coastal regions and other vulnerable parts of India, could be rendered homeless by the end of this century.'[8]

Generally, in the monsoons, the rivers swell up and cause devastating floods in the Sundarbans. Strong winds and rising sea level surges huge volumes of saline water over the dykes in most of 54 human-inhabited islands of the Sunderbans. The flooding severely damaged, particularly during high tides, standing paddy crops, led to flight of the fishes from the ponds, flattened mud houses, killed livestock and made the farmland saline—all led to shortages and threatening livelihoods.

Thus the alarm bells have been ringing for a while in the Sundarbans. Rise of the sea level has been felt here continuously for at least twenty years—so has been the devastating impact of coastal erosion. In the past two decades, four islands in the Sundarbans—Lohachara, Kabasgadi, Suparibhanga and Bedford—have been eaten away by the sea, displacing 6,000 families (about 35,000 to 40,000 people). Two other islands—Ghoramara and Mousuni—are fast going under, threatening another 40,000 people with displacement.[9]

The 20,000 sq.km Sundarbans forest delta stretches across the lower reaches of the Bengal basin—60 per cent falling in Bangladesh and the rest in the Indian state of West Bengal. Satellite imagery shows that the sea level in the Sundarbans has risen at an average rate of 3.14 cm a year over the past two decades—much higher than the global average of 2mm a year. Scientists believe that in the next 50 years, a rise of even 1 m in sea level would inundate 1,000 sq.km of the Sundarbans.

'The Sundarbans appears to be a lost cause,' says Professor Sugato Hazra, Director of Jadavpur University's School of Oceanographic Studies (JUSOS), Kolkata, which runs a project in the Indian Sundarbans. 'Creating a mangrove forest on the riverfront is the only way to stop embankment erosion and save lives. Mangroves hold the soil in the thick network of roots and soak more carbon dioxide from the atmosphere.'[10] Islanders are slowly realizing the need to grow and protect the mangrove species like Baine, Geona, Hetal, which otherwise they would cut off and use as firewood or as logs for construction. As monsoon ends, the residents of Madanganj village go out to collect the floating seeds of mangroves from the rivers and estuaries to plant them. Men collect mangrove seeds, dig trenches to collect mud beds on the riverfront during high tide and women plant the germinated seeds on the mud beds when the river ebbs. Sunderbans Development Board and several NGOs have come forward to give money and technical expertise to the villagers to plant mangroves, which is being considered as the main protector of the dykes.

But this may be a losing battle for Sundarbans' villagers. Researchers at JUSOS stated that in another fifteen years the sea will submerge a dozen islands in the Sunderbans, six of which are populated, rendering about 70,000 people homeless. (These predictions are part of a study that was conducted over several years to assess the vulnerability of the ecologically sensitive Sunderbans island system vis-à-vis climate change.[11]) The team found erosion and submergence at its most severe in the twelve sea-facing southern islands of the Sunderbans in West Bengal, including the largest island of Sagar where a large number of pilgrims gather at Kapilmuni Temple during the Ganga Sagar fair in January. The western bank of the islands is more vulnerable and the Sagar Island has lost 30 sq. km. The original temple was devoured by the sea during British rule. A new one had to be built several kilometres inland, but now the sea is closing in on that as well.

The Sunderban Islands are home to more than four million people who live in the high risk zone of cyclone and storm surges. According to Hazra, the rate of rise of sea level is currently approaching 3.14 mm per year near Sagar Island and this could increase to 3.5 mm in the next few years due to global warming. 'The rate is higher in case of Bangladesh's part of Sunderbans, due to higher rate of deltaic subsidence,' he says.

The panic is as acute in the Bangladesh Sundarbans as in the rest of the coastal region of the low-lying country. Mohon Kumar Mondal, the executive director of the Local Environment Development and Agricultural Research Society (LEDARS) operating in the country's south-west coastal region sounded the alarm during a Greenpeace press conference on 25 March 2008. 'I don't want to see the day I lose my home to the sea and the saline desert where people have to live without clean water. It can be prevented and we are the last generation that can stop it.'[12] Mondal then went on to predict that if large parts of coastal Bangladesh went under the sea, 'India would certainly be the first country to experience a huge inflow of refugees.'

The world has finally woken up to the threat of climate change, but the true enormity of the future crisis it will cause in South Asia has not yet fully dawned on the governments and the peoples of this rather highly populated region. Some studies, like the one released by Greenpeace, have assessed the dangers of climate change in South Asia, leading to growing awareness in the academic and the activist communities of the possible havoc that climate change will cause in the region. Climate change is no longer an issue for the distant future. Climate change is already taking place and the South Asian countries, particularly the poorest people, are most at risk.

The impacts of higher temperatures, more variable precipitation, more extreme weather events and sea level rise are felt in South Asia and will continue to intensify. These changes are already having major impacts on the economic performance of South Asian countries and on the lives and livelihoods of millions of poor people. The impacts result not only from gradual changes in temperature and sea level but also from increased climate variability and extremes, including more intense floods, droughts and storms.

FUTURE IMPACTS ON SOUTH ASIA

The FAR of IPCC[13] provided specific information for South Asia concerning the nature of future impacts. Some of the future manifestations of climate change in South Asia are listed below:

- Glacier melting in the Himalayas is projected to increase flooding and will affect water resources within the next two to three decades;
- Climate change will compound the pressures on natural resources and the environment due to rapid urbanization, industrialization and economic development;
- Crop yields could decrease up to 30 per cent in South Asia by the mid-twenty-first century;
- Mortality due to diarrhoea primarily associated with floods and droughts will rise in South Asia;
- Sea-level rise will exacerbate inundation, storm surge, erosion and other coastal hazards.

The impact of such environmental change in South Asia would include:

- Decreased water availability and water quality in many arid and semi-arid regions;
- Increased risk of floods and droughts in many regions;
- reduction in water regulation in mountain habitats;
- Decrease in reliability of hydropower and biomass production;
- Increased incidence of waterborne diseases, such as malaria, dengue and cholera;
- Increased damages and deaths caused by extreme weather events;
- Decreased agricultural productivity;
- Adverse impacts on fisheries;
- Adverse effects on many ecological systems.

As a result of these changes, the achievement of many of the Millennium Development Goals (MIDGs), including those on poverty eradication, child mortality, malaria and other diseases and environmental sustainability might be hampered. Much of this damage would come in the form of severe economic shocks. In addition, the impacts of climate change will exacerbate existing social and environmental problems and lead to migration within and across national borders.[14]

Though the Fifth Assessment Report is due in 2013/14, the IPCC has come up with its Special Report on Renewable Energy Sources and Climate Change Mitigation (SRREN). The Summary for Policy Makers was approved line by line and the final draft of the report was accepted at the Eleventh Session of the Third Working Group held in Abu Dhabi, United Arab Emirates from 5–8 May 2011. The Special Report was accepted in its entirety at the 33rd IPCC Plenary Session held also in Abu Dhabi from 10–13 May 2011. SRREN is important because of the following reasons:

- It presents an assessment of the literature on the scientific, technological, environmental, economic and social aspects of the contribution of six renewable energy (RE) sources to solve problems related to climate change. It is intended to provide policy relevant information to governments, intergovernmental organizations and other interested parties.
- It deals in detail, about the type of technology, market development and the environmental and social impacts for each renewable source of energy including bioenergy, direct solar energy, geothermal energy, hydropower, ocean and wind energy. Prospects for future technological innovation, cost reduction and deployment of RE are also explored.[15]

Climate change is clearly not just an environmental issue but one with severe socio-economic implications in South Asia. As Sir Nicholas Stern said: 'From the Himalayas, which feed water to a billion people, to the coastal areas of Bangladesh, South Asian countries must prepare for the effects of global warming, even as they work to combat the human causes of climate change.'[16] Needless to say, climate change is already impacting on environment in parts of South Asia, like in the Sundarbans delta. It is submerging low-lying islands and coastal region and sending thousands of refugees looking for safer places to stay. In some other areas, it is causing gradual environmental degradation leading to slow-onset disasters such as droughts or sudden disasters like floods and cyclones.

Some have already realized the dangerous consequences of climate change on countries such as Bangladesh. The Bangladesh government itself has launched an action plan to fight climate change that prioritizes adaptation and reduction of disaster risks, also addresses low carbon development, mitigation, technology transfer, and the provision of adequate finance. The 2009–2018 plan aims to build the capacity and resilience of the country to meet the challenge of climate change. Drawing from the National Programme of Action, Bangladesh's Ministry of Environment and Forests has been working out the cost of implementing the action plan that was devised in consultation with non-profits, research groups and the private sector.[17] The UK has promised 75 million pounds ($133 million) to fund this action plan to help Bangladesh prepare for the impacts of climate change. The money will go on measures 'such as protecting houses, schools and farms against flooding and in introducing new crop strains'.[18]

Bangladesh, due to its location, is falling prey to cyclones resulting not only in human casualties and loss of property but also perpetual floods. The cyclones Sidr (2007), Nargis (2008), Aila (2009) and Laila (2010) had disastrous impact. An indigenous research in Dakshin Bedkashi (Koyra Upazila) reveals that tidal flood water level had risen by 1 m during 2004–2008, but it rose by an additional 1m in 2009 alone and in 2010 it continued to rise further, thereby making twelve districts at the south of Bangladesh, namely Satkhira, Khulna, Bagerhat, Pirojpur, Barguna, Patuakhali, Bhola, Laxmipur, Feni, Noakhali, Chittagong and Cox's Bazar, really vulnerable.[19] As Mallick predicts over 35 million will be climate refugees in Bangladesh by 2050.[20]

In Bangladesh, villagers have been making floating vegetable gardens to protect their livelihoods against flooding.[21] Oxfam has been helping families to raise their homes above flood levels, build flood-proof latrines, provide communities with seeds that can grow and flourish in floods and working tirelessly to ensure that the poor people are less at risk.[22] Aid agencies have welcomed the move but say poorer countries like Bangladesh need much more funds to adapt to climate change. The UK's International Development Secretary Douglas Alexander observed while announcing this assistance: 'Climate change is today's crisis, not tomorrow's risk and is already affecting millions of people in Bangladesh.' Some of the UK funding will go into, among other things, setting up classrooms on stilts and floating platforms, so that schools remain usable in spite of heavy flooding.

Dhaka is also planning to use these funds to build multi-purpose cyclone shelters that could also act as clinics or schools. Other proposals in Bangladesh's climate action plan include raising the level of polders (sea defences) in the Bay of Bengal, increasing the height of embankments that protect residential areas or lands where crops are grown, and introducing seeds tolerant to salt or arsenic.

While welcoming the UK government's plans to fund Bangladesh's efforts to wrestle with adverse climate change, John Magrath, an Oxfam researcher, raised a vital issue, calling for more such funding: 'But more money will be needed to combat impacts of climate change—that's indisputable—and it should be new money, because it should be compensation for changes we've caused through our industrialization'.[23] This is one example about the growing awareness of the possible fallout of adverse climate change in South Asia and to help some of its least developed countries like Bangladesh. Such efforts are only beginning; as Magrath says, much more need to be done. This chapter focuses on migration patterns that will result from adverse climate change in South Asia, and the kind of conflicts it could possibly cause.

BANGLADESH-TO-INDIA MIGRATION: THE POSSIBLE FALLOUT

Nearly 130 million people currently live in the 160,000 sq.km LECZ in India, Pakistan and Bangladesh; 75 million of these people live in Bangladesh, 50 million in India.[24] The Blue Earth report estimates that nearly 120 million of these people may have to move out of their present habitats by 2100 in a worst-case scenario of sea level rise of 5 m above the present level. The report projects that 23 million people would be displaced in India by sea level rise of 1 m by 2100 against 41 million Bangladeshis in a similar scenario. But if little is done to arrest climate change and if the sea level rises by 3 m by 2100, 33 million Indians and 58 million Bangladeshis will be displaced in the LECZ area. According to the report, if the sea level rise is 5 m by 2100, 43 million Indians and 74 million Bangladeshis will be displaced.

In 2005–2007 estimates of Bangladesh's population range from 142 to 159 million, making it the seventh most populous nation in the world. With a land area of 144,000 sq.km, the population density is remarkable. A striking comparison is offered by the fact that Russia's population is slightly smaller even though Russia has a land area of 17.5 million sq.km, at least 120 times bigger than Bangladesh. Bangladesh has the highest population density in the world, excluding a handful of city states.

Most of those displaced by climate change in Bangladesh will move to India.[25] Political parties and regional groups across India, especially in states like Assam which border Bangladesh, are already crying hoarse over illegal migration from Bangladesh into India. On 6 January 2003, Advani addressed state chief secretaries and directors-general of police and said that 11,500 Pakistani nationals and as many as 15 million Bangladeshis have been overstaying the duration of their visas in India; they deserved to be deported.[26]

Former Indian intelligence official Bibhuti Bhusan Nandy, who handled a secret intelligence project in the late 1990s to document illegal migrants from Bangladesh, says: 'Illegal migration from Bangladesh has acquired the proportions of a demographic invasion years ago. Thanks to bureaucratic ineptitude and the lack of political will, successive govern-ments slept over the problem. The presence of 15–20 million aliens—besides signalling a total breakdown of border management and immigration control—has imposed a crushing socio-economic burden on the country and is posing a serious threat to India's national security.'[27]

If most of the 40 to 75 million 'climate migrants' from Bangladesh (under various projected scenarios as above) were to move into India by 2100, it would add hugely to the population burden of India, which itself will be affected by climate change in a big way. Some details about the climate migrants from Bangladesh who were recently intercepted by Indian border guards while crossing into India have been listed towards the end of this chapter. That will provide some insights into the way climate change is going to affect people in South Asia's LECZ and the problems it will cause.

The maximum initial flow of this displaced Bangladesh population will be towards West Bengal, where people speak the same language and where the migrants are expected to find kinship support. Since much of West Bengal will also be affected by adverse climate change in much the same way as Bangladesh, it is unlikely that the climate migrants of Bangladesh would find much by way of land or livelihood in West Bengal. West Bengal's density of population is already one of the highest in India because of the impact of Partition and the continuous flow of refugees and migrants from erstwhile East Pakistan, now Bangladesh. So many of these Bangladeshis will be forced to northern India and also into northeast India, especially Assam, which has been one of their favourite destinations. These displaced Bangladeshis will slowly start moving further inland into northern and western India, where there will be livelihood opportunities for them at least at the bottom of the unskilled labour markets.

West Bengal

Since much of these migrants from Bangladesh into West Bengal will be Muslims, that could lead to a growing Hindu–Muslim divide in West Bengal, right-wing Hindutva parties and groups will seek to use the divide to increase their influence. Hence, the contours of West Bengal's politics will change and a real danger that the fight for scarce resources will trigger conflicts over land and livelihood sources. Such a conflict may lead to religious polarization, as in pre-Partition Bengal. The situation may be further complicated by the growing number of Hindu migrants, who would leave Bangladesh as much for economic reasons as for fears of persecution. These new Hindu migrants from Bangladesh are much more anti-Muslim than their predecessors, and their increasing presence in West Bengal will bolster the Hindutva forces.

But religious polarization will take time. As the resource crisis aggravates, a mass of dispossessed peasants from coastal regions of West Bengal will start moving inland, looking for work. They will join those who have already lost land to river erosion in large numbers. Most of these land-losers will move to cities like Kolkata and join the urban underclass. Those who remain in rural areas will join the ranks of sharecroppers and wage labourers, undoing the benefits of land reforms that have happened in a limited way so far. Localized conflicts between peasantry desperate to hold on to land and governments trying to acquire them for industrial projects will also multiply. The government in West Bengal argues that it will have to acquire land for speedy industrialization to generate more employment, but such employment rarely benefits unskilled rural people who have therefore opposed acquisition of croplands. The conflict over such intended possessions will further intensify and create an intense rural-urban divide, along with a possible religious divide.

Northeast India

Rising migration from Bangladesh into Northeast India would lead to more intense migrant-native conflicts in Assam and elsewhere in the Northeast, where the migrants from Bangladesh—or second-generation settlers from that stock—have begun to settle down. Since the migrants already dominate at least eight to ten districts of Assam in the lower reaches of the Brahmaputra, they would be bolstered by the growing flow of their co-religionists from across the border and would seek to consolidate their political position, sparking a huge Assamese-tribal backlash both in Upper and Lower Assam. Riots such as the one that rocked Udalguri and Darrang in October 2008 have exponentially multiplied, where both the settlers and the indigenous population groups, evenly matched in numbers, combat for resources.

The conflicts have also spread to states like Meghalaya, Nagaland and Tripura, where the recent migrants are at a receiving end. In such a situation, desperate migrants would seek to move further to other states in the region, where land is more readily available like Arunachal Pradesh. The whole of Northeast India would become a battleground between migrants and indigenous peoples and matters would be made worse by the religious divide. Protracted migrant–native conflicts could create a 'free-for-all' civil war situation in Assam and adjoining states that would seriously undermine legislative and administrative capacity and weaken governance because the ethno-religious polarization would be likely to affect bureaucracy, politics, police and even business.

If the backlash against the migrants from Bangladesh follow the polarized contours of a religious divide, there would be a strong possibility of a sharp growth of Islamic radicalism, sustained from across the border in Bangladesh but essentially fuelled by home-grown fundamentalists reacting to the growing power of Hindutva.

North and West India

Since it will be impossible for most of these climate migrants from Bangladesh to find land and livelihood in West Bengal and Northeast Indian states, they will slowly but steadily push further inland into northern and western India. They will first try settling down in 'enclaves' where some of their people have already found shelter and work, but as their numbers grow, they will spread into areas, wherever they find some livelihood, even if it is at the lowest rungs of the Indian labour market.

The migrants, mostly Muslims, will come into serious conflict for livelihood opportunities with Indian climate refugees—those who would be forced to abandon their ancestral homes in coastal India due to sea-level rise consequent on global warming and also those who would be forced out of mountains and spreading deserts following a sharp drop in water resources over large parts of India. In many areas of north and west India—or even in the south—where Hindu and Muslim Bengalis from West Bengal are joined by those from Bangladesh in seeking livelihood, the conflicts may grow along local-outsider fault lines with distinctive linguistic overtones. The kind of conflict we now see between Marathis and 'North Indians' over jobs in Maharashtra may multiply. The fault lines will vary from place to place but at the root it would be the conflict for control over scarce resources and livelihoods.

In many places, the conflicts may develop along the Hindu-Muslim divide and create unmanageable levels of religious schism. Hindutva forces will exacerbate this divide because that will further cause political mobilization in their support. This process is already discernible in the hounding of Bangladeshis in several north and west Indian cities after the serial explosions in Delhi, Bangalore, Hyderabad and Jaipur. Terrorists from Bangladesh may—or may not—have been involved in the explosions, but the entire migrant population from Bangladesh has been targeted. Some state administrations have even isolated these migrants and put them on trains for deportation back to Bangladesh through West Bengal.

So far, local Muslims have not come out in support of the migrants, but as resentment among Indian Muslims grow over harassment after bombings and terrorist actions, the migrants might secure local Muslim support because of radicalization within Indian Muslims. That would exacerbate the religious divide in mainland India and might lead to the process of 'enclaving' across the country: polarized religious or ethnic groups living separately in enclaves in cities or semi-urban, perhaps even rural, areas in a state of perpetual conflict. This in turn would severely weaken India's polity along religious and ethno-linguistic divides and create deep fissures undermining its national unity. A free-for-all conflict scenario, like what happened during the Lebanon civil war of the 1980s and the Balkan conflicts during the 1990s cannot be ruled out for India. Much would depend on how the federal and provincial government tackles the resource crisis but it will not be easy.

Foreign relations

Relations between India and Bangladesh would go from bad to worse. India would raise the pitch on the migrants issue. Frequent conflict between border guards of the two countries would multiply sharply during Indian attempts to deport illegal migrants forcibly from Bangladesh whenever they were intercepted at the frontier or picked up from states further inland. India would reinforce and expand its border fencing and there would be huge pressures on India to sever its surface communication links with Bangladesh. Many migrants would try to reach India by sea and rivers and the frequent use of armed action by Indian coastal guards would multiply. India's worsening relations with Bangladesh could affect its relations with other Islamic countries, on whom India depends much for its energy needs. It would further complicate its relations with Pakistan.

But at this point, it is not possible to foresee much migration from Pakistan to India due to climate change, though some parts of Pakistan's coastal regions are likely to be affected by submergence caused by sea-level rise. So the migrant issue that is a major irritant in India–Bangladesh relations will not per se affect India–Pakistan relations. Those displaced may try to relocate themselves in Pakistan or may seek refuge in neighbouring Iran. The problem may be further complicated within Pakistan because movement of climate migrants from coastal Sindh into inland areas like Balochistan or Punjab may exacerbate ethnic conflicts which has already affected Pakistan.

CLIMATE MIGRANTS FROM BANGLADESH: RANDOM PROFILES

Mohammed Abdul Majid's[28] ancestral village is in Bangladesh's south-western district of Khulna. River Shagberia runs through their village, Jorsingh. Majid, along with his wife and three kids, crossed over to West Bengal a couple of months back (in 2008), illegally, like thousands of his fellow countrymen. Till a couple of years back, his family was quite happy. He had about one-third of an acre of fertile land where he used to grow paddy. The rice produced from his land was enough to feed them for almost half the year. For the rest of the months, he depended on the Sunderbans forest. He used to collect honey and forest wastes and went out fishing in the river and other water bodies.

River Shagberia that flows into the sea was once a lifeline for the villagers of Jorsingh. But now it often overflows and fills the village's fertile land with saline water. With the increase in salinity, nothing can be grown on his land. Even coconut and other trees around his house have dried up. Many of the big landlords have switched over to prawn cultivation, converting agricultural land into huge fisheries. Prawn cultivation needs much less labour than farming. So there's no work from most of them. As entering into the Sunderbans is banned, Majid has also lost his income from the forests. Because of the seepage of saline water into the groundwater level, drinking water is also fast becoming scarce. Majid and his wife had hardly any choice but to leave their motherland.

Scientists say that all these are the results of climate change and global warming. Majid is the first of the new generation of 'climate migrants' from Bangladesh, which, according to the Greenpeace report, will produce anything between 40–75 million migrants owing to sea-level rise. None in authority has told Majid about climate change—but he knows it is happening—and that things would go from bad to worse in his ancestral abode. The process has already made him a 'marginal', an economic migrant.

From a self-reliant farmer-fisherman, Majid has become a rag picker in his land of refuge. But he is new to rag picking and cycling. So, at Rajarhat, where the state's government has built a huge 'mega-city', and where he stays in a shanty, Majid plies his cycle van, joined by his eldest son, who has discontinued his primary school education after crossing over into India. The father–son duo search the municipal waste bins for their picks, earning around Rs 50 (1 US$). Majid's two other children and his wife stay at home. Maybe they will also work on some of Rajarhat construction sites to augment the family income, as the entire family is sometimes forced to skip meals.

Majid's neighbour is Abdur Rahim. He came to India about three years back (2005), has a kid and wife. He lives in a 10 sq.ft shack, surrounded by waste papers, plastic bottles and what not! To Abdur and many others, these aren't wastes. They earn their living from these municipal wastes. He is also a rag picker like Majid. He leaves home around 3 o'clock in the morning so that he doesn't lose the 'best available' waste.

His father was a well-to-do rice trader in Bangladesh. They used to trade in one of the finest quality of rice, Gobindabhog. They had about an acre of fertile land, where they used to grow paddy twice a year. But Rahim lost everything. Their entire land is full of saline water, even drinking water tube-wells now bring up only saline water. During the high tides, their lands get submerged by the saline water that comes up the river from the sea. Prawn cultivation (owned mostly by big businessmen) added to their woes. So people like Rahim went to Dhaka—the capital of Bangladesh—to get some work. He says Dhaka is costlier and hard to survive.

So they decided to leave their motherland and come to West Bengal in India. He still does not have any kind of document to prove his 'Indian' identity. Rahim and his neighbours allege that often police arrives at their doorstep to pick them up. 'You'll either have to shell out huge amount of money to manage them or else land up in jails with cases against you. We don't have that kind of money, so many of our neighbours have landed in jails.'

Fazlu Mian and his family live in the shanty next to Rahim's. His story is almost same: from a self-reliant farmer in his own country to a destitute in a foreign land. Barindra Mandal from Harinagar village in Satkhira is a brave man. Owing to erosion caused by the River Malancha, adjacent to his farm, he lost much of the land. Only one-third of an acre land remains with him, but cultivation was not easy with saline water all over. So he used to venture out in the deep forests for collecting honey and other forest products and go for fishing. During one of his trips into the forest along with his friend, a royal Bengal tiger attacked them. The tiger grabbed Barindra's friend by his neck, but Barindra hacked away at the tiger with his sharp implements. The man-eater finally left them, but with deep wounds. After this incident, the local women decided their menfolk would not go into the forests.

Barindra lost the land to the saline water, now the family won't allow him to go to the forest. So Barindra and his friend, along with their families, landed up on a shallow pond full of hyacinths on the eastern fringes of Kolkata. Their shack is built on the pond, upon a bamboo structure. The only 'road' that leads to their 'home' is a bamboo track. One has to be an acrobat to walk on that. During monsoon, the drainage canal near their 'home' overflows and the filthy water remains in their home for at least two months. Now Barindra does odd jobs once in a while, but his wife and two daughters work as house maids. His younger daughter, aged 16, works in four households in a day. At one of her workplaces, there's a girl, aged around 17, who goes to college and to parties quite often. Barindra's daughter was almost in her tears when she told him, 'If we were in our native village, I would have also gone to college like that girl.'

Binoy Krishna Mondal and his wife are luckier than most of their other countrymen fleeing climate change. Binoy's native village was in Satkhira. He crossed over about seven to eight years ago (in 2000). He had the same story to tell—fertile agri-cultural land growing some of the best and most expensive rice lost to growing salinity due to ingress of sea water (possibly due to sea-level rise), forcing them to decide on migration. Initially he used to stay in a shanty next to a drainage canal. He quickly picked up a job of a mason's assistant. 'At that time, there were plenty of jobs, as very few Bangladeshis were around and the labour demand was just beginning to pick up at the start of the mega-city project,' said Binoy. Though he was new to the trade, he picked it up quickly and became a stand-alone mason in a couple of years. Then he bought a small piece of land in a newly built colony.

'How did you manage to buy a land? You were not an Indian citizen?' I asked him.

Binoy laughed at me.

'If you have the right contacts inside the ruling party—CPI(M)—and if you are ready to pay, everything is possible here . . . I caught hold of a CPI(M) leader and managed a ration card—the primary requirement to become an Indian citizen. Then slowly I got a voter identity card and then I bought a small piece of land—all with the help from the party.'

But Binoy resented the CPI(M)'s overbearing ways, though he kept joining their rallies and poll-time mass meetings. But as a Hindu migrant from Bangladesh, he, like many other Hindu migrants, went over to the Hindu fundamentalist BJP, a few years ago. In fact, people like Binoy were responsible for the victory of Tapan Sikdar, the first BJP member of parliament from West Bengal.

In the recent panchayat (village council) elections in West Bengal, the BJP routed the ruling CPI(M) in Binoy's area. Though Binoy is friendly to the Muslim migrants in the area and people like Fazlu are close to him, his politics may well lead to a religious divide at some point. In 2008, after eight years, Binoy has finally settled down in India. He has a *pucca* house—with a television set, electricity and a mobile phone. Mobile phones could be seen with almost everyone in the locality. Even rag pickers and rickshaw pullers have got one. Many people from his ancestral village from Bangladesh come to Binoy, to explore possibilities of crossing over.

A few weeks after I had spoken to these 'climate migrants' in their colony in Rajarhat , the Indian Border Security Force (BSF) intercepted 150 illegal migrants who were trying to cross into India in three boats across River Ichhamati. The detainees were in Hasnabad, North 24 Parganas district. The BSF called up the media and declared this was the single largest 'catch in a day'. The border guards took me deep inside the Sunderbans—on the Rayamangal and Ichhamati Rivers—where one boat-full of 'climate migrants' were waiting since morning. They travelled for more than 48 hours to reach the Indian border—only to be caught by the border guards. Most of them were women and children. They only had some khichri, rice and lentils to eat. The children were crying—some of them were so tired—they were asleep on their mothers' laps. They didn't know what was the problem why had they left their village and why had the policemen kept them confined inside a boat throughout the day.

I spoke to Mohammed Azid, who had come from a village in Shyamnagar Police Station area of Satkhira district in Bangladesh. Azid wasn't crossing the border for the first time. He had already migrated. He is a rag picker and has a shanty in Ultadanga area in northern Kolkata. He went back to his village to attend the last rites of his mother-in-law. While coming back he got caught. He didn't have any land to till in Bangladesh. Everywhere in his ancestral village, there's saline water. 'No one can grow anything on that land—it's prawn farming haven . . . they have used almost every inch of our land for prawn cultivation.'

Another of Azid's fellow villagers, Rafikul Gazi said, 'Once the agricultural land has been taken for prawn cultivation, there's excess labour. We tried going inside the Sunderbans to catch fish, even that has become dangerous. Our families persuaded us not to venture into the jungles. On the other hand, the prices are sky-rising. Rice is 35 taka per kg, potatoes are 17–18 taka a kilo in Bangladesh and we could not earn anything any more. So we were compelled to cross the border.' Rafikul was crossing the border for the first time; surely, he was not the last of his countrymen to do so.

MIGRATION WITHIN INDIA: THE FALLOUT

While the flow of climate migrants from Bangladesh to India might have caused serious conflict between them and the natives of Indian states where they relocated themselves, clashes would also result from inter-state and within-the-state migrations in India itself, due to the impact of climate change. Such migrations and the discord they would create might further complicate the scenario caused by the influx of climate migrants from Bangladesh. In India, climate change would cause *(a)* migration within states; *(b)* migration from one state to another; *(c)* migration from one region to another.

Migration within states

Inhabitants of the coastal areas in Andhra Pradesh or those occupying the mountains as well as plains, as in West Bengal, might exacerbate conflict between regions within a state, especially if the regional demography fitted the ethnic divide. For instance, in West Bengal, one can clearly see an aggravation of the Gorkha-Bengali conflict (that is already raging over the Gorkhaland statehood issue), which will further increase if more Gorkhas start moving into the plains of North Bengal, as they are already doing, as the capacity of Bengal's Himalayan region to sustain its existing population level has sharply declined due to climate change. Again, Bengali farmers and fishermen displaced from coastal Bengal would be likely to move up into northern Bengal, where, they would cross paths with Gorkhas moving down the mountains into the same area. One can clearly see areas like the North Bengal plains and foothills region like the Dooars emerging as a flashpoint, primarily due to the varied manifestation of climate change. Such forced migration due to climate change would also be accompanied by high levels of human misery—food shortages leading to starvation, diseases leading to mass deaths and the like. Inland forest regions of many Indian states would come under severe pressure due to climate change displacements—and many forests would be decimated by unwelcome population flows, seriously jeopardizing local environment. Further, floods, like the Kosi flood of 2008, might also complicate the existing situation.[29]

Inter-state migration would also lead to ethnic and nativist-outside conflicts on a large scale. As climate migrants move out of coastal states into those further inland, seeking livelihoods, they would cause huge pressures on the local labour markets and demographic patterns closely linked to electoral political structures. Parochial political groups could multiply to encash on possible demographic change, especially if such rivalries have some history of conflict. For example, Tamil-Kannadiga conflict might intensify, if a large number of Tamil fishermen or farmers move into Karnataka due to loss of livelihood on the coast. Local concerns born out of local resource conflicts would lead to possible multiplication of localized politics marked by high level of parochialism.

Migration within regions

This would also lead to similar conflicts and lead to much the same kind of political impact; only the scale of the conflict could get bigger and more complicated if religious differences accentuated ethnic ones or otherwise. Cities like Kolkata would grow in size with people pouring in from other parts of the country as well as across borders.[30] If Kolkata became flooded by fast sea-level rise, the out-migration volume would be unmanageable and cause huge conflicts. If the pace of sea-level rise were high, causing floods to the southern environs of Kolkata, like the Sundarbans, the metropolis would come under a huge pressure of population and end up as an unmanageable urban nightmare. The same could happen in some other large coastal Indian cities, which are among the world's highly populated cities.

Thus, adverse climate change has the potential to unleash very high levels of domestic conflict on religious, ethnic, linguistic and class lines all across India. Even the remote peaceful islands of the Andaman-Nicobar archipelago, where India is building one of its largest naval air bases, would not be spared of such a conflict. As the low-lying Nicobar islands might go under the sea, its indigenous population would seek to move into higher islands in the Andamans where land and livelihood is already monopolized by settlers from the mainland—mostly Bengalis and Tamils. Weapons are easily available in Southeast Asia. Proximity to the sea/ocean makes it easy to smuggle weapons into one's country.

The flashpoints of the conflicts would be located in cities and provinces that represent India's economic success story because migrants from areas affected by climate change would seek to move to areas perceived as presenting livelihood opportunities rather than to areas which would be perceived as lacking them. Mumbai, itself on the coast, is India's financial capital, but it is already home to high levels of both religious conflict (Hindu-Muslim) and nativist-outsider conflict (earlier between 'South Indians' and Marathis and now between 'North Indians' and Marathis). That process, as mentioned earlier, might be repeated in many of India's great urban growth centres in years to come as millions displaced by climate change from India—and its neighbouring countries like Bangladesh—desperately move about in search of livelihood and shelter. Such conflicts, if they multiply, would seriously jeopardize the capabilities of India's federal government and its writ would begin to get weaker and weaker. Disputes between states over water resources—like the Cauvery water dispute—would multiply and the federal government would find it difficult to control them.

THE CHINESE SHADOW

India and Bangladesh may spar with each other on the migrants issue, but they might have to join hands to combat China's water diversion designs from the Tibetan plateau that would have a serious bearing on lower riparian nations of South Asia. Tibet's vast high-altitude glaciers are the source of many of Asia's greatest river systems—the Indus, Brahmaputra, Karnali, the Mekong and the Salween, and the Yangtze and the Yellow rivers. Only the Ganges originates from the Indian side of the Himalayas. These rivers are lifelines of the world's two most populous countries—China and India—but also of some other highly populated countries like Bangladesh, Pakistan, Burma, Cambodia, Laos, Thailand and Vietnam, besides the smaller Himalayan nations like Bhutan and Nepal. These countries account for 47 per cent of the global population.

Although home to more than half of the human population, Asia already has less fresh water—3,920 cubic metre per person—than any continent other than the Antarctica. Climate change and environmental degradation in the form of shrinking forests and swamps would lead to chronic flooding and droughts once the Himalayan snow melt process, that feeds Asia's great rivers, is accelerated by global warming. 'While intra-state water-sharing disputes have become rife in several Asian countries—from India and Pakistan to Southeast Asia and China—it is the potential inter-state conflict over river-water resources that should be of greater concern.'[31] The uneven availability of water within some nations has given rise to grand ideas—from grand river-linking project in India to the Chinese grand plan for diverting the fast-flowing Brahmaputra northward to feed the arid areas in its heartland. Chinese leaders like Jiang Zemin called it the 'Xibu Da Kaifa' (Great Western Extraction), a bold plan first conceptualized by hydrologist Guo Kai who called it the 'shuo-tian' (reverse flow). A 1999 survey by China, covering an area of 13,600 km, calculated that 600B cubic metre per year of the Brahmaputra waters were being wasted in Tibet.[32]

The idea of a Great South-North Water Transfer Project diverting Tibetan river waters had the full backing of President Hu Jintao, a hydrologist himself. The first phase of this project called for building 300 km of tunnels and channels to draw waters from the Jinsha, Yalong and Dadu rivers, on the eastern rim of the Tibetan plateau. In the second phase, the Brahmaputra waters might be rerouted northward, destroying one of the main river systems of northeast India and Bangladesh. In November 2005, China's military and water resources ministry adopted a strategy manual '*Save China through Water from Tibet*'. The same year, China Hydropower Engineering Consulting Group began analysing the hydro potential on sectors of the Yarlung Tsangpo. In February 2006, the detailed planning for the 'Tsangpo Project' was approved by the state council with the full support of Hu Jintao. Professor Chen Chuanyu was put in charge of the project. Recently, Beijing has identified the bend where the Brahmaputra forms the world's longest and deepest canyon just before entering India as holding the largest untapped reserves for meeting its water and energy needs.[33]

Lack of water resources in northern China has compelled Beijing to toy with massive inter-basin and inter-river water transfer projects from Tibet. After building two dams up-stream, China is building at least three more on the Mekong, stirring passions in Vietnam, Laos, Cambodia and Thailand. Several Chinese projects in west-central Tibet have a bearing on river-water flows into India, but Beijing is secretive about its plans. Having extensively contaminated its own major rivers through massive industrialization, China now threatens the ecological viability of river systems tied to South and Southeast Asia in its bid to meet its thirst for water and energy.

If China's north–south water transfer project materializes and the Yarlung Tsangpo (as the Brahmaputra is called in Tibet) is diverted to northern China, it would deal a cataclysmic blow to the environment of India's northeast and adjoining areas of Bangladesh, sharply reducing water availability and affecting agriculture, fisheries and other livelihoods. It would doubtlessly be the beginning of Asia's first water war. With Western support, India and several South and Southeast Asian nations could gang up against China in a repeat of the Cold War scenario of the 1960s.

This is a classic example about how the climate change and resource crisis in the neighbourhood—in this case, China—could affect South Asia and trigger environmental degradation and huge resource crisis for a huge area within this region. The process of adverse climate change has to be fought at global and regional levels. South Asia will not only have to take urgent measures to stem the tide in areas likely to be worst affected by climate change but its governments have to do a lot of advance planning to *(a)* identify areas to relocate those displaced by climate change; *(b)* identify alternate livelihoods for those displaced, and going by past evidence, this is not easy, as coastal fishermen cannot be expected to pursue gainful livelihood if settled in a sparsely populated mountain zone; *(c)* evolve strategies to avoid local-settler conflicts resulting from displacement caused by climate change; *(d)* implement effective population control measures to reduce pressure on scarce resources. Unless that is done, the conflicts will reach unmanageable levels and put huge pressure on the local polity and economy.

CRISIS IN PAKISTAN AND ITS IMPACT ON THE BORDERS

In the recent past, Pakistan has faced a series of displacement crises due to natural disasters and armed conflict. Nineteen million people have been displaced by earthquakes and flooding.[34] In December 2011, more than half a million people were still displaced following the flooding of the Indus in September.[35] The flood had led to a crisis in the refugee situation in Pakistan. Pakistan has 1.7 million Afghan refugees and more than 1.5 million of these are in affected provinces. Dozens of Afghan refugee villages have been damaged, and several destroyed completely. In Khyber Pakhtunkwa province alone, more than 12,000 dwellings in refugee villages have been swept away leaving almost 70,000 people homeless.[36] It is very important to mention that any crisis within the territory of Pakistan will impact its borders.

Not all environmental disasters are equally sudden and drastic in nature. While the Aila of 2009 or the Sindh Floods of 2011 were sudden events, one can notice slow but steady changes in the nature, which affects millions. Slow but protracted natural calamities often lead to protracted displacements of human beings. River bank erosion in

Malda and Murshidabad in West Bengal and that along the banks of River Bramhaputra are two cases in point. For many today, the process of displacement is a continuous one. Many take refuge in a place, however, to be uprooted again with further changes in the course of the river. The worst victims in such situations are the marginal sections of the society—the poorest of the poor, women and children and those physically challenged. Unfortunately, this leads to a sudden increase in the rates of sexual abuses, trafficking of women and children, and a general rise in the levels of violence in the areas affected by some environmental disasters. It is important that state authorities, NGOs, civil society, media and the political parties work together for the betterment of this vulnerable section of the society.

NOTES

1 An Abrupt Climate Change Scenario and Its Implications for United States National Security, October 2003 http://www.greenpeace.org/international/Global/international/planet-2/report/2006/3/an-abrupt-climate-change-scena.pdf last accessed on 14.2.12
2 Michael Byers and Nick Dragojlovic, 'Darfur: A Climate Change-Induced Humanitarian Crisis?', Human Security Bulletin, October 2004. For more details see: www.humansecuritybulletin.info/October:2004/Editorials/en/index.php.
3 Mesarovic and Pestel, Mankind at the Turning Point: The Second Report of the Club of Rome (New York: E P Dutton, 1974).
4 Mike Davies, Late Victorian Holocausts: El Niño Famines and the Making of the Third World (NY/London: Verso, 2001).
5 'Impacts, Adaptation and Vulnerability', for details see: http://www.ipcc.ch/publications_and_data/publications_and_data_ reports.shtml; last accessed on 14.02.12.
6 W. J. Mc G. Tegart, G. W. Sheldon and D. C. Griffiths (eds.),

'Climate Change The IPCC Impacts Assessment'; for more details see: http://www.ipcc.ch/publications_and_data/ar4/wg2/en/contents. html; last accessed on 27.11.12.

7 Cited in Nick Robson, 'Climate Change in South Asia: A Precursor for Conflict?' South Asian Strategic Stability Unit. For more details see: http://www.sassu.org.uk/html/Climate Changeand Conflict.htm; last accessed on 27.11.12.

8 Sudhir Chella Rajan, 'Blue Alert: Climate Migrants in South Asia: Estimates and Solutions', ritimo, Greenpeace, 2008.

9 Subir Bhaumik, 'Fears Rise for Sinking Sundarbans', BBC Online; for details see: http://news.bbc.co.uk/2/hi/south_asia/3102948.stm; last accessed on 12.02.12.

10 'Vulnerability Assessment in a Climate Change Scenario: A Pilot Study on Ecologically Sensitive Sunderban Island System, West Bengal', P. I. Prof. Sugata Hazra, School of Oceanographic Studies, Jadavpur University, Sponsor: National Communication Programme of the Ministry of Forests and Environment, Govt. of India (NATCOM: I) 2007.

11 Cited in 'Vanishing Islands', Down to Earth, 15 January 2007. For further details see: http://afishandabird.com/wordpress/wp-content/uploads/DTE-Sunderbans-Cover-Story.pdf.

12 'New Zealand Coal Shipment Blockaded', Greenpeace International; for further details see: http//www.greenpeace.org/international/en/news/features/nz-coal-ship-blocked080325/; last accessed on 26.11.12.

13 http://www.ipc.ch/SPML3apr07.pdf; last accessed on 12.02.12.

14 'Managing Climate Risk: Integrating Adaptation into World Bank Group Operations', World Bank, 2007; for further details see: http://web.worldbank.org/WBSITE/EXTERNAL/COUNTRIES/SOUTHASIAEXT/0,,contentMDK:21469804~menuPK:2246552~pagePK:2865106~piPK:2865128~theSitePK:223547,00.html.

15 'Renewable Energy Sources and Climate Change Mitigation'; for more details see: http://srren.ipcc-wg3.de/report/IPCC_SRREN_Full_Report.pdf

16 'Climate Change in South Asia: A Conversation with Sir Nicholas Stern'; for details see: http://web.worldbank.org/WBSITE/EXTERNAL/COUNTRIES/SOUTHASIAEXT/0,,contentMDK:21220691~pagePK:146736~piPK:146830--theSitePK:223547,00. html 2007.

17 BBC: 'Down to Earth', 23 October 2008.

18 Richard Black, 'UK Gives Bangladesh Climate Help'. For further details see: http://news.bbc.co.uk/2/hi/science/nature/7606024.stm; last accessed on 27.11.12.

19 'Latest News on Climate Displacement in Bangladesh', see: http://displacementsolutions.org/?p=547, last accessed on 3.1.12.

20 'Growing Environmental and Climate Refugees in Bangladesh: Urgent Actions are Required', paper presented by Dwijen L. Mallick (Research Fellow in Bangladesh Centre for Advanced Studies) at the C40 Tokyo Conference on Climate Change-Adaptation Measures for Sustainable Low Carbon Cities.

21 http://practicalaction.org/floating-gardens; last accessed on 26.11.12.

22 http://www.oxfam.org.uk/oxfam_in_action/emergencies/bangladesh-floods.html; last accessed on 26.11.12.

23 John Magrath is an Oxfam researcher; for more details see: http://news.bbc.co.uk/2/hi/science/nature/7606024.stm; accessed on 14.02.12.

24 Sudhir Chella Rajan, 'Blue Alert: Climate Migrants in South Asia: Estimates and Solutions'.

25 As claimed by Mohan Kumar Mondal, executive director of the Local Environment Development and Agricultural Research Society (LEDARD), operating in Bangladesh's south-west coastal region of LEDARD, Bangladesh.

26 'Beggaring the Neighbour', *Frontline*, 28 February 2003; For more details see: http://insaf.net/praful/archives/20030228.fl.htm) last accessed on 26.11.12.

27 http://www.preventgenocide.org/prevent/news-monitor/2003feb.htm; last accessed on 26.11.12.

28 The study has been compiled by Amitabh Bhattasali, a BBC correspondent. The study came out as a report in BBC and it was in Bengali. He had studied the impact of global warming on Sunderbans (Bangladesh). The study was conducted early 2008.

29 It had displaced many people; lot of property was lost. There was a shortage of resources.

30 'World Urbanization Prospects. The 2011 Revision', *Economic and Social Affairs*. For details see: http://esa.un.org/unup/pdf/WUP2011_Highlights.pdf; last accessed on 26.11.12.

31 Brahma Chellaney, 'China-India Clash over Chinese Claims to Tibetan Water', *The Asia-Pacific Journal: Japan Focus*, 2007. http://www.japanfocus.org/site/view/2458; last accessed on 20.12.12.
32 Li Ling, 'How Tibet's Water Will Save China', (Beijing: Zhongguo Chang'an chu ban she, 2000).
33 Brahma Chellaney, 'China-India Clash over Chinese Claims to Tibetan Water'. www.japanfocus.org/site/view/2458; last accessed on 20.12.12
34 http://www.internal-displacement.org/countries/pakistan; last accessed on 26.11.12.
35 Ibid.
36 http://www.unhcr.org/4c6e762b9.html; last accessed on 3.1.12.

PART III

Institutions

11

PROTECTION AS RECOVERY: A Commentary from Sri Lanka

JEEVAN THIAGARAJAH

This chapter highlights the responses, to date, on the part of the Government of Sri Lanka and humanitarian and development organizations working within the country. Additionally it outlines the challenges and obstacles faced in addressing the IDP situation in efforts to portray the scale and considerations that need to fall into the devising of protection strategies. To conclude, it illustrates how the Guiding Principles on Internal Displacement can play a positive and key role in supporting a potential government legislation and policy to safeguard the rights of IDPs.

The conflict in Sri Lanka has displaced more than 300,000 persons following escalated hostilities after 2006, which excludes the hundred thousands displaced over the last two decades. The tsunami disaster caused further displacement, creating approximately one million IDPs. From 2006 the renewed conflict displaced more than 308,000 persons, equivalent to the 312,000 persons displaced prior to the 2002 ceasefire. As of December 2007, the government estimated 577,000 IDPs in Sri Lanka.[1] Thus in terms of the proportion of its population, Sri Lanka has one of the world's largest IDP populations. There have been large-scale efforts on the part of both national and international actors to respond to the needs of the IDPs, but internal displacement still poses a huge challenge.

The government's response over the last two decades, in terms of schemes to assist, has seen many approaches; however, a lack of proper legislation or a national policy focusing on the needs of the IDPs has hampered effective and durable responses to their situation. A process of rectification is being undertaken now. Humanitarian and development organizations also have a potential role to play in furthering protection, both by being aware of human rights issues as well as maximizing protection through their own assistance programmes.

When looking to address the issue of protection it is important to note the different areas that contribute to protection mechanisms. The protection of basic human rights should immediately indicate the different areas which come into the discussion of 'protection', which is heavily linked to the notion of physical security and safety alone. Issues pertaining to definition of the IDPs, IDP registration, land issues, access to information, IDP consultation and participation, access to livelihoods and health ought to be considered as significant attributes that shape effective protection strategies. Furthermore, initiatives which capture protection of the right to development, we argue, should encapsulate the regime of 'protection'.

GOVERNMENT RESPONSE: FROM EARLY YEARS TO CURRENT PREVAILING IDP SITUATION

The frameworks for assistance in Sri Lanka showed the government responding to the IDP situation prevailing in the country from the 1980s onwards as a result of the civil war. Whilst the LTTE controlled certain areas in the north and east, the government managed to maintain skeletal administration structures in these areas, registering the IDPs and managing government-provided humanitarian assistance. In the government-controlled areas, the IDPs and resettled families were also able to receive some government assistance for shelter, as well as food rations and food stamps. [2]

The Unified Assistance Scheme (UAS)[3] also sought to include returnees (from abroad as well as those IDPs returning or resettling) such that they were able to benefit from government grants and loans, in a long-term vision of hoping to support their ability to be self-sufficient. The UAS, however, was weakened in both its structure and maintenance.[4] The government established several rehabilitation and reconstruction programmes throughout the country, which in the past brought in much international financial assistance and other forms of support. However, criticisms of early strategies by the government noted the lack of participation amongst target groups and beneficiaries when such approaches had been recommended.[5]

To date, Sri Lanka does not have a specific law or policy which seeks to address displacement comprehensively; however, a law on the protection and assistance of the IDPs has been in the thinking pipeline over the last couple of years. Existing provisions to address critical issues for protection have been scattered and non-systematic. But from as early as 1987 there have been several significant rehabilitation and relief-oriented programmes/projects to respond to the needs of the IDPs. In 1988, the Government of Sri Lanka, with the assistance of several donor agencies, launched a massive Emergency Reconstruction and Rehabilitation programme (ERRP-I) to be implemented in the north and east, as well as the bordering districts. However, due to increasing hostilities in 1990, the success of the programme was hampered and it was largely confined to cleared areas and border districts.[6] Between 1988 and 1994 the programme saw a total expenditure of Rs. 22.65 billion, with allocations towards compensation, dry rations and other food (Rs. 12 billion) and a further

13 per cent being spent on housing grants, grants towards production enterprises and settling allowances. All funds were provided mainly by external donors.[7]

More persistent efforts to resettle and relocate the IDPs came in 1994 with the inauguration of a Resettlement Scheme in Kapalturai in Trincomalee district. Following this, a further 23 resettlement schemes were implemented.[8] In 1994–1995, efforts were made to continue the initial reconstruction programme (budget of Rs. 67 billion), with an additional Rs. 39 billion to be invested in an ERRP specifically for the Northern Province. However these programmes could not be implemented due to increasing hostilities.[9]

By 2002, the National Framework for Relief, Rehabilitation and Reconciliation (NFRRR) was formulated by various bodies such as government departments, the diplomatic community, UN agencies, donor agencies and international NGOs and provincial administrative officials. The NFRRR was established in response to the government's recognition of the responsibility to provide assistance, development support and essential services to the conflict-affected populations. Several committees and village-level committees were formed to implement the triple R projects.[10]

In 2002–2003, the government and the UN prepared a Joint Strategy to meet the immediate needs of the returnees which approximated to more than 100,000 persons. The strategy encapsulated a reintegration which sought to support the initial reintegration phases, assisting communities whilst protecting the IDPs through essential services such as food and non-food relief items, water and sanitation, health, education and immediate employment, mainly in agriculture and fisheries.[11] The strategy addressed the issue of landmines and unexploded explosive ordinances, in furthering emphasis on the protection of the IDPs. It also called for strengthening of government capacities at the national, district and local levels to coordi-nate successfully the Resettlement and Reconstruction programme.[12] Furthermore, in 2002, the government, along with the UN and World Bank, embarked on a larger Resettlement and Reconstruction programme than that of 1988. This programme was based on projects funded by donor agencies. It provided income support grants (Rs. 25,000/per family) and food rations for 15 months. The programme was estimated to amount to more than US$ 600 million, being fully funded, and covered areas of livelihoods, health and education.[13] In 2004, the government made concerted efforts to relocate the IDPs without land. The programme relocated more than 2500 families in Kilinochchi, Vavuniya and Mannar. A further 17 schemes were planned for Kilinochchi yet only two were implemented due to funding.[14]

In 2005, the President of Sri Lanka outlined his policy document—the 'Mahinda Chintana Towards a New Sri Lanka' —pledging to pay a temporary allowance to people who had to leave their homes as they were in the high security zones. It also emphasized that all those displaced would be resettled in their villages and all associated damages and destruction caused to the infrastructure in terms of education, health services, transport, roads, markets, power and energy needs will be rehabilitated.[15] It also emphasized on the revival of the eastern area.[16]

In 2006, the Consultative Committee on Humanitarian Assistance (CCHA) established by the Ministry of Disaster Management and Human Rights continued to bring together key decision makers across the government level as well as international and national partners and representatives from embassies and the European Union. A commitment to the safety and welfare of Sri Lankan civilians was at the core of these open dialogue sessions, practical issues were discussed and action decided upon.[17]

The listed programmes and efforts on the part of the government side by side with development partners and international NGOs show good intentions, yet there is still a need for a more binding law; for example, the NFRRR is not a binding law though the cabinet approved it as a policy document, which essentially does not provide any practical legal protection to the IDPs. It adopts the Guiding Principles on Internal Displacement without noting the requirements to make the principles effective, that is, it must be understood that the degree to which these could be translated to consolidate the development of legislation, the provisions and directives at the national level and also to reflect the country's situation, which would determine the success in safeguarding the rights of the IDPs. Also, consequently, the NFRRR carries only two references to displacement and thus fails to grasp the reality of the country's situation in this context.[18]

Parallel to this, the common laws which exist to respond to IDP entitlements are for the most part authority-forming decrees, and additionally the lack of accountability of and the under-funding by the authorities, have also raised the question of the effectiveness of these acts in supporting the IDPs. Several acts are deemed special and only serve as temporary provisions in humanitarian responses as opposed to offering long-term solutions. Existing legislation does not take into consideration all phases characteristic of internal displacement, notably the pre-displacement circumstances, the displaced phase and post-displacement.[19] However, there are authorities such as the Resettlement Authority that are in place which aim to deal with the IDPs and refugees, with several functions in place. The Resettlement Authority was established in April 2007, and led to the creation of a national legal framework to uphold the rights of IDPs and refugees and provide them with durable solutions to their displacement. The Resettlement Authority Act No. 9 seeks to facilitate the resettlement or relocation of IDPs and refugees in efforts to rehabilitate and assist them. The Resettlement Authority primarily seeks to resettle the IDPs and refugees in their original homes or to relocate them to new state land and provide them with immediate humanitarian assistance, including temporary shelter, food, water and sanitation.[20]

The key functions of the Resettlement Authority are to:

- Formulate and implement the resettlement policy for displaced persons and refugees.
- Coordinate government, donor agencies, international NGOs, civil society organizations or companies with the necessary mandates and resources in efforts to end displacement of persons.
- Plan and implement specific programmes and schemes for resettlement and new settlements.
- Assist IDPs and refugees to obtain legal documents such as birth, marriages and/or death certificates, as well as national identity cards, deeds and other documents from respective government departments.
- Assist in providing infrastructure, health and educational facilities.
- Implement resettlement programmes including housing schemes for facilitating resettlement and new settlements.[21]

HUMANITARIAN ORGANIZATIONS: PROTECTION STRATEGIES

On the part of the humanitarian community, several organizations have extensive experience and knowledge on the protection of the IDPs, and the interlinking circumstantial considerations that need to be acknowledged. However, the role of the government in assisting and supporting the humanitarian community, and vice versa, is a notable fact when reviewing the efficiency of responding to IDP needs in a timely and appropriate manner.

In some instances, international organizations and NGOs show some reluctance to raise or become involved in protection issues in fear of provoking restrictions on their access and attacks on their personnel, or because they lack experience or expertise in these issues. However, when the physical security and fundamental human rights of the people benefiting from their assistance are threatened, to ignore the issues at hand would only undermine the assistance programmes themselves. International organizations and NGOs could alternatively seek to enhance the IDPs security by designing assistance programmes to enhance protection, which is referred to as preventive protection.[22]

CURRENT CHALLENGES IN ADDRESSING AND RESPONDING TO IDPs

The following sections outline the key challenges faced in attempting to address the needs of the IDPs. In some cases the issues are those faced by those trying to assist (such as the government and humanitarian actors) or the IDPs themselves. These issues must be recognized as having overarching significance in ensuring proper protection and assistance for the IDPs.

Definition

One of the most pertinent elements in the discourse on responding to the IDPs is the definition of the IDP itself, as Sri Lanka has experienced protracted and multiple displacements over the past two decades. In failing to agree to one common definition of 'IDP', the lack of common standards would arise and would make humanitarian and administrative responses difficult at different phases of displacement. Additionally accurate data would be harder to obtain and this would have an overriding impact on the effective management of practical issues such as registration/de-registration, statistics and beneficiary lists. Finally, assessing whether durable solutions have been achieved for a protracted IDP situation would be harder.[23]

Registration/Statistics

Another key challenge is that of registration and statistics. Registration of the IDPs is the key way of protection for IDPs as it marks their right to protection, humanitarian assistance and assistance in pursuing durable solutions to their displacement. It is also useful for the government and the humanitarian community in planning and delivering assistance.[24]

Assistance

Whilst Sri Lanka has extensive systems to register and collect data, there are varying standards across different districts and areas, and one of the most difficult areas to establish clear figures is when the IDPs are staying with friends and families and for those who originate from areas which have been proclaimed as safe for return. Additionally IDPs who have been displaced more than once, who try to register in the new place of displacement, often face the problem of 'de registering' from their previous place of displacement.[25]

In the provision of assistance lies another challenge in the variation of policies, schemes and standards. Where different standards are being used, such as the government dry ration scheme and the emergency assistance scheme of the World Food Programme (WFP), such standards are not based on the assessment of needs, yet are guided by set standards. Additionally other schemes such as grant assistance schemes saw significant variations in the assistance afforded to those affected by the tsunami in comparison to those affected by conflict. Furthermore those affected by conflict were also divided into two groups in terms of assistance, that is, those displaced prior to 2006 and those displaced after 2006.[26]

Land

A traumatic after-thought, and second to being displaced, is that of losing one's home or property. For most IDPs the possible return home is hope of returning to normalcy, however, where the reality of loss or damage to property and land is discovered in returning home, the trauma of displacement is felt even more. Property or land is the key issue and concern when attempting to respond to IDP situations as land is noted as the single largest resource for returning IDPs.[27]

Return and relocation: Several obstacles within these areas

SECURITY

Security issues faced by the IDPs in the northern and eastern regions revolve around occupation of property or land, the presence of landmines in several areas and the establishment of High Security Zones.[28] In such instances, the IDPs and returnees are prevented from accessing their houses and/or their agricultural lands in these areas.

LEGAL/DOCUMENTATION

Legal issues arise with the lack, loss or damage of land title documents, which are very common in instances, of displacement. This renders many at a loss, unable to provide evidence of title to the property where they lived, prior to the displacement, and they find it difficult to return. Women feel the struggle of claiming land or property even more as they face much difficulty during and after displacement, with regard to the inheritance of land or property; again, this is due to missing or a lack of necessary legal documents.[29]

SECONDARY OCCUPANCY

Secondary occupancy has also been a long-standing issue for the IDPs in Sri Lanka where, their property has been occupied during their displacement either through encroachment or with the occupiers obtaining prescriptive title after having been in possession for a period exceeding ten years. Secondary occupants, who have lived in an abandoned property for at least ten years, can obtain prescriptive title to that property which makes it difficult for the original owners to reclaim the property. In addition sometimes the IDPs themselves are the secondary occupants.[30]

Compensation

Housing compensation remains an important yet somewhat complex issue within the discourse on IDPs. Sri Lanka has established several schemes to respond to housing and property concerns as early as 1987, in efforts to provide compensation. The amounts themselves have varied greatly over the years since 1987, with the tsunami disaster of 2004 pushing the government to raise the amount afforded to conflict-affected IDPs[31] to match that provided for tsunami-affected IDPs due to increasing debates around the subject.

Consultation with IDPs, their participation and access to information

A common experience in Sri Lanka has been that the IDPs have not been consulted on their needs, interests and concerns in key areas on a regular basis, in terms of plans for assistance, return, compensation and other issues affecting durable solutions. Additionally, access to information remains strained.[32] Systematic approaches to ensure the participation of the IDPs in the decision making regarding their lives are essential to ensuring the long-term sustainability of any decisions reached. Access to information will also enable the IDPs to make informed choices as well as enhance their level of self-sufficiency.

Physical security

IDP camp security remains a slightly controversial matter, as in some areas the IDPs are kept under tight security measures both for overarching security reasons as well as for their welfare. However, severe military presence and heavy procedures to register the IDPs in camps seriously restrict the movement of IDPs and tends to undermine their own sense of security.

On a wider level, increased police and military presence in areas of tension and areas vulnerable to sudden instability, leads to insecurity in civilian populations. This is especially evident where there are communication and language gaps between authorities and civilian populations. Confidence Building and Stabilization Measures (CBSM) have been used previously within Sri Lanka; to a great degree they were successful in easing relations and understanding between the respective parties. Hence in general, looking to enforce CBSM would increase the confidence and security of the IDPs in police and/or armed forces.[33]

Livelihoods/health

During displacement, livelihoods and basic health are often severely affected and are temporarily remedied by emergency assistance and thereafter by more long-term support. With regards to livelihoods, it is vital that considerations be made to the specific activities the IDPs were engaged in prior to displacement, such that allowances and support can be given, where possible, for them to gain some form of income in their place of displacement should they wish to do so. In addition to this, preparations should be made well in advance of returns to support the rehabilitation of lost livelihoods where possible.

Psychosocial support

In some cases, it would not be surprising to note that the psychological trauma experienced by them has been overlooked or forgotten, in the rush to respond to their physical needs and basic nutritional and hygiene requirements. The trauma caused during pre-displacement, during displacement and post-displacement requires thought, and sufficient mechanisms to respond to psychosocial needs should be carefully established. This is especially critical when addressing the needs and future of children; maximum efforts should be invested to safeguard a healthy emotional state for their futures.

Recovery programmes/development

It is essential to recognize the significant role played by inducing recovery programmes, not from the obvious immediate role these play, but rather the more sustainable potential they carry. In ensuring that adequate recovery programmes are in place, more concise and appropriate measures will be taken to safeguard long-term protection of the IDPs. Parallel to this, humanitarian assistance should not be the only focus, development efforts should be coupled with the former in order to enhance the lives of citizens, let alone the IDPs. A development focus will carry the lives of individuals and communities further than short-term humanitarian programmes, and protection is further maximized in doing so.

THE GUIDING PRINCIPLES ON INTERNAL DISPLACEMENT: A STEPPING STONE TO PROTECTION STRATEGIES

While the Guiding Principles are exceptional on their own, they require the endorsement of respective countries experiencing internal displacement in order to materialize durable outcomes for the IDPs. The critical need is for a national legal framework for the IDPs in Sri Lanka, which would establish their rights. The act which set in place the Resettlement Authority decrees the government's responsibility to uphold the rights of the IDPs and establish a basis of reference for a national policy, whilst reflecting national commitment towards internal displacement.[34]

Sri Lankan citizens have the right to all the guarantees under international human rights and international humanitarian law, given with the state's endorsement of both. It is also important to note that the IDPs have needs and vulnerabilities which are distinct from the non-displaced populations; these needs can be responded to through the effective implementation of well-planned protection and assistance mechanisms.[35]

The presence of several national and international humanitarian agencies in Sri Lanka provides the government with immense opportunity to coordinate efforts to ensure that optimum efforts to ensure the protection and assistance to the IDPs are being used. As noted in Guiding Principle 3, the IDPs have the right to request and receive protection and assistance from the government, hence where the government has insufficient capacity or the lack of means to do so, several experienced actors amongst the humanitarian community are worthy to fulfil the needs of the IDPs.[36] However, reinforcing protection should extend to recognizing human rights as a central concern or function, yet this is not always the case. Humanitarian and development organizations are positioned such that any violations of rights and further information of such incidents could potentially be forwarded on to relevant bodies. The recognition and willingness to do just that must be present. On the other hand, it would also be beneficial, as mentioned above, to strengthen protection by working directly with the displaced and with local communities and authorities in finding solutions.[37]

CONCLUSION

The creation of the Guiding Principles has responded to a global need to have a wholly inclusive document which details methods to cover gaps in the international protection system for the IDPs. The principles serve to press all involved parties, from states, international and national organizations to insurgent parties, to recognize their role at the different stages (as well as their role in the root causes of internal displacement). Additionally, the principles promote enhanced accountability on the part of state actors whose prime responsibility is to ensure the protection of its citizens, including the IDPs.

For protection strategies to be appropriately planned, fundamental understanding of existing human rights and protection gaps is clearly needed. If this is not the case, such gaps will remain, especially where relevant actors do not recognize the importance of physical safety. Combined legal, institutional and practical measures would appropriately serve to address situations of internal displacement.

Sri Lanka should actively seek to establish legislation which focuses only on the IDPs and heavily incorporates the Guiding Principles on Internal Displacement, given the scope and detail of the Guiding Principles. Collaborations and coordination with relevant actors, such as international and national humanitarian and development organizations must be sought to enhance the efficiency and long-term sustainability of any response to safeguard the rights and dignity of the IDPs.

In making these recommendations, negotiations amongst many intervening parties need to be borne in mind. IDP situations are largely the results of the efforts of men and, in some measure, women, establishing environments of conflict. National security and counter measures become a reality. Likewise those who fund and conduct programmes have their own expectations. Added to this cast are the IDPs, government officials, multilateral and intergovernmental institutions and non-state parties. Negotiating with principles with such a cast requires acumen not found in any manual. It nevertheless remains a crucial element in the quest for protection.

(Research by Nayomi Dharmatileke, Consortium of Humanitarian Agencies, Sri Lanka)

NOTES

1 W. Kalin, 'Report of the Representative of the Secretary-General on the Human Rights of Internally Displaced Persons', Mission to Sri Lanka Geneva, UN, 2007.
2 K. Van Brabant, *Internally Displaced Persons: A Global Survey*, J. Hampton (ed.) (London: Earth Scan, 1998).
3 Ibid.
4 Ibid.
5 K. Van Brabant, *Internally Displaced Persons*.
6 Ministry of Disaster Management and Human Rights, 2008, Durable Solutions for Old Internally Displaced Persons (IDPs); Achievements 1983–April 2006, Sri Lanka.
7 Ibid.
8 Ibid.
9 Ibid.
10 Ibid.
11 Ibid.
12 Ibid.
13 Ibid.
14 Ibid.
15 Housing grants increased from Rs. 250,000 to Rs. 325,000 per house.
16 Ministry of Disaster Management and Human Rights, 2008, Durable Solutions.
17 Ibid.
18 A. Angel, 'IDPs: Need for a National Legal Framework in Sri Lanka, Institute for Peace and Conflict Studies, for details see: www.reliefweb.int/rw.rwb.nsf/db900oSID/ONIN-7HFQYF? 2008.
19 Ibid.

20 Ministry of Resettlement and Disaster Relief Services, 2008. Background Paper, Resettlement Authority and Its Activities,
21 Ibid.
22 R. Cohen and F. M. Deng (eds), *Masses in Flight: The Global Crisis of Internal Displacement*; *The Forsaken People: Case Studies of the Internally Displaced* (Washington, DC: Brookings Institution, 1998).
23 UNHCR, 2008, 'The Challenge of Assessing and Responding to the Protracted IDP Situation', Background Paper, National Consultation on the Status of Internally Displaced Persons.
24 Ibid.
25 Ibid.
26 Ibid.
27 Consortium of Humanitarian Agencies, 2008, 'IDP Land, Property and Compensation Issues', Background Paper, National Consultation on the Status of Internally Displaced Persons.
28 Either legally by gazetting them such as in Trincomalee District or in practice like in Jaffna.
29 Consortium of Humanitarian Agencies, 2008, 'IDP Land, Property and Compensation Issues'.
30 Ibid.
31 Assistance provided to conflict-affected IDPs has been largely infrequent, with compensation being provided more on an ad hoc basis, in response to particular incidents.
32 W. Kalin, 'Report on the Human Rights of Internally Displaced Persons', 2007.
33 Ibid.
34 A. Angel, 'IDPs: Need for a National Legal Framework in Sri Lanka', 2008.
35 Ibid.
36 The state also has an obligation to request assistance from others where it deems it appropriate and where it will not interfere with internal affairs of the given country (Guiding Principle 25).
37 R. Cohen and F. M. Deng (eds), *Masses in Flight* and *The Forsaken People: Case Studies of the Internally Displaced*. See no 22.

12

POLICIES AND PRACTICES OF THE NATIONAL HUMAN RIGHTS COMMISSION (NHRC) ON THE INTERNALLY DISPLACED PERSONS (IDPs) IN NEPAL

SHIVA K. DHUNGANA

The phenomenon of forced displacement and the violation of the human rights of displaced persons, families and communities have been one of the most debated issues in the recent global humanitarian arena.[1]

The crisis brought about by the incidence of forced displacement, especially of the poor in Asia and Africa, has reached an alarming stage. They are among the most vulnerable victims and constitute arguably the largest at-risk population in the world.[2] People all over the world are constantly being forced to leave their homes for many reasons: natural calamities, human-made disasters, state sponsored population transfer, terrorism, abuse of human rights and threat of violence from state and non-state forces, giant commercial projects, major infrastructure development projects such as dams and national parks and wildlife reserves, and as a result of political, ethnic, religious or other conflicts.[3] While an estimated 25 million people are displaced worldwide by conflict, the number of people uprooted by development projects is estimated to be much higher. A study published in 2000 estimated that between 40 and 80 million people were forcibly displaced by that time because of large hydroelectric projects alone. Other development projects are also forcing millions of people to be evicted from their home each year.[4] In the past few decades, the countries of South Asia are also facing the displacement of their large populations at a serious level mainly because of political, religious, ethnic conflicts or a state of lawlessness, partition of the country and major development projects such as dams and other commercial infrastructure projects.

INTERNAL DISPLACEMENT IN NEPAL

Nepal experienced a serious crisis brought about by the forced displacement of population only recently. The issues of protection and promotion of rights of the internally displaced persons (IDPs) in Nepal were never taken seriously before the birth of the Maoist armed struggle called 'Peoples' War' in early 1996, despite the existence of large number of such people as a result of development projects and natural disasters, which were 'recorded' as early as the 1960s. It also caught the attention of the international community, especially the UN, when the wider implications of the armed conflict found space in the international debate as a result of heavy casualties caused by the state and the insurgents. The conflict-induced displacement in Nepal saw another dimension with the birth of ethnicity-based violent activities launched by political and armed groups in the eastern hills and southern plains, the Terai region, of Nepal. The magnitude of displacement and the vulnerability of certain ethnic communities in the region have increased manifold after ethnic violence erupted in early 2007 in the region.

Further, hundreds of thousands of Nepalis have been displaced since the construction of hydroelectric projects and national parks and wildlife reserves.[5] Many displaced families were resettled by the government in different locations under 'land for land' packages. However, many of them could not stay there for long because of the poor quality of the soil[6] and other socio-cultural and livelihood difficulties and were forced to move to other parts of the country. No official information is available about their recent status and whereabouts.

Natural disasters have been another persistent cause of involuntary displacement of people since time immemorial in a country with rugged mountains and high hills where every monsoon brings many cases of landslides and flash floods and hundreds of thousands of people are forced to leave their homes when floods and landslides sweep away their houses and agriculture lands. The Koshi River floods in eastern Nepal[7] and flash floods in far eastern Terai of Nepal in the Monsoon of 2008 are examples of how natural disaster struck the lives and livelihoods of poor villagers in rural Nepal. Many of them never return to their villages as the landslide and flood make the place permanently inhabitable.[8] Moreover, many families affected by natural disasters in the remote areas hardly receive any compensation or logistical support for their relief, rehabilitation or resettlement and are left to face the crisis on their own.

There are more than 50,000 Kamaiyas (bonded labourers), who were declared free by the government in 2000 and their outstanding family loans with the rich landlords were written off. They worked generation after generation on the land of the landlords to pay the interest of the inter-generational loans, without being paid wages.[9] The government promised to provide small parcels of land for their livelihood once they were released from the slavery of the masters. However, the promise was merely lip service and they are fighting for their survival and are still organizing sit-in protests in Kathmandu. The government does not seem to be bothered to fulfil the promise of 'reasonable' resettlement and is leaving them to live in the wilderness of poverty and frustration.[10]

There is no accurate database of the IDPs in Nepal. In the absence of globally accepted definition, comprehensive registration of IDPs and of any systematic monitoring of population movements by national authorities or by international organizations, it is difficult to provide any accurate estimates on the total number of people displaced. Thus, the estimation of the IDPs in Nepal is one of the most complicated tasks compared to the estimation of other conflict induced IDPs belonging to other countries, because of the provision of the 'open border' between Nepal and India and the age-old practice of seasonal and long-term economic migration, especially from the western hills of Nepal.

The UN has estimated around 50,000-70,000 conflict-induced IDPs at the end of 2007. However, the government had registered only 35,000 IDPs by 2008.[11] Additionally, an unknown but substantial number of Nepalis have been displaced to India through the porous open border. There is no formal recording of data regarding internal displacement caused by development projects as well as human-made or natural disasters. Further, there is no official information regarding those displaced by the ethnic violence taking place in the southern plains and eastern hills of Nepal. Many of the displaced do not want to reveal themselves as IDPs because of the security vulnerability as well as the social stigma associated with their status as IDPs.

The status of the people displaced to India through the open border is a tricky one. By the 1951 UN Convention on Refugees, these people are Nepali refugees in India, but they are never given the status of refugees in India because of the provision of the 1950 Treaty of Peace and Friendship between the two countries which stipulates that the Nepali people can travel to India (as do Indians to Nepal) without any documentation and theoretically share the same legal rights, with the exception of voting, as citizens. This provision of the treaty nullifies the chances of the Nepalis fleeing the conflict to India to be considered as refugees, and they remain in the 'state of statelessness' in India.

There is no authentic information on the status and suffering of people displaced to India, except for some case-specific information. However, some media and NGOs reporting from both sides of the border point to a pathetic condition of those displaced to India. The actual situation could only be assessed through reliable research among the displaced Nepalis in India. The problem lies in the manner the Nepali and Indian governments define the status of economic and forced migrants as the same under the Treaty of Peace and Friendship, 1950.

IDPS AND THEIR RIGHTS

The UN Guiding Principles on Internal Displacement, 1998, and National Policies on IDPs, 2007, clearly stipulate that '*all displaced persons have the right to return voluntarily, in safety and with dignity, to their homes or places of habitual residence, or to resettle voluntarily in another part of the country*', but it is never honoured by the conflicting and/or responsible parties. There is a selective 'approval' process practised by the CPN(M) cadres for the return of the conflict-induced IDPs in many parts of the country. They have categorized the IDPs into three groups which serve as the basis of the 'approval process'. While IDPs belonging to the third group—those who quietly left in anticipation or in fear of the conflict—were welcome to return, those belonging to the second group—those accused by the Maoists of some 'wrongdoing'—had to accept conditions imposed by the Maoists before being allowed to return. These included paying a 'donation' or appearing before a 'People's Court' to explain their displacement and apologize for actions committed before being displaced. The IDPs belonging to the first group are seen as responsible for 'serious crimes' and not welcome back.[12] The state of lawlessness prevailing in the country, to date, makes the situation even worse for the safe and dignified return of the IDPs as they have to be totally dependent on the pleasure of the Maoist cadres. The near absence of the government mechanism outside district headquarters has led to the lack of protection and reconciliation mechanisms and provisions for basic support service and facilitation for the returnees. Hence the burden has been taken up by the local NGOs to facilitate the return and reintegration of IDPs, with limited authority and resources.

STATE PROTECTION MECHANISMS

Though the UN Guiding Principles on Internal Displacement came into effect in 1998 with the unanimous approval of the UN General Assembly, the government authorities in Nepal never paid attention towards the Principles in protecting the victims of forced displacement. It could be because the majority of the displaced until that time were victims of government actions and atrocities. When pressured by the international community, the government set aside some funds, broadly defining conflict-induced IDPs as those victimized only by the rebels, denying the IDP status to those displaced by the atrocities of the state security forces. The highly unjust definition of IDPs nullified the minimal government effort and was severely criticized by NGOs, civil society and the international community. There was no national policy on the IDP until then and the government was dealing with the issue on an ad hoc basis.

For the first time, the Twelve-Point Agreement signed between the Seven Party Alliance (SPA) and the CPN(M) in November 2005 acknowledged the problem of the IDPs. Article 5 of the Twelve-Point Agreement signed in November 2005 specifically mentions:

> The CPN(M) has expressed its commitment to create an environment allowing the political party activists of the democratic parties displaced during the course of the armed conflict to return to their homes and live with dignity, return their land and other properties confiscated by their cadres

and carry out their activities without hindrances (Twelve-Point Agreement 2005, INSEC 2005: 2).

However, the article in the agreement came as a CPN(M) commitment to allow (only) activists of the 'democratic' political parties[13] to return to the districts without any hindrances.

Further to this, Article 18 of the Twenty-Five-Point Ceasefire Code of Conduct (CCC) signed by the SPA Government and the CPN(M) on 25 May 2006 has committed to: 'Provide help in the rehabilitation of and extend cooperation to displaced people to return to their respective homes in a peaceful, comfortable and respectable manner'.

Similarly, Article 19 makes a commitment on the return of properties of the IDPs which stipulates that: 'The CPN(M) will return the properties of the leaders of political parties, activists and civilians, which were seized, locked up or prohibited from being used during the period of the conflict, to concerned persons or their families. Problems arising while returning the properties will be resolved through mutual agreement'.

It was only in March 2006, that the then government issued National Policies on IDPs,[14] but as with the previous document, the latest failed to comply with international standards (as prescribed by the UN Guiding Principles on Internal Displacement) as it only recognized those displaced by the actions of Maoists as IDPs, depriving the larger mass of the IDPs displaced by the actions of the state forces, not to mention the IDPs who had fallen into this status by development projects and natural disasters. Even after the success of the April 2006 People's movement the mainstream political parties failed to realize the gravity of the problem and never made the issue of internal displacement as an inherent component of the peace process. Only the Comprehensive Peace Accord (CPA) signed by the government and the CPN(M) on 21 November 2006 incorporated an article to ensure the 'right to return' of every individual displaced as a result of the armed conflict. Article 5.2.8 says: 'Both parties express the commitment to allow without any political prejudice the people displaced due to the armed conflict to return back voluntarily to their respective ancestral or former residence, reconstruct the infrastructure destroyed during the conflict and rehabilitate and socialize the displaced people into the society.'

Similarly, Article 7.3.3 ensures the freedom of movement of the IDPs as well as their right to return or reintegration: 'Both parties shall respect and protect the individual's freedom to move freely and the right to choose a place to reside within the legal periphery, and also expresses commitment to respect the right of the people who have been displaced to return home or to live in any other place they choose.[15]

With increasing pressure from the national and the international communities, the Interim Government developed and adopted new National Policies on IDPs on April 2007, almost one year after its formation. The Policy defines an IDP as

> Person who is living somewhere else in the country after having been forced to flee or leave one's home or place of habitual residence due to armed conflict or situation of violence or gross violation of human rights or natural disaster or human-made disaster and situation or with an intention of avoiding the effects of such situations.

Thus, the government, for the first time, has been able to incorporate the spirit of the UN Guiding Principles on Internal Displacement in a local policy document. The policy has shifted 'the mandate to deal with the issues of IDPs from the Ministry of Home Affairs (MoHA) to the Ministry of Peace and Reconstruction (MoPR). The ministry formulated the Procedural Directives for the smooth implementation of the newly adopted IDP policy.

In the meantime, the national attention shifted towards the election of the Constituent Assembly (which was postponed twice). The focus on elections followed by the prolonged conflict on power sharing among political parties for the election of the first president and the prime minister of the Federal Democratic Republic of Nepal may explain delays in approving the directives on the implementation of the National Policy on the IDP (which is pending in the cabinet since February 2008).[16] The political actors do not seem to have realized the gravity of the problem and its possible implication in the entire peace process and have, so far, failed to approve the directives and develop an effective implementation mechanism to materialize the spirit of these documents into action.

INTERNATIONAL NGOS (INGOS), UN AGENCIES AND ETHICS OF CARE

Many human rights organizations and UN agencies are also working towards addressing the vulnerability of the IDPs and protecting and promoting their right to return, rehabilitation, reintegration and reconciliation. Many NGOs working in the field of human rights have been implementing holistic programmes for return, reintegration, rehabilitation and reconciliation by ensuring the personal security of individual IDPs throughout the process. Most of the organizations have focused their activities in the districts of mid- and far-western Nepal, where a large number of people were displaced during the conflict. Those organizations focused their activities in providing the IDPs with logistical support for their return or rehabilitation, providing relief, support, organizing 'farewell meeting' at the place of displacement and 'reconciliation meeting' at the place of origin, and accompanying the IDPs during the return process to ensure their physical safety. They are present to address the vulnerability of certain IDPs, such as women, children and senior citizens during the travel from the place of displacement to the place of their origins. These organizations also provide financial and logistical support to IDPs to start their lives and livelihood anew. Further, NGOs involved in protecting the rights of people such as Informal Sector Service Centre (INSEC), Human Rights Organization of Nepal (HURON), Human Rights Alliance, Centre for Victims of Torture (CVICT), Human Rights Home, Himalayan Human Rights Monitors (HimRights), INHURED International monitor the human rights violations of people, including IDPs, and draw attention of national and international community towards their plight.

Since 2005, the international community has intensified its assistance efforts to provide protection to the displaced population. A Common Humanitarian Action Plan (CHAP) was devised in mid-2005 among international agencies and served as the basis for Consolidated Appeal Process (CAP) launched in October 2005 and which requested $66 million. As of the end of September 2006, almost 75 per cent of the total sum had been given, with the protection sector particularly well funded; but many projects aimed at addressing the needs of the IDPs and conflict-affected people in the sectors of agriculture, education, economic recovery and water and sanitation had not received any funding.[17] The revised requirements for the Appeal are US$ 104 million. In 2008, the UN stated 39 per cent funding has been raised to meet these needs, and $63 million to fund the gaps was still required.

To contribute to the safe and sustainable return of the IDPs, UNHCR has been organizing and conducting various programmes—with support from the Office of the High Commissioner for Human Rights (OHCHR), Office for the Coordination of Humanitarian Affairs (OCHA), the National Human Rights Commission (NHRC), the Norwegian Refugee Council and many other organizations—such as workshops, awareness campaigns through locally based programmes and media. The national and international organizations/ agencies, especially the UNHCR and the Norwegian Refugee

Council in Nepal, played major roles in formulating the National Policies on IDPs and the Procedural Directives to implement the policy and raise awareness among the people about the documents and the UN Guiding Principles on Internal Displacement.

When the Ministry of Peace and Reconstruction requested the international community for technical assistance, OCHA, on behalf of the IDP Protection Working Group, supported the ministry with technical assistance to formulate the Procedural Directives of the IDP Policy.[18] The monthly meeting of the IDP Protection Working Group, chaired by OHCHR and UNHCR and whose members are from the UN, NGOs, INGOs and donor agencies, provides a platform for in-depth and wide discussions on protection issues related to the IDPs in Nepal. This includes assessment of needs, planning and strategy development, identification of key partners, and standard setting and information sharing on the protection concerns of displaced persons.[19] Hence, the UN and other international agencies are coming out to support the IDPs in their relief, rehabilitation and protection whereas the NGOs, both local and international, are assisting in their return, reintegration and legal assistance. However, all such efforts are not very effective because of the lack of governance in the most part of the country, lack of protection mechanism supported by integrated reintegration approach and lack of willingness of the government authorities to coordinate and collaborate with non-state sectors.

POLICIES AND PRACTICES OF NHRC

For most of the time during conflict, the majority of the conflict-induced IDPs were looked as the enemy of the state authority. The state was never concerned about the human rights violation of IDPs and they were not given fair treatment, not to mention the special treatment. There were hardly any cases filed leading to the protection of the rights of the IDPs.

The NHRC also remained without commissioners for almost two years during the height of the conflict because of the unwillingness of the royal government to make it operational and during the post-conflict period because of the political bickering of the political parties in the appointment process. There are no specific legal provisions to protect the rights of the IDPs till date. Most of the promises have remained as mere lip-service. All the government authority and the judicial organs of the state are dealing with the issues of the IDPs or conflict victims within the general framework of the legislations related to human rights violation and criminal offence. However, many IDPs are not willing to identify themselves as IDPs because of possible stigmatization created by the state; it is unlikely that their plight reaches the judiciary or the NHRC.

The National Policies on IDPs 2007 calls for some specific legislations and implementing mechanisms to protect the social, political, economic and other fundamental rights of the IDPs. However, there are no formal attempts to put such necessary legal provisions in place. Even after 18 months of endorsement of the Policy, the government has not been able to come up with implementation guidelines to convert the policy into practice.

Since the NHRC was established only in 2000, while the problem of internal displacement was basically looked from the armed conflict perspective, it never paid attention towards the existence of the large number of IDPs caused by other reasons. When the issue of human rights violations of conflict victims and the IDPs came into discussion the NHRC started to look into the affair with a general human rights monitoring perspective. Later, it considered the guarantee of human rights of IDPs as one of its most important responsibilities and has given high priority to the issues of human rights violation of the IDPs. In its Strategic Plan (2004-2008), the Commission has given priority to the IDP problem and included it as the first strategic objective.

> The National Human Rights Commission (NHRC), Nepal is an independent and autonomous constitutional body with its slogan of 'Dignity, Equality and Justice for all'. It was established in the year 2000 as a statutory body under the Human Rights Commission Act 1997 (2053 BS). The Commission is created in response to the 1991 UN-sponsored meeting of representatives of national institutions held in Paris, which laid down a detailed set of principles on the status of national institutions commonly known as the Paris Principles. These principles, subsequently endorsed by the UN Commission on Human Rights (Resolution 1992/54 of 3 March 1992) and the UN General Assembly (Resolution 48/134 of 20 December 1993, annexure) have become the foundation and reference point for the establishment and operation of the National Human Rights Commission of Nepal as well. The Interim Constitution of Nepal, 2007, elevated it to the constitutional body from the earlier statutory status. The provision of NHRC, Nepal, has been mentioned in the Article 15 (Section 131, 132 and 133) of the Interim Constitution of Federal Democratic Republic of Nepal. Primarily, the Commission is responsible for the protection, promotion, respect for and enforcement of human rights in Nepal (NHRC Strategic Plan 2008-2010).

In the post-conflict scenario, the NHRC developed its Strategic Plan (2008-2010) for the protection, promotion, respect for and fulfilment of the human rights of the people of Nepal. The NHRC has identified nine core values of human rights. The values include *Accessibility, Accountability, Diversity, Equality and Equity, Impartiality, Independence, Integrity, Participation and Transparency*. NHRC endeavours to comply and consider these values in a wide range of its activities in order to protect the rights of every individual, including those of IDPs. Considering the deep-rooted and deteriorating conflict dynamics and social, economic, cultural, civil and political rights situation in the country, the Commission identified major areas of focus of which following, to some extent, deal with the concern of the IDPs.[20]

Ending the culture of impunity

Impunity is a serious problem that the country has faced for a long time. The lack of fear of punishment, inadequate laws, politics of power and ineffective law enforcement mechanisms are the major causes behind the persistence of the state of impunity. During the armed conflict situation, thousands of people lost their lives and millions suffered due to displacement, disappearance and torture. The government has planned to establish the Truth and Reconciliation Commission and Peace and Reconstruction Commission to address the grievances involved and bring the perpetrators of the past human rights abuses to justice as per the CPA. The Commission plans to actively involve through the effective monitoring of activities directed to end the state of impunity.

According to an estimate, approximately 13,000 people died during the decade-long violent conflict. Many more have been the victims of injury, enforced disappearances, abduction, torture, among other atrocities. The exact figure of victims such as the widows, orphans and cases of internal displacement caused by the conflict is hardly available yet. In the recent days, the process of victimizing has indeed declined in figures, but not ended, even after commitment shown through the CPA signed between Government of Nepal and CPN(M).

Establishment of right to life, liberty and security of the people

Despite the Peace Accord between the Government of Nepal and the then rebel CPN(M) and the victory of CPN(M) in the Constituent Assembly elections, life, liberty and security of the people are under severe threat in different parts of the country. NHRC has frequently received complaints that various ethnic, criminal and armed outfits are largely involved in killing, abduction, torture, extortion, forced eviction and disappearance in the central and eastern part of the Tarai and eastern hill region. NHRC has shown grave concern on the degrading condition of human rights' violations and has frequently monitored the situation and recommended to the Government of Nepal to restore law and order in the country.

Establishment of truth on disappearance, IDPs and victims of conflict and justice to survivors and their families

The CPA and Twenty-three-point agreement signed between the Government of Nepal and the CPN(M) has mandated the NHRC to monitor the implementation status and ensure realization of enjoyment of right to acquire, own and dispose of private property. In this context, the Commission would frequently monitor the situation of the IDPs and recommend effective implementation of the CPA. However, the NHRC is of the opinion that both the parties are found to be less serious in making the names and whereabouts of the missing persons known. The Commission therefore asks the former conflicting parties to make public the whereabouts of these individuals and provide interim relief and compensation to the victims' families and to make the perpetrators accountable for the crimes committed. In this context, the Commission supports the idea of the establishment of the Disappearance Commission and expresses its willingness to work together in the complimentary basis to make the concerned organizations and individuals accountable for their involvement in the human rights abuses and to ensure adequate compensation to the conflict victims by the Government of Nepal.

The Commission has identified seven strategic objectives and corresponding areas of interventions. Out of the seven objectives, the first objective deals with the concerns of the IDPs in Nepal. It intends to *strengthen the rule of law, culture of human rights and peace to end impunity and the violation of human rights*. The strategic objective has identified the following areas of strategic intervention (among others) that are directly or indirectly related to the concern of the IDPs:

(a) Monitor implementation of HR aspects of various agreements signed by the Government of Nepal:
- Review of the existing IDP policy of the Government of Nepal and monitor its effective implementation;
- Publish reports on the status of implementation of various agreements signed by the Government of Nepal;
- Conduct impact study on IDPs, disappearances and land mines.

(b) Ensure Implementation of the NHRC recommendations by the Government of Nepal.
- Develop a systematic monitoring mechanism for the implementation of the NHRC recommendations and policy directives and guidelines in practice;
- Work with civil society/HR organizations to develop a victim-oriented approach to HR investigations and monitoring;
- Publish reports of non-compliance of the NHRC recommendations.

(c) Review and strengthen the monitoring and investigation mechanisms for HR protection
- Conduct monitoring and investigation on incidents of human rights violation;
- Facilitate to develop witness and victim protection mechanism;
- Apply innovative and standard methods for investigation;
- Extend and strengthen NHRC capacity on investigation of HR violation cases and follow up the implementation of recommendation in practice;

- Organize public hearings on cases of gross violation of human rights;
- Publish and disseminate overall human rights situation report periodically.

Based on the earlier Plan of Action (2004-2008) and the recently approved Strategic Plan (2008-2010), the Commission is slowly moving towards institutionalizing the mechanisms and implementing activities to protect the rights of IDPs in the country.

Further, with the increased magnitude of internal displacement and the cases of violation of human rights of the IDPs as a result of the Maoist rebellion in the past few years, the Commission established a Focal Point within the Protection and Monitoring Division in the head office in Kathmandu and in all regional offices to pay special attention to the protection and promotion of human rights of the IDPs. The desk regularly monitors the IDP situation by desk reviewing, news analysis and filed visits in the areas with larger numbers of IDPs. Based on the analysis, the Commission also takes suo moto action on issues related to the violation of rights of the IDPs. It also puts regular pressure to those accountable for the plights of the IDPs by issuing press statements and organizing discussions with responsible actors for their rehabilitation and return.

The Commission, till date, has carried out regular awareness campaign on the rights of IDPs, monitoring of the IDP camps and other IDP settlements in different parts of the country. It also regularly organizes workshops/interactions among concerned national and international organizations on issues of the IDPs and prepares database, facilitates the flow of related information through press conferences, press statements, e-bulletins and website. It is also active in receiving complains regarding the human rights' violation of the IDPs, investigating the cases and recommending to the government for appropriate legal actions. Further, it promotes different stakeholders to coordinate their activities related to the relief of the IDPs and works towards increasing their awareness about special rights of IDPs as well as the UN Guiding Principles on Internal Displacement across the country. However, due to the government inability of appointing the chair and commissioners for a long time, the majority of the recommendations made by the Commission have not been enforced at all. This is a serious concern and illustrates the government's indifference towards protecting the human rights' of civilians, especially the IDPs.

NHRC programmes related to IDPs

The IDP Focal Point established in the central and regional offices as guided by the Strategic Plan 2004-2008 has been converted into IDP Unit under the Protection and Monitoring Division. Following are the activities carried out by the IDP Unit.[21]

- HR sensitization and awareness-raising activities to the conflicting parties during field visits, investigation and monitoring on occasional basis. However, these activities were not IDPs-specific.
- Interaction/meetings with stakeholders on promotion of several of rights with special focus on the right to return, rehabilitation and resettlement.
- Pilot research on IDPs in Dhanusha district, May 2006.
- Rapid assessment and research on conflict-induced IDPs for facilitating and advocating their right to return, resettlement and reintegration.
- Continuously receive complaints from the IDPs regarding their human rights' violations. Until July 2008 (from 2000), the Commission has received 307 complains (concerning around 1,000 individuals) of which 13 were against the state and 294 were against the CPN(M). Despite the massive human rights' violations from the state security forces, the

complaints received at the Commission against the state are negligible as compared to those received against the then rebel party. The causes of displacement, as reported by the victims in the complaint forms, are internal armed conflict, natural disasters, bonded-labourers and government development projects.

- Continuous monitoring of the IDPs activities and their human rights' violation by the state and other actors. Following are the monitoring activities carried out by the Commission.
  - *(a)* IDPs Temporary Shelters in various parts of Kathmandu, May 2005;
  - *(b)* Demonstration of IDPs to draw the attention of the government and other stakeholders towards their plights in Kathmandu, May 2005;
  - *(c)* Monitoring and interaction with the detained IDPs at Bhaktapur, June 2005;
  - *(d)* Monitoring and Interaction with IDPs taking shelter in Gopal Dharmashala and Mandal Kuti in Janakpur, 2006;
  - *(e)* Monitoring of the IDPs demonstration in front of the government secretariat (Singhadurbar), March 2007;
  - *(f)* Monitoring of the demonstration of IDPs in front of Nepal Food Corporation, OHCHR, NHRC and offices of major political parties, during February and March 2007;
  - (g) Monitoring of human rights' situations of victims of Koshi River flood and flash flood in Kailali district completed and recommendations submitted to the government for swift actions for their relief and rehabilitation;
  - *(h)* Completed IDPs-specific situation monitoring in Doti, Surkhet, Baglung, Dhading, Dolakha, Ramechhap, Bara, Dhanusha, Banke, Kailali, Kapilbastu and Saptari districts, 2006-2007. Besides, the local offices of NHRC in the regions and district monitor HR vio-

lation in their respective working areas on regular basis. The NHRC has completed monitoring of human rights' situation in 73 districts till date during which the staff collected cases of human rights' violations of IDPs as one of the components of the entire monitoring process. The cases related to the human rights' violations of IDPs received separate space in the monitoring reports prepared by the Commission.

(i) Continued monitoring of the CPA and drawing attention of the non-compliance of the provisions mentioned specifically for the right to return and return of the properties confiscated during the war. However, such effort has not been given due respect by the government or the concerned political party.

After completing the monitoring, the team prepares the monitoring report and submits to the Commission for its review, which discusses the report with the team and puts it to the meeting of the Commission for formal approval. Based on the report, the Commission submits written recommendations to the government for necessary actions. Upon receiving the written recommendations, the concerned body or authority shall take action as required by the Commission, or if such action cannot be taken, the concerned body or authority shall send its report of the action taken within three months from the date of receipt of the intimation from the Commission.[22] In case of non-compliance by the concerned authority, the Commission shall publish names of violators; draw attention of legislators; lobby and recommend for necessary changes in constitution and laws; file litigation of cases; and publish report on non-implementation of NHRC decisions. The same process applies for the findings of the investigation of cases related to human rights' violations of people. The Commission has already submitted at least 12 cases related to the violations of human rights of IDPs, but no action has been taken by the government till date.

Investigating cases of human rights' violations of the IDPs on complaint as well as on suo moto basis[23] such as people displaced by flood in Chitwan district (2004), murder of an IDP in Bardiya and Janakpur, displacement of indigenous Chepang community in Dhading district (2006) because of stone quarrying by Hetauda Cement Factory and backlog cases investigation in Ramechhap, Dolakha, Sindhuli and Chitwan during 2006/2007. As a result of the monitoring, the Commission recommended the government to provide the IDPs with facilities in accordance with the UN Guiding Principles on Internal Displacement and existing Nepali laws. It also urged the government to provide food, shelter, clothing, medical treatment and medicine, employment and education to IDPs.

The Commission has also submitted a recommendation to the Government of Nepal to take necessary and immediate action to return, rehabilitate, resettle and reintegrate IDPs, not to use excessive force during peaceful demonstrations. It also recommended to the government for immediate and unconditional release of IDPs detained during the peaceful demonstration.

The Commission follows up with specific complaints with the concerned Government of Nepal and CPN(M) authorities, but there has never been any response from either side to NHRC concerns.

It organized a workshop on the UN Guiding Principles on Internal Displacement in collaboration with the Brooking Bern Project on Internal Displacement during 2004 (for all concerned stakeholders) and in 2006 (for the staff of NHRC).

The Commission has been actively engaged in pursuing the government to formulate the National Policies on IDPs. It submitted recommendations for the immediate formulation of the policies, took part in the meeting organized by the Ministry of Peace and Reconstruction (MoPR), it reviewed the draft policy document and submitted its recommendations to the government through MoPR.

As a result of the monitoring and the investigation, the Commission refers cases for legal aid (to Nepal Bar Association, legal aid NGOs such as Legal Aid and Counselling Centre (LACC) and Forum for Women, Law and Development (FWLD); cases in immediate relief to the Government of Nepal, Nepal Red Cross Society, World Food Organization (FAO) and International Red Cross and Red Crescent (ICRC); cases in need for return, resettlement and reintegration, education and trauma healing to NGOs such as Caritas and Informal Sector Service Centre (INSEC),[24] Child workers in Nepal (CWIN) and Centre for Victims of Torture (CVICT).

Problems faced by the NHRC in protecting the rights of IDPs

Despite various policy level efforts made and corresponding activities implemented by the Commission, it faces many weaknesses and challenges in effectively and efficiently implementing the protection strategies to address the human rights (HR) violations of the people in general and IDPs, in particular.

The Commission lacks a holistic approach in addressing the issue of IDPs as it focuses on protecting the rights of conflict-induced IDPs. The latest Strategic Plan does not say anything about the protection of the rights of people forced to move out of the ancestral places as a result of government (and other) projects and natural disasters.

The Commission has limited reach to monitor regularly the HR violations in a comprehensive manner. It has only four regional offices and five contact offices (of an ad hoc nature), which are not capable of monitoring the HR violation cases throughout the country by making its presence felt instantly in the places of violence or other HR violation incidents. Further, the Commission lacks staff with a minimum required knowledge on issues of forced migration and the vulnerability associated with it. The limited number of staff in its head-quarters and four regional offices along with some staff (of an ad hoc basis) in the five district-offices are too small in number and capability to focus their work on the issues of IDPs, which is one of the components of a broader human rights violation framework. As a result, the IDP-related activities of the Commission are sporadic in nature and lack continuity and are also first-hand experiences in many cases. The NHRC staff depends on the media and other NGOs as sources of information of HR violation to take decision on further action. It also leads to a situation where the NHRC is out of reach of many victims because of the lack of formal presence of the Commission in their close proximity.

Despite having upgraded to constitutional status, the recommendations submitted by the Commission to the government and other parties are rarely addressed. Despite carrying out investigation on cases of serious human rights violations such as the brutal killing of innocent people by the Maoist and mass disappearance of (suspected) 65 Maoist cadres from the army detention, the Commission has not been able to go into further details to investigate the violation of the rights of IDPs and their sufferings. Further, the lack of respect for the NHRC among the political stakeholders in general and the government, in particular, is the major problem in paralyzing the effectiveness and efficiency of the Commission. Many senior government officials consider the human rights issue to be of less importance—especially if the offender is closer to them by political ideology or some other relationship—and tend to ignore their accountability towards the mandate and decisions of the Commission.

The political decision has prevailed over the unbiased and independent nature of the Commission, which is reflected, to some extent, in the appointment of the commissioners and strong political domination and sharing of the appointments among the loyalists of the political parties, rather than based on meritocracy. The NHRC suffered a serious setback in 2005-2006 when the government, during the king's rule and the subsequent government led by political parties, did not bother to appoint the chairperson and commissioners for almost two years, once the term of the earlier Commission was over. In that duration, the Commission remained as a mere spectator of the human rights violations of people.

The issue of human rights violation of IDPs has been unnecessarily politicized by different political parties based on their vested interest, despite the (so-called) firm commitment expressed in the Comprehensive Peace Accord (CPA) and other accords, agreements, decisions and Ceasefire Code of Conduct. Most of the IDPs still living in limbo are Maoist victims and were displaced by Maoists cadres during the war. Many claim that their fixed assets, including land, have been captured by the Maoists and redistributed among the poor and marginalized people from the same localities. Once the Maoists ascended to the power, the issue became more complicated because of the Maoists' tendency of ignoring the outcry of the IDPs and the opposition's (especially Nepal Congress) tendency of politically and emotionally highlighting the issue as much as possible, to gain political benefit and to denounce the CPN(M) among the public. The NHRC is also helpless in this regard and it limits its activities to monitor the activities of the Maoists and issue press statements as both the government and the opposition are focused on taking political benefit out of the human rights violations of the people, rather than focusing on restoring their pride.

One of the weaknesses of the NHRC is the data management system. The Commission has not been able to develop a consolidated data management system. As a result, all the complaints received from the victims, various findings of the monitoring and investigation, record on compliance and non-compliance of the recommendations made by the Commission and the number of individuals included in the complaints have not been summarized yet. Further, there is a lack of database linkage between the headquarters and the regional and district offices.

Most of the recommendations regarding the IDPs are

focused on compensation and rehabilitation. However, the lack of appropriate basis impacts on deciding the level of compensation for the victims in the existing NHRC Act, 1997, and NHRC (Complaints, Action and Fixing Compensation) Guidelines. Thus, compensations recommended by the Commission, at times, become controversial and too small to be considered as a fair compensation. Since these documents were passed long before the formation of the Interim Constitution, 2007, and the National Policies on IDPs, the Act and Guidelines are considered to be outdated.

The Commission is also trying to develop strong linkage with media as guided by its Strategic Plan (2008-2010) to highlight the issue of HR violations of IDPs. It organizes press conference to disseminate the findings of its monitoring and investigations. However, the Commission has not been able to motivate the media to pay enough attention towards the plights of IDPs. Most of the time, the media picks issues from the NGOs which publish their reports overnight on the issues of HR violations, whereas the Commission publishes its report a few days after the incident has taken place, after proper and detailed investigation. As a result the issue does not remain a saleable issue for the media.

Despite such challenges and shortcomings, the National Human Rights Commission, Nepal, believes that it has got recognition of being the strongest Commission in the South Asia Region because of its constitutional status and its experience of the comparatively lower level of political intervention by the government. Following are some of the general recommendations to make it further effective in protecting human rights of IDPs/victims.

- The NHRC should revise the section related to IDPs in its strategic plan, make it holistic by including all types of IDPs in its protection framework and should make itself sole campaigner for protecting the rights of people displaced by causes other than the People's War.

- The Commission needs to plan and work for expanding its coverage by establishing offices in more districts and geographic regions to increase its immediate reach as well as to make its presence felt by the victims.
- Further, the Commission should work in building the capacity of staff responsible for implementing activities related to IDPs, assist them in acquiring more knowledge on the issue of IDPs, their knowledge on UN Guiding Principles, National Policies on IDPs and the Procedural Directives as well as the vulnerability associated with different groups of IDPs. Such an effort would make the staff more efficient and effective in handling the cases related to the human rights violation of IDPs.
- The Commission as well as the IDP Unit should develop a consolidated data management system which helps in developing a clear picture of the entire protection mechanism regarding the HR situation of people, in general, and IDPs, in particular.
- There is also a need for developing a rapid investigation and reporting mechanism in order to draw the attention of the media, the government and other concerned national and international stakeholders, so that authentic information is disseminated immediately after the incidents take place and superficial and unauthorized reporting does not reach the general public. This helps in minimizing further conflict in the society.
- The Commission should work closely with civil society and NGOs to make the ruling authority realize its importance and its mandate and press the government for implementing its recommendations. It needs to develop strategies towards making the political stake-holders and the government more accountable towards its mandate and the recommendations. As a constitutional Commission,[25] it needs to establish its constitutional authority firmly so that the government is compelled to implement the recommendations and not drag its feet.

- The Commission should mobilize civil society and the NGO sector to increase awareness regarding its potential role in protecting the human rights of people as well as in raising awareness on various important documents such as the UN Guiding Principles on Internal Displacement, National Policies on IDPs (yet to be approved), Procedural Directives to implement the Policy, and other international humanitarian laws to which Nepal is a party.
- The commissioners should be highly accountable towards the ethics of care and work independently by raising themselves over the vested agendas of the political parties. The Commission should be alert in pointing out the politicization of the plights of IDPs by the political parties and should make its voice heard strongly against such acts, regardless of the political parties.
- Finally, there is an urgent need for revising the existing NHRC (Complaints, Action and Fixing Compensation) Regulation 2000, to embrace the spirit of the UN Guiding Principles of Internal Displacement and National Policies on IDPs 2007. Moreover, there is also the need for increasing and specifying the amount of compensation in the Guidelines to make the compensation of the HR violation of the individual or the family fair and just.

NOTES

1 Paper prepared for the 'Dialogue on Protection Strategies for People in Situations of Forced Migration' organized by Mahanirban Calcutta Research Group (MCRG) in collaboration with the UNHCR, as a special part of the Sixth Annual Winter Course on Forced Migration, on 14 and 15 December 2008 in Kolkata.
2 Global IDP Project, 2005.
3 SAFHR 2005.
4 Ibid.

5 See Dixit 1994; Pandey 1998; Bhattarai 2001; Dhungana 2007.
6 Bhattarai 2001.
7 Dhungana 2007. The Koshi River flood displaced around two million people in Bihar, India, alone.
8 Ibid.
9 Some people even estimate the number of bonded labourers to be as high as 200,000. See Dhungana, 2007.
10 Ibid.
11 UN, 'Nepal: Common Appeal for Transition Support Mid-Year Review' (Kathmandu: UN, 2008).
12 UNHCR 2006; OCHA 2006.
13 Doesn't mention anything about the displaced ordinary citizens and activists of other political parties not belonging to the Seven-Party Alliance (SPA). Twelve-Point Agreement signed between the Seven Party Alliance (SPA) and the CPN(M). New Delhi: 22 November 2005 www.peace.gov.np.
14 Article 4.1 of National Policies on IDPs, March 2006 has provision on 'Identification of the Conflict Displaced Person or Family', which stipulates:
   (i) Joint family dependent on the person killed by the terrorists;
   (ii) Dependent family of the of the person kidnapped and subsequently disappeared or declared dead by the terrorists;
   (iii) Persons who have received serious threats or have been forced out of their villages after their property was seized by the terrorists;
   (iv) Persons or families who have been mentally or physically tortured by the terrorists;
   (v) Persons or families who house has been destroyed by the terrorists;
   (vi) Persons who have shunned terrorist activities and surrendered but cannot live in the place of their residence from the security point of view;
   (vii) Dependent families of innocent persons killed during encounters;
   (viii) Persons who have been displaced due to damages to their property during clashes.
15 CPA, 2006.
16 UN, 'Nepal Common Appeal', 2008.
17 IDMC, 2006.

18 UN/IASC, 2007.
19 UNIP, 2006.
20 NHRC, 2008: 15-18.
21 Based on the information provided by the IDP Unit, Protection and Monitoring Section of NHRC.
22 Government of Nepal 1997. The NHRG of Nepal was established on 26 May 2000 under the Human Rights Commission Act, 1997. The Interim Constitution of Nepal, 2007, elevated its status to a constitutional body and broadened its mandate regarding protection, promotional and respect for human rights.
23 The IDP unit has investigated 7 cases of human rights violations of IDPs till 2008.
24 INSEC is in all 75 districts of Nepal for civil monitoring of the Human rights violations of people.
25 The NHRC as a Constitutional Commission, needs to establish its constitutional authority firmly so that the government is compelled to implement the recommendations without dragging its feet.

Bibliography

Bhattarai Ananda M., *Displacement and Rehabilitation in Nepal: Law, Policy and Practice,* Kathmandu: Anmol Publications, 2001.

Dhungana, Shiva K., 'The Policy of the Government of Nepal towards the Internally Displaced Persons; in *Limits of the Humanitarian: Studies in Situations of Forced Migration, Policies and Practices,* no. 17, Kolkata: Calcutta Research Group, December, 2007.

Dixit, Ajaya. 'Water Projects in Nepal: Lessons from Displacement and Rehabilitation', *Water Nepal* 4, 1. Kathmandu: Nepal Water Conservation Foundation, 1994, pp.74-85.

Global IDP Project, *Internal Displacement: Global Overview of Trends and Developments in 2004.* Geneva: Norwegian Refugee Council, 2005.

Government of Nepal. Ceasefire Code of Conduct Signed between the Government of Nepal and CPN(M), 25 May 2006,Kathmandu: Ministry of Peace and Reconstruction.

——, National Human Rights Commission Act, 2053, HMG/N. 1997, Kathmandu: Ministry of Law, Justice and Parliamentary Affairs, 1997.

——, National Policies on IDPs, Ministry of Peace and Reconstruction, April 2007. www.peace.gov.np.

IDMC, 'Nepal: IDP Return Still a Trickle Despite Ceasefire: A Profile of Internal Displacement situation Internal Displacement Monitoring Centre', Norwegian Refugee Council, 16 October 2006. www.internal-displacement.org.

Informal Sector Service Centre (INSEC), Informal: *Special Issue on IDPs*, 19, 2 & 3 (September; December 2005). Kathmandu: Informal Sector Service Centre, pp.2, 18.

National Human rights Commission of Nepal (NHRC), 'National Human Rights Action Plan 2004-2008', Kathmandu: NHRC, Pulchowk.

——, 'Strategic Plan, 2008-2010', Kathmandu: NHRC, Pulchowk.

Office for the Coordination of Humanitarian Affairs (OCHA), *Guiding Principles on Internal Displacement*, Kathmandu: OCHA, 2004.

——, *The Internally Displaced Persons: Current Status,* Kathmandu: OCHA, *Thematic Report*, issue 1, (6 September 2006).

Pandey, Bikash, *Dams and Civil Society in Nepal: Major Concerns*. World Commission on Dams, 1998. Katmandu: SAFHR, 2005.

UN, 'Nepal: Common Appeal for Transition Support. Mid-Year Review', Kathmandu: UN, 2008.

UNHCR, *UNHCR's Expanded Role in Support for the Inter Agency Response to Internal Displacement Situations.* New York: UNHCR, 2006.

UN/IASC, *Nepal 2007-Midyear Review: Common Appeal for Transition Support,* Kathmandu: UN/Inter Agency Standing Committee-Nepal, 2007, p.14.

UNIP, 'IDP Protection Sub-Group. Coordination Mechanism in Nepal', UN Information Platform, 2006. www.un.org.np/meetings /coordination.php (Accessed 27 October 2008).

13

NATIONAL HUMAN RIGHTS COMMISSIONS (NHRCs) AND INTERNALLY DISPLACED PERSONS (IDPs): The Sri Lankan Experience

MARIO GOMEZ

Although the first Human Rights Commission (HRC) was set up in Canada in 1947, HRCs received prominence after the UN began to actively promote the concept.[1]

After the endorsement by the UN Commission on Human Rights in 1992 and by the General Assembly and Vienna World Conference in 1993, of the 'Principles Relating to the Status and Functioning of National Institutions for the Protection and Promotion of Human Rights' (Paris Principles), the Office of the UN High Commissioner for Human Rights (OHCHR) initiated a programme that provides support for countries that are in the process of setting up such institutions.

Evaluations of NHRCs have been mixed. As one expert who has studied these commissions commented, 'The rapid proliferation of these institutions, though widely celebrated, is in many ways puzzling. It is unclear why some governments would create national institutions to implement international norms that they routinely violate. Nor is it self-evident why very different states would create NHRIs that are remarkably similar'.[2] Nevertheless, some human rights commissions have performed effectively. For the human rights activist the question is how national institutions can be used in a positive way. What roles and functions can they best perform? Are the roles and functions they best perform determined largely by each country's social and political context or are there general or universal roles for these institutions? Should activists engage with these institutions or ignore them? If they do engage with them, what should be the nature of the engagement and what sort of resources and energy should be put into this engagement?

THE SRI LANKAN HUMAN RIGHTS COMMISSION

In response to both international and domestic pressures, the Sri Lankan Parliament passed a legislation in 1996 establishing a permanent Human Rights Commission (HRC).[3] The Commission started functioning in July 1997. It moved cautiously in interpreting its mandate and focused mainly on receiving and resolving complaints from individual victims or persons acting on their behalf. While the Sri Lankan human rights movement had great expectations for the Commission, the latter's profile during its first three years was low and public awareness of its activities was limited. It had only a marginal impact on the advancement of human rights in the country. The new group of Human Rights Commissioners who took office in 2000 (and who for the first time included a woman) envisaged a broader role for the HRC. One of the Commission's early decisions was to examine the status of vulnerable groups and three groups were identified: women, persons with disabilities and IDPs. The Commission decided to initiate a study into the status of the IDPs, a fluctuating population between 500,000 to one million for more than twenty years.

Since displacement had been affecting the human rights of a significant part of the Sri Lankan population for a number of years, the Commission sought to generate a set of findings and recommendations that would identify a role for it in this area, help it to intervene in an effective and sustained way and to identify possible areas of collaboration between it and other organizations working in this area. Another purpose of the study was to ascertain the potential for applying the Guiding Principles on Internal Displacement in Sri Lanka. At the international level, the Representative of the UN Secretary-General on IDPs had developed Guiding Principles culled from international human rights law, humanitarian law and refugee law by analogy. These Principles constitute a set of human rights standards that should apply during the different phases of displacement: pre-displacement, during displacement and during return or resettlement and reintegration.

INTERNAL DISPLACEMENT IN SRI LANKA

For almost a million Sri Lankans, the right to freedom of movement guaranteed by the country's Constitution and the International Covenants on Human Rights has been until recently largely an illusion.[4] The IDPs, the group closest to the ethnic conflict, have had little choice in opting to remain or to flee. As a group they are identified by a common history of uprootedness and continue to have fewer opportunities to meet their basic needs than those Sri Lankans who have not been forcibly displaced. The experiences of the displaced have varied. While they share a common experience, in that they have all been uprooted and forced to flee, their experiences as displaced persons have differed depending on their geographical location, their ethnic background, the interaction they have had with local and international NGOs and their relationship with the local population.[5]

The conflict in Sri Lanka has generated at least six broad categories of displaced persons:

- Those displaced and living in camps (or welfare centres);
- Those displaced and living outside camps (or welfare cen-

tres);

- Refugees who have returned from Tamil Nadu, India and are living in transit camps;
- Those who have been resettled;
- Refugees being repatriated by Western governments; and
- Refugees outside the country.

In the early 1990s, the situation with regard to the displaced population was relatively stable. The LTTE had de facto control over most of the Jaffna Peninsula while the government forces made an attempt to regain control in the east. In 1992 and 1993 many people were re-settled in the east, in Mannar and some other areas, in a government-sponsored initiative and many returned from refugee camps in southern India in a UNHCR-sponsored initiative. Previously the state and NGOs had focused almost exclusively on providing emergency relief and assistance. This was shaped by the belief that displacement was a short-term phenomenon which needed to be addressed through short-term strategies.

However, as displacement acquired a semi-permanent character, approaches changed. The emphasis shifted to helping the displaced 'take responsibility for their lives' and trying to foster a sense of independence among the displaced. Less attention was given to 'handouts' and increased attention to activities that were geared to establishing self-reliance. Thus, access to employment emerged as a major concern. In the wake of the October 1995 offensive, the emphasis again shifted to 'relief and assistance' because of the massive displacement that took place and the humanitarian consequences that ensued.

October 1995 was a turning point. The Sri Lankan armed forces, which until that point had been content to let the LTTE control most of the Jaffna Peninsula, launched a major operation to take control of the Peninsula. Thousands left the Peninsula as a result of this operation. Many left because of LTTE pressure, while others fled the shelling and the bombing that accompanied the operation. In December 1995 the Sri

Lankan armed forces took control of a largely empty Jaffna town, and in April 1996, after a further operation, they resumed control of much of the Jaffna Peninsula. It was estimated that the Sri Lankan armed forces controlled between 60 to 80 per cent of the Jaffna Peninsula at the end of 1996. In 2000, the LTTE launched a counter operation to re-take control of Jaffna. While they succeeded in re-capturing significant portions of the territory, they failed to re-take Jaffna. The ensuing battles had adverse consequences for civilian life in the area.

The Government of Sri Lanka had assumed some responsibility towards the displaced but its policy was heavily influenced by military imperatives. The military and defence apparatus had played a crucial role in determining the extent and nature of the humanitarian response to the displaced, including the range and quantity of supplies that would reach the conflict areas. Almost all supplies sent to the conflict areas required clearance by the Ministry of Defence, which sometimes took many months, resulting in delayed deliveries of food and medicines.

WOMEN AND DISPLACEMENT

In a report released in January 1994, the US Committee for Refugees (USCR), a Washington-based NGO, quoted a female NGO worker who observed:

> The people most affected by this conflict have been women—morally, physically, financially. Some lost not only their husbands, but also their grown sons. Many women are traumatized, they don't know for sure if their husbands [disappeared or] are dead or alive; some have been in and out of camps since 1985.[6]

In Sri Lanka, the number of displaced women exceeds those of the men significantly. In addition to the problems shared by other IDPs, women also face gender-based discrimination and are exposed to gender-specific violence and exploitation.[7] In 1993, the Representative of the Secretary-General reported that some women had been raped prior to being displaced.[8] Incidents of rape in the conflict areas continued to increase.[9] An Amnesty International report noted a 'marked rise' in allegations of rape by police, army and navy personnel in 2001 and observed that among the victims of rape by security forces were 'many internally displaced women'.[10] The UN Committee on the Elimination of Discrimination against Women (CEDAW Committee), in its Concluding Comments on Sri Lanka, noted with alarm 'the high and severe incidences of rape and other forms of violence targeted against Tamil women by the police and security forces in the conflict areas'.[11]

The USCR team which visited Jaffna in November 1996 reported that many instances had not been reported because of the fear of retribution and the social stigma attached to rape.[12] The collapse of community and family structures, including the support provided by the extended family, had made displaced women even more vulnerable. The UN Special Rapporteur on Violence against Women observed that lack of access to health care and food had been one of the main problems faced by refugees and the internally displaced women generally.[13] In some cases women had lost their husbands and thus the burden of carrying on with family life had fallen exclusively on them.

Displacement has affected the human right to privacy in significant ways.[14] The conditions of existence of most of the residents in camps resulted in particularly severe invasions of privacy, especially for women. Their 'areas' of habitation were sometimes cordoned off only by old saris and other pieces of rags. A representative of a donor agency who visited Vavuniya in November 1996 observed that at least two women had been forced to give birth in the overcrowded, unhygienic detention centres in Vavuniya town. USCR observed that two babies were still-born in the Vavuniya detention centres in 1996.[15]

KEY FINDINGS OF THE STUDY

According to the study, in Sri Lanka, every single right spelled out in the Guiding Principles on Internal Displacement was not being fully complied with. While different segments of the IDP population experienced violations differently, harassment, arrests, abductions, rapes, torture, executions, exploitation and imprisonment were part of their general existence. Certain categories of displaced people, such as females and single heads of households, the elderly and the disabled, were particularly vulnerable. The study concluded that these people's special needs were not being effectively addressed and their rights to life and dignity were being violated.

Another key conclusion was the lack of a coherent policy on displacement. According to the study:

> Without doubt the most worrying concern is the lack of a governmental framework on displacement or of a clear division of responsibilities among Government Departments and Aid Agencies. No ministry has overall responsibility for the welfare of the IDPs nor are there comprehensive policies or guidelines on displacement. Various departments, ministries and aid agencies are responsible for various aspects of relief, protection and assistance. The allocation of ministerial areas of responsibility appears to be driven by political motives, such as securing a vote base.

The study observed that one of the biggest obstacles was the lack of vision on the part of the government. In addition, a number of state entities were involved with little coordination among them. There were some areas, especially with regard to arrest and detention, in which the IDPs were particularly vulnerable. Amending the Prevention of Terrorism Act and the Emergency Regulations to bring them into line with international human rights principles was a matter of priority and the study recommended that this was an intervention that the HRC was well placed to make.

What was most lacking was the political will to respond to the needs of the IDPs based on a recognition of their rights. What was also highlighted was the discrimination that resulted from the operation of a complex 'pass' system. Those living in 'uncleared areas' or areas controlled by the LTTE had to obtain permission from both the LTTE and the government to travel south. Many were virtual prisoners in the Vanni as the LTTE imposed stringent restrictions on the movement of civilians in areas under its control. Compulsory training and forced recruitment into its ranks, inclusion of children, was widely reported. Those who lived in the transit point of Vavuniya, which was technically under the control of the state, had to obtain clearance from the security forces to proceed further south.

The lack of coordination among the different aid organizations in the distribution of food and other relief was also highlighted. Security concerns, including frequent arrests and abductions, contributed to the vulnerability that the IDPs faced. The role of paramilitary groups that until recently officially assisted the Sri Lankan army was highlighted and the study observed that both the army and the paramilitary groups were responsible for an unacceptable number of arbitrary arrests, illegal detentions, torture, rape and 'disappearances'. Abduction and extortion of money by the LTTE were also highlighted.

The plight of the displaced was made worse by the then existing government policy regarding the provision of relief and other assistance. Only 50 per cent of the dry food rations needed was reported to reach affected areas. Other food items to be sold in Multi Purpose Co-Operative Society outlets were overpriced and in very short supply. The study noted that recurrent shortages, delays and sudden blockades had given rise to the allegation that the Sri Lankan army was using food as a method of combat. The LTTE was also accused of diverting food and other items meant for displaced populations.

According to the study, malnutrition was reportedly very severe in the areas under LTTE control. The embargo on so-called 'war related items' further affected the welfare of those populations. Restricted items reportedly included kerosene, fertilizers, fishing equipment, construction materials, batteries, books, maps and ink, among others. Medical equipment and medicines were also subject to embargoes as well as delays and shortages. Poor hospital and transport facilities further affected the health of civilians in those areas.

The study also issued findings with reference to the role of the regional network of the HRC. The study concluded that the Commission's regional coordinators were not equipped to deal with the problems of the IDPs. The lack of a special desk or unit in the HRC's main office in Colombo was another factor highlighted in the report. IDP complaints were grouped with other complaints, and until recently, the Commission did not focus on IDPs as a distinct category. The study concluded that both the main office in Colombo and its regional offices did not possess the sensitivity or capacity to respond to IDP concerns effectively.

RESPONSE TO THE STUDY

Subsequent to the publication of the study, UNHCR committed itself to help develop the capacity of the Commission to respond to IDPs. The first step it took was to invite two consultants to examine how the Commission could begin to address IDP concerns seriously. It then went a step further with the decision to support the establishment of a unit at the Commission's main office in Colombo and desks in select regional offices that had within their jurisdiction large numbers of IDPs.

The NGOs that collaborated on the study had also begun to explore the possibility of specific projects aimed at the Commission. The Consortium of Humanitarian Agencies

(CHA), which interviewed regional coordinators for this study, looked into the possibility of conducting regular training programmes for Commission's field office staff as well as developing programmes of legal aid for the displaced. UNHCR and the Bar Association of Sri Lanka also began to look at developing a legal aid programme aimed specifically at the displaced.

The ceasefire and the possibility of a negotiated solution to the ethnic conflict were likely to require additional responses and solutions. In the event that peace did return, displacement policy would need to shift from a focus on emergency relief and assistance to a focus on return, reintegration and resettlement. Other questions such as compensation for past abuses would also need to be addressed by the Commission unless another mechanism is set up as part of the peace settlement.

THE POTENTIAL OF NHRCS

Although a human rights commission is an institution set up by the state and funded by the state, it is supposed to possess autonomy so as to enable it to investigate the conduct of the state. The Commission should therefore have the power to monitor and scrutinize the state's performance in terms of human rights criteria and develop the capacity to challenge state actions when the situation so warrants.

In 1998 the UN Committee on Economic, Social and Cultural Rights adopted a General Comment on the role of NHRCs in the protection of economic and social rights.[16] The committee noted that national institutions have a potentially crucial role to play in promoting and ensuring the indivisibility and interdependence of all human rights.

Many commissions have had to function in political contexts in which the commitment to human rights is poor and governments are sensitive to any criticism of their record.

In some countries, commissions have been constrained by narrow mandates and precluded from examining sensitive areas of governmental action.

At the same time, some commissions have taken effective steps, as in the case of Sri Lanka's Commission, innovatively extending its work to encompass IDPs. Of course, there has to be a compelling domestic reason for HRCs to address the rights and concerns of the IDPs. Where the rights of large numbers of IDPs are under threat, this clearly warrants priority attention from the HRC.

HRCs are part of a larger global trend of 'institution building'. Globally, a variety of institutions have been set up to advance human rights and democracy. Human rights commissions, truth commissions, ombudspersons, women's commissions, election commissions, commissions to deal with corruption and entities dealing with the rights of children and the application of humanitarian law are part of this larger global trend. In one sense, this process of global institution building is an attempt to occupy some of the space that courts have occupied. In many countries, although not in all, courts have occupied a peculiar space between state and civil society. This process of global institution building has been at least partly an attempt to create 'court like' institutions, but without many of the procedures and trappings that constrain courts. This process of global institution building has attempted to create independent and autonomous institutions with a procedural flexibility that will enable them to pursue multiple strategies in their methods of work. The ideal human rights commission would be an entity that is on a solid legal foundation, financially secure, independent of government and possessing a capacity to engage in strategies that NGOs frequently use. Their location inside the government, yet independent of the government, places them in a position to help develop human rights capacities within the government.

While the powers of NHRCs in different countries vary,

there seems to be a 'core' concept emerging. One possible consequence of this 'globalization' of HRCs is the cross-fertilization of ideas and jurisprudence that may take place. Like courts, commissions will hopefully borrow from one another's jurisprudence and ideas. The integration of national institutions into regional and global networks will provide ways of internationalizing their work and provide some measure of protection from 'unfriendly' political regimes.

NHRCS AND INTERNAL DISPLACEMENT

A recent report of an International Colloquy on the Guiding Principles on Internal Displacement noted that internal displacement was often a critical aspect of the human rights situations that fall within the mandates of human rights commissions and should be an essential part of their work. The report went on to state:

> Considerable scope exists for making use of the Guiding Principles in the four areas of work typical to national commissions: investigating individual complaints; monitoring government compliance with treaty obligations; providing advice to government officials and legislators on draft legislation; and engaging in raising awareness and human rights education, especially among national and local authorities, the police and the military. Two general strategies were proposed for facilitating the inclusion of the Guiding Principles into these four areas, notably, mainstreaming the Guiding Principles into the work of national commissions, especially at the field level; and promoting their use in policy formulation and advocacy work, for example through their inclusion in draft laws and in dialogue with governments. —'Report of the International Colloquy on the Guiding Principles on Internal Displacement', Vienna, 21-23 Sept 2000, Brookings Institution Project on Internal Displacement, p.26.

The experience of the Sri Lankan Human Rights Commission with IDPs raises several questions for HRCs worldwide. Do these commissions possess the potential to begin looking at the rights of the IDPs in a sustained and systematic way? What comparative advantage do they have over other institutions? Their comparative advantage lies in their location within the government and this gives them access to a wide range of actors who are either involved in the conflict or in providing relief and assistance to the displaced. It also comes from their ability to engage in a wide range of intervention strategies, both on their own and in combination with other actors. Their location within the government gives them the opportunity to use both strategies of shame and strategies of negotiation to advance the rights of the displaced. Their status as a national institution enables them to critique government policy and to go public with their findings, which are likely to have more impact than the pronouncements of NGOs.

With regard to internal displacement, there are a number of activities that HRCs are well positioned to do, including:

- Monitor access to the displaced and their ability to receive basic supplies such as food and medicine;
- Visit camps and other places where the displaced are located and obtain accurate assessments of the conditions under which they live;
- Conduct broader field surveys on a periodic basis, which would include gathering information on how the displaced populations are interacting with the local population, the state of basic services in those areas;
- Receive complaints and mediate or adjudicate them;
- Go to court where necessary, to enforce recommendations, especially where the Commission makes a finding that rights have been violated;
- Engage with the military to ensure that the civilian populations are spared the consequences of the conflict and that

military imperatives do not prevent assistance from reaching IDPs;

- Engage with non-state actors where this is possible to minimize the consequences of the conflict on civilians;
- Assist policy makers in framing policy that takes into account the rights and needs of the displaced;
- Develop legislation beneficial to the displaced, based on the Guiding Principles on Internal Displacement;
- Engage with the relevant government institutions responsible for providing assistance and protection to the displaced;
- Provide a conduit for displaced populations and humanitarian organizations to hold a dialogue with governments and state institutions;
- Develop a human rights capacity within state institutions, especially a capacity to respond to IDP rights and a sensitivity to their needs.

In some contexts, its stature as a 'national institution' will enable HRCs to engage with the parties to the conflict: the state and the non-state actor or actors. This will depend to a large degree on the public credibility and stature of the commissioners.

At the normative level, the Guiding Principles on Internal Displacement should provide the framework to guide commissions in their actions. One innovative regional initiative being undertaken to achieve the integration of internal displacement and the Guiding Principles into the work of NHRCs has been launched by the Asia Pacific Forum of National Human Rights Institutions. Indeed, it was partly because of the Forum's encouragement that the Sri Lankan Commission was led to study the role it could play with IDPs. The Forum could also act as a conduit between its member commissions and the OHCHR, where technical and human resource support may be available. Where development-induced displacement is the concern, the Forum could provide specific support to local commissions to negotiate with the multilateral or bilateral donors supporting the 'displacement causing' project to ensure that standards are met.

CONCLUSION

IDPs clearly count among society's most vulnerable groups. Displacement affects in important ways the quality of education, health care, housing and water to which the displaced have access. Little opportunity exists for their cultural activity; where capacity and ability to work have been affected. And at a different but also important level, their ability to participate in and influence the political process may be restricted. In effect, a broad range of the IDPs' rights: civil, political, economic, social and cultural, have been infringed. Yet few national commissions have sought to address the plight of the internally displaced. At a theoretical level, national commissions remain very exciting institutions. At a practical level, they have a long way to go. The few success stories do raise the possibility that commissions can emerge as effective institutions over a period of time with the support of the domestic and international human rights community. While governments may have been motivated by their own political agendas in setting up these institutions, the institutions have the potential to take on a life of their own, depending on the social and political contexts, the personalities and staff that direct the institutions and the type of engagement that civil society actors have with these institutions.

As the Sri Lankan experience shows, national human rights commissions provide one way of responding to the concerns of IDPs. As we have seen, their location within the government enables them to interact with government entities on a variety of human rights themes in a way that few other institutions can do. Their status as a national institution positions them well to conduct inquiries into systematic violations and to publish reports and recommendations with regard to the displaced. These reports and recommendations have the potential to have impact, if the inquiries have been conducted transparently and in consultation with local constituencies. Their location also enables them to begin to build human rights capacity and sensitivity within government institutions, including government ministries and departments. This is essential to the commissions' ability to act effectively.

Indeed, the creation of HRCs has generated expectations on the part of domestic human rights movements. Yet, most commissions lack the resources and capacity to respond to even half of what local activists expect of them. At the same time, in many societies, these institutions have not exploited their position to do what might be reasonably expected of them even within their limited capacities. For national human rights commissions, the challenge would be to generate the capacity within the institution to perform these tasks.

NOTES

1 Excerpted from a larger paper of the same title. The Brookings - SAIS Project on Internal Displacement (Washington, DC: Brookings Institution, July 2002).
2 Excerpted from a larger paper of the same title. Sonia Cardenas, 'Adaptive States: The Proliferation of National Human Rights Institutions,' Working Paper (Cambridge, Ma: Carr Center for Human Rights Policy, Harvard University, 2001).
3 The legislation establishing the Commission provided it with a broad range of powers that included investigating and mediating human rights complaints, advising government departments on incorporating human rights criteria into legislation and administrative practices, engaging in human rights education,

reforming existing legislation, initiating investigations on its own initiative, and generating research and documentation. Among the other powers of the Commission was the authority to intervene in ongoing litigation and to initiate new litigation. If an investigation by the Commission disclosed an infringement or an imminent infringement of a fundamental right, it could refer the matter to a court having jurisdiction over the matter. The Commission could also undertake investigations at its own initiative or on the receipt of a complaint of a violation of one of the rights in the fundamental rights chapter of the Constitution as a result of 'executive or administrative action.' The Commission was also authorized to make recommendations to the government on the signing of international treaties or other instruments.

4 The number of IDPs has fluctuated between 500,000 and 1,000,000 since the 1980s. Sri Lanka's ethnic conflict escalated in the early 1980s after anti-Tamil riots in 1983. The riots saw Sri Lanka descend into a spiral of violence that has wrecked the economy and torn apart its social fabric. As in all internal conflicts, the heaviest casualties were civilians, and since 1980, thousands upon thousands of Sri Lankans have been uprooted and forced to flee their homes. An estimated 200,000 have fled overseas while the majority has remained displaced within the country's borders. Many of the IDPs have been displaced several times. According to statistics provided by the Commissioner General of Essential Services (CGES), as of 2 January 2002, there were approximately 174,250 persons in 346 welfare centres in the districts of Jaffna, Kilinochchi, Mullaitivu, Mannar, Vavuniya, Trincomalee, Batticaloa, Ampara, Puttalam, Anuradhapura, Kurunegala, Polonnaruwa, Colombo and Matale. A further 509,036 displaced persons were staying with friends and relatives. The IDPs outside the camps are also eligible to receive rations from the state. According to the CGES statistics, there were a total of 683,286 persons displaced as of 2 January 2002, both within and outside camps. However, these statistics do not capture the total number of displaced people who either are not eligible to receive dry rations due to economic reasons or have not registered with the government and who are living in other areas, including the city of Colombo.

Numbers Displaced (estimated)

Dec 1994	525,000
Oct 1995	649,049
Dec 1995	1,017,181
May 1996	839,161
Oct 1996	770,837
Dec 1996	768,356
Mar 2001	707,215
Jan 2002	683,286

Source: Ministry of Rehabilitation and Reconstruction/ Commissioner General of Essential Services (CGES).

5 In 1990 approximately 100,000 Muslims were evicted from Jaffna and Mannar by the Liberation Tigers of Tamil Eelam (LTTE) who gave them 24 hours in which to collect their belongings and flee. Almost twelve years later they continue to live the lives of displaced people in Puttalam, Anuradhapura and Kurunegala.

6 'People Want Peace' (Washington DC: US Committee for Refugees, 1994), p.12.

7 Preliminary Report of Radhika Coomaraswamy, the Special Rapporteur on Violence against Women, E/CN.4/1995/42, 22 November 1994, para. 294.

8 Report of the Representative of the UN Secretary-General on Internally Displaced Persons, Francis M. Deng, *Internally Displaced Persons*, UN Document E/CN.4/1995/50, February 2, 1995, para. 30.

9 See also University Teachers for Human Rights (Jaffna), 'Jaffna: The Contest between Man and The Beast Within,' Special Report No. 7, 29 August 1996, pp.16-18.

10 Amnesty International, *AI-index*, ASA 37/001/2002, 28 January 2002.

11 Committee on the Elimination of Discrimination against Women, 26th Session, CEDAW/C/2002/I/CRP.3/Add.5, 30 January 2002, para. 31.

12 Hiram Ruiz and Katie Hope, 'Conflict and Displacement in Sri Lanka' (Washington DC: US Committee for Refugees, 1997), p.12.

13 Preliminary Report of Radhika Coomaraswamy, the Special Rapporteur on Violence against Women, E/CN.4/1995/42, 22 November 1994, para. 310.

14 Article 12 of the UDHR and Article 17 of the ICCPR.
15 Ruiz and Hope, 'Conflict and Displacement in Sri Lanka,' p.32.
16 The role of NHRIs in the protection of economic, social and cultural rights, General Comment No. 10 of the Committee on Economic, Social and Cultural Rights, E/C.12/1998/25, adopted by the Committee at the 51st meeting (nineteenth session) in December 1998.

APPENDIX

DIALOGUE ON PROTECTION STRATEGIES FOR PEOPLE IN SITUATIONS OF FORCED MIGRATION

(A conference organized by the Mahanirban Calcutta Research Group, in collaboration with UNHCR,
14–15 December 2009)

RECOMMENDATIONS

1. Stressing the importance of sustained dialogue on emerging trends in the realm of prevention, protection and reintegration of refugees and internally displaced persons (IDPs) and the need for identifying sustainable solutions, the group of South Asian experts gathered in the Conference titled 'Protection Strategies for People in Situations of Forced Migration' (thereafter the Conference) proposes to transform itself into a Working Group on Challenges of Displacement in South Asia (thereafter the Working Group). The Working Group, with the assistance of a Secretariat to be established at the Mahanirban Calcutta Research Group, will *(a)* serve as an open forum for discussion and debate across countries and regions; *(b)* convene in regular intervals; and *(c)* help translate research findings of displacement in South Asia into region-specific laws and policies. Such an initiative would aim at establishing a broad-based dialogue on the existing and emerging protection needs of people affected by displacement, including as a result of conflict, development and environmental degradation, with a view to informing policy making.

2. Being aware of the historical and geographical limitations of the term 'refugee' as framed in the Refugee Convention (1951) and stressing the need of capturing new social phenomena in the realm of protecting vulnerable populations, in particular with respect to climate change, the Conference invites a dialogue, inspired by South Asian experiences, among state governments, international organizations and civil society that looks beyond the refugee definition contained in the Refugee Convention.
3. Recognizing that *non-refoulement* is one of the principal pillars of any comprehensive protection strategy, the Conference encourages the states in the South Asian sub-continent to consider signing and ratifying the Refugee Convention as well as the Optional Protocol (1967) and to put in place national legislation to enforce the principles enshrined in these two instruments, inspired by the model law on refugees (2007) initiated by the Eminent Persons Group. The Conference further invites the governments of the states of South Asia to work towards a regional framework for protection under the auspices of the South Asia Association for Regional Cooperation (SAARC).
4. Emphasizing the importance of durable solutions in the face of new displacement paradigms and upholding the fundamental right to freedom of movement, the Conference calls on the states in the South Asian sub-continent to ensure that conditions are established for refugees and IDPs to make informed choices from a range of options, including voluntary return in safety and dignity, local integration and relocation to a third place.
5. In light of a significant increase of IDPs in the world and South Asia, the Conference invites a dialogue, in close coordination with people affected by displacement and with the active involvement of the epistemic community, among stakeholders in South Asia on the effective implementation of the 'UN Guiding Principles on Displacement' (1998) by way of adopting national legislation, or addressing the protection needs of IDPs by other comprehensive measures ensuring clear benchmarks and minimum standards.
6. Mindful of the need to sensitize all segments of society on protection needs of displaced populations as well as the linkages of marginalization and forced migration, the Conference calls on the electronic and print media to assume its responsibility

for *(a)* clarifying in the discourse the definition of refugees, IDPs as well as migrants; *(b)* providing independently researched, comprehensive and balanced information on displacement situations; and *(c)* refraining from all reporting potentially jeopardizing displaced persons, their families or the population hosting them.

7. In this context, the Conference *(a)* emphasizes the potentially beneficial role of local language media to advocate protection strategies; *(b)* encourages reporting from a distinctively South Asian perspective, tapping into existing regional media outlets and possibly creating new media structures for that purpose; and *(c)* notes the increasing influence of the new media in shaping public opinion.
8. Taking note of the UNHCR Ten Point Plan of Action titled 'Refugee Protection and Mixed Migration' (2007), the Conference proposes to identify suitable topics for consideration in upcoming meetings and conferences of the Working Group-to-be. One set of issues that emerged from discussion as a pertinent theme for further deliberation would be the fencing of borders, its impact on displacement and possible solutions. Other themes include the prospects and limitations of state institutions, including Human Rights Commissions (HRCs), and the involvement of civil society in devising new policies and strategies.
9. In recognition of the fact that the majority of refugees, IDPs and trafficked persons are women and children, the Conference highlighted the need for gender and age sensitive assistance, protection and capacity-building policies and programmes and will feed its findings into the activities of the Working Group.
10. In light of the findings of the Fourth Assessment Report from the Intergovernmental Panel on Climate Change and their likely implications for migration and internal displacement, the Conference underlined the need for a South Asian dialogue and a regional Action Plan on Climate Change based on the principles of human security as well as justice and equity on issues of environmental concern. The Conference also stressed the importance of devising a framework for redressing issues pertaining to the impact of growth-oriented development on sections of society vulnerable to displacement.

BIBLIOGRAPHY

Afzal, Mehreen, ' "A Violation of His or Her Human Security" – New Grounds for the Recognition of Refugee Status: A Proposal for Reform', Research paper no. 140, UNHCR, December 2006.

Agamben, Giorgio, *Homo Sacer: Sovereign Power and Bare Life*, Stanford: Stanford University Press, 1998.

Agarwal, Anuja (ed.), *Migrant Women and Work*, New Delhi: Sage, 2006.

Akol, Joshua and John Rogge, 'Repatriation: Its Role in Resolving Africa's Refugee Dilemma', *International Migration Review*, 22, 2, 1989: 184–200.

Alam, Shah, 'International Refugee Law: A Critical Review', *Bangladesh Journal of Law*, June 1997.

Allen, Timothy Gordon, (ed.), *In Search of Cool Ground: War, Flight and Homecoming in Northeast Africa*, Institut de recherche des Nations Unies pour le développement social, Londres: Africa World Press and James Currey, 1996.

Andrews, Geoff, *Citizenship*, London: Lawrence and Wishart Limited, 1991.

Angel, A., 'IDPs: Need for a National Legal Framework in Sri Lanka', Institute for Peace and Conflict Studies, 2008, for details see: www.reliefweb.int/rw.rwb.nsf/DB900oSID/ONIN-7HFQYF?

Areeparampli, Mathew, 'Displacement Due to Mining in Jharkhand', *Economic and Political Weekly*, 15 June 1996.

Austin, Granville, *Working a Democratic Constitution*, New York: Oxford University Press, 1999.

Bader, Veit (ed.), *Citizenship and Exclusion*, New York: St. Martin's Press, 1997.

Banerjee, Paula, Sabyasachi Basu Ray Chaudhury and Samir Das (eds), *Internal Displacement in South Asia: The Relevance of the UN's Guiding Principles*, New Delhi: Sage, 2005.

Banerjee, Upala Devi, 'Sexual Exploitation and Trafficking of the Girl Child: The Indian Scenario', *Migrant Labour and Trafficking of Women: Workshop Report*, Nepal: National Network against Girl Trafficking,

1999.

Banerjee, Subharati, 'Bharat Bangladesh Simanta Samasya: Char-meghna, Shikarpur o Nasirerparar Porjalochona' (Problems in Bengal–Bangladesh Border: A Discussion of the Three Villages of Charmeghna, Shikarpur and Nasirerpara), unpublished M.Phil thesis, Department of South and Southeast Asian Studies, University of Calcutta, 2000–2001.

Banerjee, Parthasarathi and Frank-Jurgen Richter (eds), *Economic Institutions in India*, New York: Palgrave Macmillan, 2002.

Banerjee, Kishna and Purna Banerjee, 'Lives Delimited by Barbed Wires', *Refugee Watch*, 13, April 2003.

Banerji, Arun Kumar, (ed.), *Integration, Disintegration and World Order: Some Perspectives on the Process of Change*, Calcutta: Allied, 1995.

Bardhan, Pranab, *The Political Economy of Development in India*, New Delhi: Oxford University Press, 1984.

Barnett, Tony and Alan Whiteside, *AIDS in the Twenty-First Century: Disease and Globalization*, New York: Palgrave Macmillan, 2002.

Basch, Linda, Nina Glick Schiller and Cristina Szanton Blanc, *Nations Unbound: Transnational Projects, Postcolonial Predica-ments, and Deterritorialized Nation-States*, Luxembourg: Gordon and Breach, 1994.

Basu Ray Chaudhury, Anasua, 'Sabarmati: Creating a New Divide?' *Economic and Political Weekly*, 24 February, 2007.

Barkey, Karen and Sunita Parikh, 'Comparative Perspectives on the State', vol. 17, *Annual Review of Sociology*, New York: Columbia University, 1991: 523–49.

Baubock, Rainer, 'Migration and Citizenship', *New Community*, 18, 1, 1991.

——, *Immigrations and the Boundaries of Citizenship, Monographs in Ethnic Relations*, Coventry: Centre for Research in Ethnic Relations, 1992.

——, *Transnational Citizenship Membership and Rights in International Migration*, Northampton, MA: Edward Elgar, 1994.

Behera, Navnita Chadha (ed.), *Gender, Conflict and Migration*, New Delhi: Sage, 2006.

Beissinger, Mark and M. Crawford Young (eds), *Beyond State Crisis? Postcolonial Africa and Post-Soviet Eurasia in Comparative Perspective*, Washington DC: Woodrow Wilson Centre Press, 2002.

Benhabib, Seyla, *Democratic Equality and Diversity: Political Identities in Global Era*, Princeton NJ: Princeton University Press, 2002.

——, *The Rights of Others: Aliens, Residents, and Citizens*, Cambridge: Cambridge University Press, 2004.

Berezin, Mabel and Martin Schain, *Europe without Borders: Remapping Territory, Citizenship and Identity in a Transnational Age*, Baltimore: John Hopkins University Press, 2003.

Bhabha, Homi K., 'Narrating the Nation', *Nation and Narration*, Homi K.

Bhaba (ed.), New York: Routledge, 1990.

Bhatt, Pushpa, 'Trafficking of Nepali Girls in India and AIDS', *Women's Voice*, report published by National Network against girl trafficking, Kathmandu, n.d.

Bhargava, Rajeev, 'India's Secular Constitution', *India's Living Constitution Ideas, Practices and Controversies*, Zoya Hasan (ed.), London: Anthem Press, 2005.

Bhattarai, Anand Mohan, *Displacement and Rehabilitation in Nepal: Law Policy and Practice*, New Delhi: Anmol, 2001.

Bose, Tapan and Rita Manchanda (eds), *States, Citizens and Outsiders: the Uprooted Peoples of South Asia*, Kathmandu: South Asia Forum for Human Rights, 1997.

Bosniak, Linda, 'Universal Citizenship and the Problem of Alienage', *Northwestern University Law Review*, 94, 3, 2000.

Bourdieu, Pierre, *On Television and Journalism*, Pluto Press, 1988.

Brubaker, Roger, *Citizenship and Nationhood in France and Germany*, Cambridge: Harvard University Press, 1992.

Byers, Michael and Nick Dragojlovic, 'Darfur: A Climate Change-Induced Humanitarian Crisis?' *Human Security Bulletin*, 2004.

Cardenas, Sonia, 'Adaptive States: The Proliferation of National Human Rights Institutions', Working Paper, Carr Center for Human Rights Policy, Harvard University, 2001.

Castles, Stephen, 1992, 'The Australian Model of Immigration and Multiculturalism: Is It Applicable in Europe?' *International Migration Review*, 26, 2, 1992.

——, 'Multicultural Citizenship: the Australian Experience', *Citizenship and Exclusion*, Veit Bader (ed.), The Netherlands: University of Amsterdam, 1997.

Castles, Stephen and Alastair Davidson, *Citizenship and Migration: Globalization and the Politics of Belonging*, New York: Routledge, 2000.

Chanda, Nayan, *Bound Together: How Traders, Preachers, Adventurers, and Warriors Shaped Globalization*, Yale University Press, 2007.

Chatterjee, Partha, 'The Nation and Its Fragments: Colonial and Postcolonial Histories', Princeton, NJ: Princeton University Press, 1993.

—— (ed.), *State and Politics in India*, New Delhi: Oxford University Press, 1997.

——, *The Politics of the Governed: Reflections on Popular Politics in Most of the World*, New York: Columbia University Press, 2004.

Chellaney, Brahma, 'China–India Clash over Chinese Claims to Tibetan Water', *The Asia- Pacific Journal: Japan Focus*, 2007.

Chimni, B.S. (ed.), *International Refugee Law: A Reader*, New Delhi: Sage, 2000.

——, *The Law and Politics of Regional Solution of the Refugee Problem: The Case of South Asia*, Colombo: Regional Centre for Strategic Studies, 1998.

——, 'Globalisation, Humanitarianism and the Erosion of Refugee Protection, RSC', Working Paper, 3 February 2000, University of Oxford.

Coles, Gervase, 'Voluntary Repatriation: a Background Study', Paper prepared for the Round Table on Voluntary Repatriation, San Remo, Italy: International Institute of Humanitarian Law/UNHCR, 1985.

——, 'The Human Rights Approach to the Solution of the Refugee Problem: A Theoretical and Practical Enquiry', *Human Rights and the Protection of Refugees under International Law*, Alan Nash (ed.), Montreal: Canadian Human Rights Foundation/The Institute for Research on Public Policy, 1987.

——, 'Approaching the Refugee Problem Today', *Refugees and International Relations*, Gil Loescher and Laila Monahan (eds), New York: Oxford University Press, 1989.

——, *Appeal to Donor Governments*, Asmara: Commission for Eritrean Refugee Affairs, Provisional Government of Eritrea, 1992.

—— *Approaches and Strategies in the Repatriation of Eritrean Refugees*, Asmara: Provisional Government of Eritrea, 1992.

Coomaraswamy, Radhika, 'Preliminary Report Submitted by the Special Rapporteur on Violence against Women', E/CN.4/1995/42, 22 November 1994.

Crisp, Jeff, 'Refugee Protection in Regions of Origin: Potentials and Challenges', Migration Information Source, Washington DC, December, 2003.

Das, Veena and D. Poole, (eds), *Anthropology in the Margins of the State*, New Delhi: Oxford University Press, 2004.

Das, Samir Kumar (ed.), *Blisters on Their Feet: Tales of Internally Displaced Persons in India's North East*, New Delhi: Sage, 2008.

Davies, Mike, *Late Victorian Holocausts: El Niño Famines and the Making of the Third World*, NY/London: Verso, 2001.

Davis, Kingsley, 'India and Pakistan: The Demography of Partition', *Pacific Affairs*, 22, Vancouver, 1949.

de Silva, K.M. and G.H. Peiris (eds), *Pursuit of Peace in Sri Lanka: Past Failures and Future Prospects*, Kandy: ICES, 2000.

Deng, Francis M., Report of the Representative of the UN Secretary-General on Internally Displaced Persons, UN Document E/CN.4/1995/50.

Desbarats, J. 'Indochinese Resettlement in the United States', *Annals of the Association of American Geographers*, 75, Routledge, 1985.

Dhungana, Shiva K., 'The Policy of the Government of Nepal towards the Internally Displaced Persons', *Limits of the Humanitarian: Studies in*

Situations of Forced Migration, Policies and Practices, 17, MCRG, 2007.
Dillon, Michael, 'The Asylum Seeker and the Stranger: An Other Politics, Hospitality and Justice', Paper presented in International Studies Association Conference, Chicago, 1995.
Dixit, Ajaya, 'Water Projects in Nepal: Lessons from Displacement and Rehabilitation', *Water Nepal*, 4, 1, Kathmandu: Nepal Water Conservation Foundation, 1994.
Doerfel, Jan, 'The Convention against Torture and the Protection of Refugees', *Refugee Survey Quarterly*, 24, 2, 2005.
Dyryldaev, Ramazan, 'Citizen of Kyrgyzstan Perished from the Mine Explosion at the Border', Press release by the Kyrgyz Committee for Human Rights in Exile, 26 April 2001.
Eder and Giesen (eds), *European Citizenship between National Legacies and Postnational Projects*, Oxford: Oxford University Press, 2001.
Evans, Peter, Dietrich Rueschemeyer and Theda Skocpol (eds), *Bringing the State Back In*, Cambridge: Cambridge University Press, 1985.
Feller, Erika, Volker Turk and Frances Nicholson, *Refugee Protection in International Law*, Cambridge University Press.
Fonseka, Bhavani, 'A Profile on Internally Displaced Persons Living with Host Families', for details see: http://www.nrc.no/arch/_img/9293518.pdf.
Frankel, Francine R., Zoya Hasan, Rajeev Bhargava and Balveer Arora (eds), *Transforming India: Social and Political Dynamics of Democracy*, London: Oxford University Press, 2000.
Gardezi, Hassan N., 'Globalisation and Pakistan's Dilemma of Development', *The Pakistan Development Review*, 43, 4: I, Winter, 2004.
Gellner, Ernest, *Nations and Nationalism*, Oxford: Blackwell, 1983.
Ghosh, Partha S., *Cooperation and Conflict in South Asia*, New Delhi: Manohar, 1989.
——, *Unwanted and Uprooted: A Political Study of Migrants, Refugees Stateless and Displaced of South Asia*, New Delhi: Samskriti, 2004.
Gizewski, Peter and Thomas Homer-Dixon, *Environmental Security and Violent Conflict: The Case of Pakistan*, New York: American Association for the Advancement of Science, 1996.
Goodwin-Gill, Guy S. *International Law and Movements of Persons between States*, Oxford: Clarendon Press, 1978.
——, *The Refugee in International Law*, Oxford: Clarendon Press, 1996.
Gorlick, Brian, 'Human Rights and Refugees: Enhancing Protection through International Human Rights Law', UNHCR Working Paper, 30, October 2000.
Gould, Carol and Pasquale Pasquino, *Cultural Identity and the Nation-State*, New York: Rowman and Littlefield Publishers, 2001.
Graham, Edward, 'Terrorism and Borders', The Middle East Information

Network, Inc., 1999–2000, for details see: http://www.mideastinfo.com/archive/paper1.htm.

Granville, Austin, *Working a Democratic Constitution*, New York: Oxford University Press, 1999.

Haider, Naima, 'Understanding the Meaning of "Persecution" from "Gender" Perspective', *The Dhaka University Studies*, F, 15, 2, December 2004.

Hammer, Thomas, 'Citizenship: Membership of a Nation and of a State', *International Migration*, 24, 1986.

——, *International Migration, Citizenship and Democracy*, Aldershot: Gower, 1990.

Hammond, Laura, 'The Making of a Good Citizen in an Ethiopian Returnee Settlement', *Coming Home? Refugees, Migrants and Those Who Stayed Behind*, Lynellyn D. Long and E. Oxfeld (eds), Philadelphia: University of Pennsylvania Press, 2004, 206–25.

——, *This Place Will Become Home: Refugee Repatriation to Ethiopia*, Ithaca: Cornell University Press, 2004.

Hampton, J. (ed.), *Internally Displaced People: a Global Survey*, London: Earthscan, 1998.

Hansen, Thomas Blom and Finn Stepputat Hansen (eds), *States of Imagination: Ethnographic Explorations of the Postcolonial State*, Durham N.C.: Duke University Press, 2001.

——, *Sovereign Bodies: Citizens, Migrants, and States in the Postcolonial World*, Princeton, NJ: Princeton University Press, 2005.

Hardgrave, Robert L. and Stanley A. Kochanek, *India: Government and Politics in a Developing Nation*, Fort Worth: Harcourt Brace Jovanovich, 1993.

Harrell-Bond, Barbara, *Imposing Aid: Emergency Assistance to Refugees*, USA: Oxford University Press, 1986.

Hasan, Mushirul, *Legacy of a Divided Nation: India's Muslims since Independence*, New Delhi: Oxford University Press, 1997.

——, *Islam, Communities and the Nation: Muslim Identities in South Asia*, New Delhi: Manohar, 1998.

Hasan, Zoya (ed.), *India's Living Constitution Ideas, Practices and Controversies*, London: Anthem Press, 2005.

Hashmi, Taj-ul Islam, 'The "Bihari" Minorities in Bangladesh: Victims of Nationalism', *Islam, Communities and the Nation: Muslim Identities in South Asia*, Mushirul Hasan (ed.), New Delhi: Manohar, 1998.

Hathaway, C. James, *The Law of Refugee Status*, Toronto: Butterworths, 1991.

——, 'The Meaning of Repatriation', *International Journal of Refugee Law*, 9, 4, 1997.

——, 'The Rights of Refugees under International Law', Cambridge:

Cambridge University Press, 2005.

Herbst, Jeffery, *States and Power in Africa: Comparative Lessons in Authority and Control*, Princeton, NJ: Princeton University Press, 2000.

Hess, Stephen and Marvin Kalb, *The Media and the War on Terrorism*, Pakistan: Oxford University Press, 2005.

Hussain, Monirul, 'State, Identity Movements and Internal Displacement in the North-East', *Economic and Political Weekly*, 16 December 2000.

——, *Interrogating Development: State, Displacement and Popular Resistance in North East India*, New Delhi: Sage, 2008.

——, 'Fear of Being Killed, Violated and Displaced: an Incomplete Dossier of Terrorism in Post Colonial Assam', Paper presented to the seminar on 'Dynamics of Identity and Intergroup Relations in North-East India', Simla: Indian Institute of Advanced Study, 12–14 November 1996.

Ishaque, Rubina, 'Migration, Acculturation and Criminality: an Anthropological Inquiry into the Effects of Forced Migration in Azad Kashmir', Unpublished thesis paper, Islamabad: Jinnah University.

Islam, Mohammad Towhidul, 'Protection of Refugees against Refoulement', *The Dhaka University Studies*, F, 15, 1, June 2004.

Jassal, Smita Tiwari and Ben-Ari, 'Eyal, Listening for Echoes, Partition in 3 Contexts', *Economic and Political Weekly*, June 2006.

Jayal, Niraja Gopal (ed.), *Democracy in India*, New Delhi: Oxford University Press, 2001.

Jayal, Niraja Gopal and Sudha Pai (eds), 2001, *Democratic Governance in India: Challenges of Poverty, Development, and Identity*, New Delhi: Sage Publications.

K.C., Bal Kumar, 'Migration, Poverty and Development in Nepal', *Asian and Pacific Migration Journal*, 13, 2, 2004: 205–32.

Kalin, W, ' Report of the Representative of the Secretary-General on the Human Rights of Internally Displaced Persons, Mission to Sri Lanka', United Nations, 2007.

Khan, Borhan Uddin, 'Towards a Refugee Law Regime in Bangladesh', Unpublished research paper, Dhaka: UNHCR, 2004.

Khanna, D.D. (ed.), *Sustainable Development: Environmental Security, Disarmament and Development in South Asia*, New Delhi: Macmillan, 1997.

Kibreab, Gaim, 'Citizenship Rights and Repatriation of Refugees', *The International Migration Review*, 37, Spring, 2003.

Klug, Heinz, 'Contextual Citizenship', *Indiana Journal of Global Legal Studies*, 7, 2, 2000.

Kohli, Atul (ed.), *The Success of India's Democracy*, Cambridge, UK: Cambridge University Press, 2001.

Köhli, Armin, 'Kurdish Landmine Plight across and along the Borders', *The Journal of Mine Action*, April 2008.

Kothari, Rajni, *Democratic Policy and Social Change in India: Crisis and Opportunities*, Bombay: Allied Publishers, 1976.

——, *Politics and the People: In Search of a Humane India*, 1 and 2, Delhi: Ajanta Publications International, 1989.

Korn, David A., *Exodus within Borders*, US: Brookings Institution, 1999.

Kumar, Chirantan, 'Development, Displacement and Rehabilitation in Bangladesh: a Comparative Study of Kaptai Dam and Jamuna Multipurpose Bridge Project', M.Phil dissertation, School of International Studies, JNU.

Kymlicka, Will and Wayne Norman, 'Return of the Citizen: A Survey of Recent Work on Citizenship Theory', *Ethics*, 102, 2, 1994.

Lahiri-Dutt, Kuntala, 'Imagining Rivers', *Economic and Political Weekly*, 35, 27, 1 July 2000.

Lahiri-Dutt, Kuntala and Gopa Samanta, 'Fleeting Land, Fleeting People: Bangladeshi Women in a *Char*land Environment in Lower Bengal, India', *Asian and Pacific Migration Journal*, Manila, 13, 4, 2004: 475-95.

Larkin, Mary Ann and Frederick C. Cuny (eds), *Repatriation under Conflict in Central America*, Washington, DC: Georgetown University, Centre for Immigration Policy and Refugee Assistance, 1991.

Lama, Mahendra P. (ed.), *India as a Refugee Host Country: Manage-ment, Practices and Policy Options*, New Delhi: SIS/JNU, 2000.

Ling, Li, *How Tibet's Water Will Save China*, Beijing: Chang'an chu ban she, 2000.

Loescher, Gil and Laila Monahan (eds), *Refugees and International Relations*, New York: Oxford University Press, 1989.

Long, Lynellyn D. and E. Oxfeld (eds), *Coming Home? Refugees, Migrants and Those Who Stayed Behind*, Philadelphia: University of Pennsylvania Press, 2004.

Malha, Monique, 'Eighteen Years in Exile: The Situation of Refugees in Pakistan', *Liberal Times*, 5, 1, New Delhi, 1997.

Malkki, L.H., *Purity and Exile: Violence, Memory, and National Cosmology among Hutu Refugees in Tanzania*, Chicago: The University of Chicago Press, 1995.

——, 'Refugees and Exile: from 'Refugee Studies' to the National Order of Things', *Annual Review of Anthropology*, 24, 1995.

Mallick, Dwijen L., 'Growing Environmental and Climate Refugees in Bangladesh: Urgent Actions Are Required', Paper presented at the C40 Tokyo Conference on Climate Change-Adaptation Measures for Sustainable Low Carbon Cities, 2008.

Manchanda R., (ed.), *Media Crossing Borders*, South Asia Forum for Human Rights, 2004.

Marshall, T. H., *Citizenship and Social Class*, Cambridge: University Press, 1949.

Maung, Shwe Lu, *Burma: Nationalism and Ideology: An Analysis of Society, Culture and Politics*, Dhaka: University Press, 1989.

Mesarovic and Pestel, *Mankind at the Turning Point: The Second Report of the Club of Rome*, New York: E. P. Dutton, 1974.

Midgal, Joel, *Strong Societies and Weak States: State–Society Relations and State Capabilities in the Third World*, Princeton, NJ: Princeton University Press, 1988.

Mooney, Erin D., 'Principles of Protection for Internally Displaced Persons', *International Migration*', 38, 6, 2000: 81–99.

Moore, S.W. *The Critque of Capitalist Democracy*, New York: A M Kelly, 1969.

Morsink, H. and T. Allen (eds), *When Refugees Go Home: African Experiences*, London: James Currey, 1994.

Mukherji, S. 'Migration in Eastern India: How Much of It Is Illegal', *The Journal of Family Welfare*, 37, 3, September 1991.

Muni, S.D. and Lok Raj Baral (eds), *Refugees and Regional Security in South Asia*, New Delhi: Konark, 1996.

Nanda, Aswini Kumar, 'Immigration from Bangladesh to India Based on Census Data', *Asian and Pacific Migration Journal*, 2005, 14, 4, 2005: 487–99.

Nash, Alan (ed.), *Human Rights and the Protection of Refugees under International Law*, Montreal, Canadian Human Rights Founda-tion/The Institute for Research on Public Policy, 1987.

National Human Rights Commission Act, 2053, Ministry of Law, Justice and Parliamentary Affairs, 1997.

Neocleous, M. 'Off the Map on Violence and Cartography', *European Journal of Social Theory*, 6, 4, November 2003.

Nicholson, Frances and Patrick Twomey (eds), *Refugee Rights and Realities*, Cambridge: Cambridge University Press, 1999.

Newman, Edward, and Joanne van Selm (eds), *Refugees and Forced Displacement International Security Human Vulnerability and the State*, New York: United Nation Press, 2003.

Norbu, Dawa, 'Refugees from Tibet: Structural Causes of Successful Settlement', Paper presented to the Fourth International Research and Advisory Panel Conference on Forced Migration, Oxford University, 5–9 January, 1994.

Nustad, Knut G. and Christian Krohn-Hansen (eds), *State Formation: Anthropological Perspectives*, UK: Pluto Press, 2005.

Olwig, Karen and Hastrup (eds), *Siting Culture: The Shifting Anthropology Object*, New York: Routledge, 1997: 17–39.

Pandey, Bikash, 'Dams and Civil Society in Nepal: Major Concerns', World Commission on Dams, 1998.

Passi, A., 'The Role of Identities and Boundaries in the Contemporary

World', for more details see: http://www.geo.ut.ee/nbc/paper/paasi.htm.
Petterson, Bjorn, 'Development-Induced Displacement: Internal Affair or International Human Rights Issue', for details see: http://www.fmreview.org/sites/fmr/files/FMRdownloads/en/FMRpdfs/FMR12/fmr12.6.pdf.
Phadnis, Urmila, *Ethnicity and Nation-Building in South Asia*, New Delhi: Sage Publications, 1989.
Philipose, P., 'The Forgotten and the Damned', *The Indian Express*, 2000.
——, 'Borders in the Mind: Bangladeshis, a Nowhere Policy for a Nowhere People', *The Indian Express*, 2003.
Rajan, Sudhir Chella, 'Blue Alert: Climate Migrants in South Asia: Estimates and Solutions', Greenpeace, 2008.
Nick Robson, 'Climate Change in South Asia: A Precursor for Conflict?' South Asian Strategic Stability Unit, for details see: http://www.sassu.org.uk/html/ClimateChangeandConflict.htm.
Rogge, John, 'A Geography of Refugees: Some Illustrations from Africa', *The Professional Geographer*, 24, 2, 1977: 186–93.
——, *Too Many Too Long: Sudan's Twenty Year Refugee Dilemma*, Totowa, nj: Rowman and Allenheld, 1985.
——, 'Repatriation of Refugee: Not So Simple "Optimum Solution", T. Allen and H. Morsink (eds), *When Refugees Go Home*, London: James Currey, 1994.
Rubenstein, Kim and Alder Daniel, 'International Citizenship: The Future of Nationality in a Globalised World', *Indiana Journal of Global Legal Studies*, 7, 2, 2000.
Rudolph, Lloyd I. and Susanne Hoeber Rudolph, *In Pursuit of Lakshmi: The Political Economy of the Indian State*, Chicago: University of Chicago Press, 1987.
Ruiz, Hiram and Katie Hope, 'Conflict and Displacement in Sri Lanka', Washington DC, US Committee for Refugees, 1997.
Sabaratnam, *Out of Bondage: The Thondaman Story*, Colombo: Sri Lanka Indian Community Council, 1990.
Sahadevan, P., 'Ethnic Conflicts and Militarism in South Asia', *International Studies*, 39, 2, 2002.
Samaddar, R., *The Marginal Nation: Transborder Migration from Bangladesh to West Bengal*, New Delhi: Sage, 1999.
——, *Refugees and the State: Practices of Asylum and Care in India*, New Delhi: Sage, 2003.
Sammadar, Ranabir, and Helmut Reifeld (eds), *Peace as a Process*, New Delhi: Manohar Publishers and Distributors, 2001.
Sassen, Saskia, *Losing Control? Sovereignty in an Age of Globaliza-tion*, New York: Columbia University Press, 1996.
——, *Guest and Aliens*, New York: The New Press, 1999.

——, *Democracy, Citizenship and the Global City*, New York: Routledge, 2000.

——. *Global Networks, Linked Cities*, New York: Routledge, 2002.

Schuck, Peter H., *Citizens, Strangers, and In-between: Essays on Immigration and Citizenship*, Oxford: Westview Press, 1988.

Schuck, Peter H. and Rogers M. Smith, *Citizenship without Consent: Illegal Aliens in American Polity*, New Haven: Yale University Press, 1985.

Schmitter, Phillipp, 'The Scope of Citizenship in a Democratized European Union: From Economic to Social and Cultural', Eder and Giesen (eds) *European Citizenship between National Legacies and Postnational Projects*, Oxford: Oxford University Press, 2001.

Schwartz and Randall, 'An Abrupt Climate Change Scenario and Its Implications for United States National Security', October 2003, for details see: http://www.greenpeace.org/international/Global/international/planet-2/report/2006/3/an-abrupt-climate-change-scena.pdf.

Shapiro, Michael, J. and Hayward R. Alker (eds), *Challenging Boundaries: Global Flows, Territorial Identities*, Minneapolis: University of Minnesota Press, 1996.

Shklar, Judith N., *American Citizenship: the Quest for Inclusion*, Cambridge: Harvard University Press, 1991.

Shrestha, Ava Darshan and Rita Thapa (eds), *The Impact of Armed Conflicts on Women in South Asia*, New Delhi: Manohar, 2007.

Sieder, Rachel, 'Rethinking Citizenship: Reforming the Law in Postwar Guatemala', *States of Imagination Ethnographic Explorations of the Postcolonial State*, Thomas Blom Hansen and Finn Stepputat (eds), Durham: Duke University Press, 2001.

Silverman, M., 'Citizenship and the Nation-State in France', *Ethnic and Racial Studies*, 14, 3, 1991.

——, *Deconstructing the Nation: Immigration, Racism and Citizenship in Modern France*, London: Routledge, 1992.

Skalnik, Peter, *Outwitting the State*, New Brunswick: Transaction Publication, 1989.

Smith, Anthony, *The Ethnic Origins of Nations*, Oxford: Blackwell Press, 1986.

Smith, A. D., 'The Problems of National Identity: Ancient, Medieval and Modern?' *Ethnic and Racial Studies*, 18, 1995.

Soguk, Nevzat, 'Transnational/Transborder Bodies: Resistance, Accommodation, and Exile in Refugee and Migration Movements on the US-Mexican Border', *Challenging Boundaries Global Flows, Territorial Identities*, Michael J. Shapiro and Hayward R. Adler (eds), Minneapolis: University of Minnesota Press, 1996.

——, *States and Strangers: Refugees Displacement of Statecraft*, Minnesota: University of Minnesota Press, 1999.

Soysal, Yasemin N., *Limits of Citizenship: Migrants and Postnational Membership in Europe*, Chicago: The University of Chicago Press, 1994.

——,'Citizenship and Identity, Living in Diasporas in Post-War Europe', *Ethnic and Racial Studies*, 23, 1, 2000.

Spate, P.H.K., *India and Pakistan: A General and Regional Geography*, London: Methuen, 1957.

Stein, Barry, Fred Cuny and Pat Reed (eds), *Refugee Repatriation during Conflict: a New Conventional Wisdom*, Dallas: The Centre for the Study of Societies in Crisis, 1995.

Steinmetz, George, (ed.), *State/Culture State Formation after the Culture Turn*, London: Cornell University Press, 1999.

Swain, Ashok, 'The Environmental Trap: The Ganges River Diversion, Bangladeshi Migration and Conflicts in India', Report No. 41, Department of Peace and Conflict Research, Sweden: Uppsala University, 1996.

Tegart, W.J. McG, G.W. Sheldon, and D.C. Griffiths (eds), 'Climate Change: The IPCC Impacts Assessment', for details see: www.ipcc.ch/ipccreports/far/wg_II/ipcc_far_wg_II_full_ report.pdf.

Thussu, Daya Kishan and Des Freedman (eds), *War and Media: Reporting Conflict 24X7*, New Delhi: Sage Publications, 2003.

Trakroo, Ragini, Aparna Bhat and Samhita Nandi, *Refugee and the Law*, New Delhi: Socio-Legal Information Centre, Human Rights Law Network, n.d.

van Brabant, K., 'Sri Lanka', J. Hampton (ed.), *Internally Displaced Persons: a Global Survey*, London: Earth Scan Publications Ltd, 1998.

van Schendel, Willem, 'Working through Partition: Making a Living in the Bengal Borderlands', *International Review of Social History*, Cambridge, 46, 3, December 2001.

——, 'Stateless in South Asia: the Making of the India-Bangladesh Enclaves', *The Journal of Asian Studies*, Ann Arbor, 61, 1, February 2002.

Warner, D.J., 'Voluntary Repatriation and the Meaning of Return to Home: a Critique of Liberal Mathematics', *Journal of Refugee Studies*, 7, 2/3, 1994.

Weiner, Myron, 'Rejected Peoples and Unwanted Migrants in South Asia', *Economic and Political Weekly*, 21 August 1993.

Whitehead, Andrew, *A Mission in Kashmir*, New Delhi: Penguin India, 2007.

Wolff, Stefan, 'German Expellee Organizations between "Homeland" and "at Home": A Case Study of the Politics of Belonging', *Refuge*, 20, 1, 2001.

Zaman, M.Q., 'Development and Displacement in Bangladesh: Towards a

Resettlement Policy', *Asian Survey*, Berkeley, 36, 7, July 1996.
Zieck, M., *UNHCR and Voluntary Repatriation of Refugees: a Legal Analysis*, The Hague: Martinus Nijhoff, 1999.

Important Documents

Amnesty International, 'An Abrupt Climate Change Scenario and Its Implications for United States National Security, Green Peace, October 2003', AI-index: ASA 37/001/2002, 28 January 2002, for details see: http://www.greenpeace.org/international/Global/international/planet-2/report/2006/3/an-abrupt-climate-change-scena.pdf.
Bangkok Principles on the Status and Treatment of Refugees of the Asian-African Legal Consultative Committee (AALCO), February 2001.
Briefing Notes, 'Nearly 190,000 People Displaced by Fighting in Pakistan's Bajaur Area', 14 October 2008, for details see: http://www.unhcr.org/48f474e52.html.
Ceasefire Code of Conduct Signed between the Government of Nepal and CPN(M), Kathmandu: Ministry of Peace and Reconstruction, Government of Nepal, 25 May 2006
Centre for Policy Alternatives, 'Land and Property Rights of Internally Displaced Persons', 2003.
——, 'Policy Brief on Humanitarian Issues', December 2007.
Central Bureau of Statistics, His Majesty's Government of Nepal, 'Population Census—1991: Social Characteristics Tables', 1, 4, Kathmandu, 1991.
Centre for Policy Alternatives and International Movement against All Kinds of Discrimination (IMADR), 'Fact Finding Mission to Trincomalee', 23–27 April 2007.
CM/ Res. 399 (XXIV) 'Resolution on Voluntary Repatriation of African Refugees of the OAU Council of Ministers', Addis-Ababa, 1975.
Climate Change in South Asia – A Conversation with Sir Nicholas Stern, 2007, for details see: http://web.worldbank.org/WBSITE/EXTERNAL/COUNTRIES/SOUTHASIAEXT/0,,contentMDK:21220691~pagePK:146736~piPK:146830~theSitePK:223547,00.html.
Complete Text of Hayrbyar Marri's Speech at the House of Lords, for more details see: http://balochhomeland.weebly.com/factsarticle6.html.
Complex Emergency Database (CE-DAT), Brussels, 7 March 2008.
Consortium of Humanitarian Agencies, 'IDP Land, Property and Compensation Issues', Background paper, National Consultation on the Status of Internally Displaced Persons, 2008.
Convention against Torture and Other Cruel, Inhuman or Degrading Treatment or Punishment, 1984.

Convention Governing the Specific Aspects of Refugee Problems in Africa, OAU, 1969.

Convention on the Elimination of All Forms of Discrimination against Women (CEDAW), 1979.

Convention on the Rights of the Child (CRC), 1989.

Comprehensive Peace Accord (CPA) 2006 signed between the Nepal Government and the CPN(M), Kathmandu: Ministry of Peace and Reconstruction, Government of Nepal, 21 November 2006, for more details see: www.peace.gov.np.

Danish Refugee Council (DRC), 'Policy on Mixed Migration', Copenhagen, May 2008.

Displacement Solutions, 'Latest News on Climate Displacement in Bangladesh', June 2010, for more details see: http://displacementsolutions.org/?p=547.

Earth Changes and the Pole Shift: Information and Discussion about the Earth Changes and the Pending Pole Shift, 16 August 2011, for more details see: http://poleshift.ning.com/prof iles/blogs/pakistan-badin-sinking.

Global IDP Project, 'Internal Displacement: Global Overview of Trends and Developments in 2004', Norwegian Refugee Council, Geneva, 2005.

Human Rights Situation Report, 'People Displaced from Village', August 2002.

Human Rights Watch, 'Return to War – Human Rights under Siege', August 2007.

IDMC, 'Nepal: IDP Return Still a Trickle Despite Ceasefire: A Profile of Internal Displacement Situation, Norwegian Refugee Council, 16 October 2006.

———, 'Pakistan: Millions of IDPs and Returnees Face Continuing Crisis. A Profile of the Internal Displacement Situation', December 2009.

———, 'India: National and State Authorities Failing to Protect IDPs, a Profile of the Internal Displacement Situation', 2 September 2010.

———, 'Pakistan: Flooding Worsens Situation for People Displaced by Conflict in North-west, A Profile of the Internal Displacement Situation', 6 September 2010.

Informal Sector Service Centre (INSEC), 'Special Issue on IDPs', 19, 2 and 3, Kathmandu, September and December 2005.

Institute of Policy Studies, 'Kashmiri Refugees: Facts, Issues and Future Ahead', Islamabad, for more details see: http://www.ips.org.pk/pakistan-and-itsneighbours/.

Inter-Agency Standing Committee (IASC), 'Conflict Related Displacement in Sri Lanka', July 2007.

———, 'Joint Rapid Assessment of the Cyclones and Flood-Affected Areas

of Balochistan and Sindh', 9–15 July, 2007.
International Covenant on Civil and Political Rights (ICCPR), 1966.
International Covenant on Economic, Social and Cultural Rights (ICESCR), 1966.
International Organization for Migration (IOM), Glossary on Migration, Geneva, 2004.
IPCC, SREEN Full Report, 'Renewable Energy Sources and Climate Change Mitigation', for details see: http://srren.ipcc-wg3.de/report/IPCC_SRREN_Full_Report.pdf.
MCRG, 'Voices of the Internally Displaced in South Asia: A Report', Kolkata, 2006.
Ministry of Peace and Reconstruction (mopr), 'National Policies on IDPs', April 2007.
National Human Rights Commission Act, 2053, HMG/N. 1997, Kathmandu: Ministry of Law, Justice and Parliamentary Affairs, 1997.
National Human Rights Commission of Nepal (NHRC), 'Sri Lanka: State of Human Rights, 1995',Colombo, 1996.
——, 'National Human Rights Action Plan 2004-2008', Kathmandu: NHRC, Pulchowk.
——, 'Strategic Plan, 2008-2010', Kathmandu: NHRC, Pulchowk.
Office for the Coordination of Humanitarian Affairs (OCHA), 'Guiding Principles on Internal Displacement', Kathmandu: OCHA, 2004.
——, 'The Internally Displaced Persons: Current Status', Kathmandu: OCHA, Thematic Report, 1, 6 September 2006.
Public Opinion Trends (POT), Nepal Series, 5, 31, 9 June 1999: 316-17.
Refugee Watch, 'News from the Indo-Bangladesh Border', 19, August 2003.
Statute of the Office of the UNHCR.
The Convention on the Prohibition, Use, Stockpiling, Production and Transfer of Antipersonnel Mines and on their Destruction, 1997.
The Indian Commission of Jurists, 'Recurrent Exodus of Minorities from East Pakistan and Disturbances in India: A Report to the Indian Commission of Jurists by its Committee of Enquiry', New Delhi: 1965.
Twelve-Point Agreement (TPA) Signed between the Seven Party Alliance (SPA) and the CPN(M), New Delhi, 22 November 2005, for more details see: www.peace.gov.np.
UN doc. A/Res/38/121,1983.
——,. E/CN.4/Sub.2/2005/17, 2005.
UNHCR, 'Convention Relating to the Status of Refugees', 1951.
——, 'Protection Guidelines on Voluntary Repatriation', 1993.
——, 'Handbook on Voluntary Repatriation: International Protection', Geneva, 1996.
——, 'Model National Law on Refugees', Fourth Regional Consultation on

Refugees and Migratory Movements in South Asia, Dhaka, 10–11 November 1997.
——, 'UNHCR's Expanded Role in Support for the Inter Agency Response to Internal Displacement Situations', New York: UNHCR, 2006.
——, 'Refugee Protection and Mixed Migration: A 10-Point Plan of Action', Geneva, 2006.
——, 'The Challenge of Assessing and Responding to the Protracted IDP Situation', Background paper, National Consultation on the Status of Internally Displaced Persons, 2008.
UNHCR and Inter-Parliamentary Union, 'Refugee Protection: a Guide to Refugee Law', n.d.
UNIP, 'IDP Protection Sub-Group. Coordination Mechanism in Nepal', UN Information Platform, 2006.
United Nations (UN), 'Human Rights and Refugees', UN Fact Sheet 20.
——, 'Nepal: Common Appeal for Transition Support', Mid-Year Review, Kathmandu, 2008.
UN Economic and Social Affairs, 'World Urbanization Prospects: the 2011 Revision', New York, 2012.
Universal Declaration of Human Rights, 1948.
University Teachers for Human Rights (Jaffna), 'Jaffna: The Contest between Man and the Beast Within', Special report 7, 29 August 1996.
US Committee for Refugees, 'World Refugee Survey', 1997.
——, 'People want Peace', Washington DC, 1994.
Worldbank Group Global Environment Facility Program, 'Managing Climate Risk: Integrating Adaptation into World Bank Group Operations', 2007.
World Migration Report, 'International Migration Trends', 2005.

News sources

Assam Tribune 'Fighting AIDS', 24 April 2004.
BBC, 'UK Gives Bangladesh Climate Help', for more details see: http://news.bbc.co.uk/2/hi/science/nature/7606024.stm.
BBC Online, Subir Bhaumik, 'Fears Rise for Sinking Sundarbans', for details see: http://news.bbc.co.uk/2/hi/south_asia/3102948.stm
Daily Mirror, 'IDPs Moved against Their Will', 20 March 2007.
Down to Earth, 'Vanishing Islands', 15 January 2007.
Frontline, 'Beggaring the Neighbour', 28 February 2003.
Hindustan Times, 'Arunachal Wakes Up To Flesh Trade and HIV Risks', 13 May 2005.
Kathmandu Post, 'Rural Women Caught in Rebels, Traffickers', 18 May 2004.

Oh My News International World, 'Attack on Girls' Education in Northwest Pakistan', for details see: http://english.ohmy news.com/articleview/article_view.asp?no=355932&rel_no=1

Meghalaya,'Perspective of Drug Abuse and HIV/AIDS in NE', 1 December 2005.

Nagaland Post, 'Advocacy Prog on HIV/AIDS for Migrant Workers', 28 March 2004.

——, 'AIDS Threat to Army in NE', 25 September 2005.

North East Reporter, 'Rising AIDS Graph Threatens Tripura', 12 April 2004.

Shillong Times, 'Human Trafficking Cases in Meghalaya Draw US Attention', 16 June 2004.

——, 'Assam, Siliguri Main Trafficking Routes in NE', 5 June 2004.

——, 'Rebels Threaten Death to Drug Addicts, Peddlers', 2 July 2004.

The Daily Star, 'Why Bangladesh Needs Refugee Law', Dhaka, 3 June 2008.

The Express Tribune Blogs,'The Disaster Waiting in Sindh's Wings', for more details see: http://blogs.tribune.com.pk/story/941/the-disaster waiting-in-sindh%E2%80%99s-wings/.

The Hindu, 'The Unchecked Influx', Madras, 17 February 1982.

——, 'The Borderlines of Caste', 4 July 1999.

——, 'Sri Lankan Tamil Refugees in Tamil Nadu', 28 July 1997

The Indian Express, 'The Forgotten and The Damned', 2000.

——, 'Borders in the Mind: Bangladeshis, a Nowhere Policy for a Nowhere People', 2003.

The Nation, 'Floods Uproot 0.4million', 16 August 2011.

The Statesman, 'AIDS: the Enemy at the Frontier', 15 October 2006.

The Times of India, 'Flesh Trade Sets Off Barak AIDS Alarm', 1 October 2005.

——, 'CRPF Men in AIDS Grip', *The Times of India*, 18 November 2006.

Relevant sites

www.internal-displacent.org
www.unhcr.org
www.peace.gov.np
http://www.actionaid.org
http://www.bbc.com